ACTOPOLIS
The Art of Action
Die Kunst zu handeln

Goethe-Institut & Urbane Künste Ruhr (eds.)

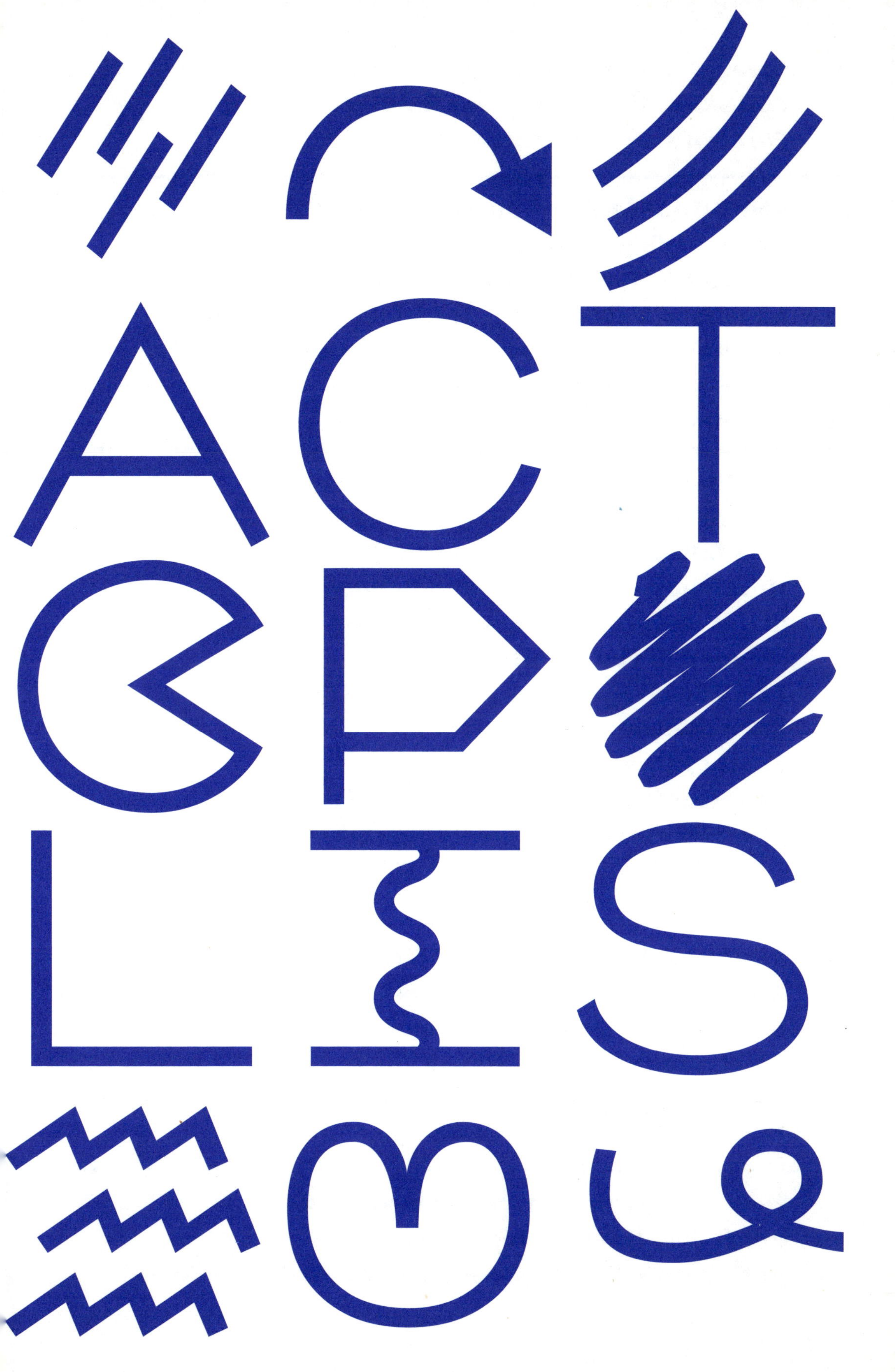

Foreword
Goethe-Institut

"We do not say that a man who takes no interest in politics is a man who minds his own business; we say that he has no business here at all."

PERICLES, Athenian politician and general (after Thucydides)

"This book [*The City in History*] opens with a city that was, symbolically, a world: it closes with a world that has become, in many practical aspects, a city."

LEWIS MUMFORD, philosopher, historian, architecture critic

Nothing provides a better example from which to study the dynamics of global change than urban development. Not only are perceptions of this term gradually freeing themselves from their Eurocentric shackles—in other words, we are abandoning the traditional idea of a city with a town hall, a market square, and a church in the centre—but the monstrous figures for urban growth in themselves also testify to the enormity of global change.

In the nineteenth century, only 10 per cent of the world's population lived in cities. By the turn of the twenty-first century, this figure had risen to around 50 per cent. And the proportion of city dwellers among the world's population is predicted to increase further to 75 per cent by 2050. Cities are hence increasingly becoming seismographs of social change, and as the principal centres of discourse they are having an impact on society, science, and culture.

The Goethe-Institut has been concerned with the connection between culture and the city for some time and has made it one of its main focuses. Branches of the Goethe-Institut the world over have initiated artistic projects that explore urban cultural themes; likewise in South-East Europe, a region witnessing rapid processes of change. One could even say that the cities of South-East Europe are in a state of continuous physical transformation.

ACTOPOLIS began its work in 2014 with some preliminary studies. Zagreb and Ankara, Bucharest and Athens, Sarajevo and Belgrade, and finally Oberhausen became the points of departure for a project involving more than seventy curators and artists from seven cities in seven countries that went into the production phase in 2016. The results are presented in condensed form here.

The cities of South-East Europe have all suffered political, economic, and ecological wounds since the Iron Curtain was lifted. The burning issues this raised are just as relevant now as they were then: Who does a city belong to? Who makes a city? Who decides how it is organised and administered? Who has access to its resources, who benefits from them? Investors? Citizens? And how do citizens become proactive? Do they all have the same recourse to the art of action in order to be heard and gain influence over THEIR city? How does the urban context determine the form of action?

These were the questions that were posed even before the project began. Hence the attitudes and principles informing this project and determining its direction are important, just like the many other projects of the Goethe-Institut. These include the exchange of knowledge and experience, encounters, and getting acquainted in the unfamiliar environment of a partner city. Experimenting jointly with different methods on-site. Experiencing reactions first-hand. Cooperating across frontiers in times when travel has become almost impossible for many creatives. Community building across borders.

Angelika Fitz developed the concept for ACTOPOLIS together with the Goethe-Institut, bringing the necessary experience and knowledge to bear. The Ruhr region in turn, with its diverse experience in dealing with migration and urban transformation processes seemed to be an ideal setting. Urbane Künste Ruhr and its artistic director Katja Aßmann were thus predestined to become our partner.

An initiative as complex as ACTOPOLIS, whose catalogue can only be a milestone on the artistic road to action, could not have evolved without the help of multiple actors. They deserve respect for their competent work, recognition for their determination, and gratitude for their personal commitment. We would like to thank all those involved and specifically the professional and highly experienced team of artistic directors Katja Aßmann, Angelika Fitz, and Martin Fritz as well as the local curators Ana Dana Beroš (Zagreb), Ștefan Ghenciulescu and Raluca Voinea (Bucharest), Danijela Dugandžić (Sarajevo), Elpida Karaba and Glykeria Stathopoulou (Athens), geheimagentur (Oberhausen), Pelin Tan (Ankara/Mardin), and Boba Mirjana Stojadinović (Belgrade). We would also like to thank our colleagues at the local branches of the Goethe-Institut, and finally the Federal Ministry of the Environment (BMUB) without whose generous support this catalogue could not have been produced in its present form.

The curators, artists, urbanists, and activists brought their creative energy, their knowledge, and their dedication to the project. We are especially indebted to them for their work and their impressive cooperation.

Athens, February 2017
JULIANE STEGNER, Director of the South-East Europe Programme, Goethe-Institut Athens
MATTHIAS MAKOWSKI, Regional Director for South-East Europe, Goethe-Institut Athens

Vorwort
Goethe-Institut

„Denn bei uns heißt einer, der an unserer Stadt keinen Anteil nimmt, nicht ein stiller Bürger, sondern ein schlechter."

PERIKLES, attischer Politiker und Feldherr (nach Thukydides)

„Einst war die Stadt das Symbol einer ganzen Welt. Heute ist die ganze Welt im Begriff, Stadt zu werden."

Nach LEWIS MUMFORD, Philosoph, Historiker, Architekturkritiker

An kaum einem anderen Beispiel lässt sich globale Veränderungsdynamik so gut studieren wie an dem der Stadtentwicklung. Nicht nur, dass sich die Perzeption des Begriffs zunehmend aus seiner eurozentrischen Gefangenschaft löst, man also Abschied nimmt von der überlieferten Vorstellung der Stadt mit Rathaus, Marktplatz und Kirche in der Mitte. Auch die allein schon monströsen Zahlen urbanen Wachstums zeigen einen monumentalen Wandel.

Noch im 19. Jahrhundert lebten nur zehn Prozent der Weltbevölkerung in Städten. An der Wende zum 21. Jahrhundert waren es bereits etwa 50 Prozent. Bis 2050 soll der Anteil der Stadtbewohner/innen an der Weltbevölkerung bei 75 Prozent liegen. Damit werden Städte immer mehr zu Seismografen gesellschaftlicher Veränderungen, sie sind die Zentren der maßgeblichen Diskurse und wirken damit in Gesellschaft, Wissenschaft und Kultur.

Das Goethe-Institut beschäftigt sich seit Langem mit dem Zusammenhang von Kultur und Stadt und hat diesen zu einem seiner Schwerpunkte gemacht. Seine Themen greifen Goethe-Institute in künstlerischen Projekten weltweit auf, so auch im Südosten Europas. Hier vollziehen sich diese Veränderungsprozesse rasant, man könnte sagen, die Städte Südosteuropas befinden sich im Aggregatzustand ständiger Transformation.

Mit Vorstudien begann ACTOPOLIS bereits 2014. Zagreb und Ankara, Bukarest und Athen, Sarajevo und Belgrad und schließlich Oberhausen waren die Ausgangsorte eines Projekts, das 2016 mit über 70 Kurator/innen und Künstler/innen aus sieben Städten und Ländern in die Produktionsphase eintrat und dessen Ergebnisse hier zusammengetragen sind.

Politische, ökonomische und ökologische Wunden taten sich in den Städten Südosteuropas auf, als der „Eiserne Vorhang" sich hob. Die Fragen stellten sich damals mit der gleichen Brisanz wie heute:

Wem gehört die Stadt? Wer macht die Stadt? Wer entscheidet über ihre Gestaltung und Verwaltung? Wer hat Zugang zu Ressourcen, wer hat einen Nutzen davon? Investoren? Bürger/innen? Und wie agieren die Bürger/innen? Bedienen sie sich alle derselben Kunst zu handeln, um sich Gehör und Einfluss in IHRER Stadt zu verschaffen? Wie bestimmt der städtische Kontext die Art des Handelns?

Schon vor Projektbeginn stellten sich diese Fragen. Deshalb sind die Haltungen und Prinzipien wichtig, die diesem Projekt wie vielen anderen Projekten des Goethe-Instituts eine Richtung geben wollen:

Wissens- und Erfahrungsaustausch, Begegnungen. Einander im Umfeld des anderen kennenlernen. Methoden vor Ort gemeinsam mit den Partnern erproben. Reaktionen selbst miterleben. Grenzüberschreitende Zusammenarbeit, gerade in Zeiten, in denen das Reisen für viele Kulturschaffende fast unmöglich geworden ist. Grenzüberschreitendes community building.

Angelika Fitz hat mit dem Goethe-Institut das Konzept für ACTOPOLIS entwickelt. Sie brachte die notwendige Erfahrung und das nötige Wissen mit. Das Ruhrgebiet wiederum erschien uns mit seinen vielfältigen Erfahrungen im Umgang mit Zuwanderung und städtischen Transformationsprozessen ein idealer Raum, Urbane Künste Ruhr und seine künstlerische Leiterin Katja Aßmann waren daher ein prädestinierter Partner.

Eine so komplexe Initiative wie ACTOPOLIS, deren Katalog nur ein Meilenstein auf dem Weg der Kunst zu handeln sein kann, entsteht nur mithilfe zahlreicher Akteur/innen. Ihnen gebührt Respekt für ihre kompetente Mitarbeit, Anerkennung für ihr Durchsetzungsvermögen und Dank für das persönliche Engagement. Stellvertretend für alle danken wir dem erfahrenen und professionellen Team der künstlerischen Leiter/innen Katja Aßmann, Angelika Fitz und Martin Fritz sowie den lokalen Kurator/innen Ana Dana Beroš (Zagreb), Ştefan Ghenciulescu und Raluca Voinea (Bukarest), Danijela Dugandžić (Sarajevo), Elpida Karaba und Glykeria Stathopoulou (Athen), geheimagentur (Oberhausen), Pelin Tan (Ankara/Mardin) und Boba Mirjana Stojadinović (Belgrad). Unser Dank gilt auch den Kolleg/innen der beteiligten Goethe-Institute und schließlich dem Bundesumweltministerium (BMUB), ohne dessen großzügige Unterstützung dieser Katalog nicht in dieser Form entstanden wäre.

Ihre kreative Kraft, ihr Wissen und Engagement setzten die Kurator/innen, Künstler/innen, Urbanist/innen und Aktivist/innen ein. Für ihr Werk und die beeindruckende Kooperation gilt ihnen unser besonderer Dank.

Athen, im Februar 2017
JULIANE STEGNER, Leiterin der Programmarbeit Südosteuropa, Goethe-Institut Athen
MATTHIAS MAKOWSKI, Regionalleiter Südosteuropa, Goethe-Institut Athen

Foreword
Urbane Künste Ruhr

Ever since it was founded in 2012, Urbane Künste Ruhr has been realising artistic projects in the many towns and cities of the Ruhr region. Not only do the various structures, existing conditions, and key issues in the Ruhr require new approaches and ideas from the municipalities themselves—collaboration with international partners has also enabled them to take a fresh look at (seemingly) recurring problems on a regular basis.

For all the wealth of experience that the many, very differently structured joint projects with other countries have yielded, ACTOPOLIS occupies a very special place in the programme of Urbane Künste Ruhr. Artists, curators, activists, and urbanists from seven different cities—in seven different countries—have spent more than three years working together and jointly addressing the same set of questions in a process of intensive exchange covering every phase of the project. In this respect, ACTOPOLIS not only occupies a unique place in the work of Urbane Künste Ruhr, it has also played a groundbreaking role for other international cooperations concerned with urban life in the future.

Although Ankara/Mardin, Athens, Belgrade, Bucharest, Sarajevo, Zagreb, and indeed Oberhausen have problems, potential, and opportunities that are specific to those cities, it has become clear in the course of the project that certain issues are of concern to all cities, including social inequality, the precarious living situations of some of their inhabitants, and the current movement of refugees to and within Europe. Yet each of the seven cities is operating under different conditions and with a different set of resources and therefore treats these issues in its own way, both on the political level and in the form of interventions staged by activists and artists.

An exchange of the kind that took place within the framework of ACTOPOLIS is of central importance for Oberhausen and the entire Ruhr region. It has afforded them a glimpse of how other cities go about tackling similar problems and thus not only offered a new perspective on how our cities are structured but also encouraged the city and region to rethink and reshape these structures via joint, small-scale interventions in a transnational process. This is precisely what made working on the ACTOPOLIS project such a valuable experience.

We would like to express our sincere gratitude to the project leader Juliane Stegner and to Angelika Fitz and Martin Fritz for their close, intensive, and fruitful collaboration. A special word of thanks too to the curators, artists, activists, and urbanists who helped to shape ACTOPOLIS in such a variety of ways.

KATJA AßMANN, Artistic Director, Urbane Künste Ruhr
LUKAS CREPAZ, Managing Director, Kultur Ruhr GmbH

Vorwort
Urbane Künste Ruhr

Seit ihrer Gründung 2012 hat Urbane Künste Ruhr in den vielen Kommunen des Ruhrgebiets künstlerische Projekte realisiert. Die unterschiedlichen Strukturen, Voraussetzungen und zentralen Themen in den Städten des Ruhrgebiets erfordern nicht nur neue Herangehensweisen und Ideen – auch die Arbeit mit internationalen Partnern liefert immer wieder einen neuen Blick auf das (scheinbar) Altbekannte.

Trotz dieser zahlreichen Erfahrungen aus ganz unterschiedlichen Projektstrukturen und der internationalen Zusammenarbeit nimmt ACTOPOLIS im Programm von Urbane Künste Ruhr einen besonderen Stellenwert ein. An dem Projekt arbeiteten Künstler/innen, Kurator/innen, Aktivist/innen und Urbanist/innen aus sieben verschiedenen Städten – und sieben verschiedenen Ländern – über drei Jahre hinweg gemeinsam an den gleichen Fragestellungen. Über alle Phasen des Projekts hinweg fand ein intensiver Austausch zwischen den unterschiedlichen Akteur/innen statt. ACTOPOLIS ist in dieser Hinsicht nicht nur einzigartig für die Arbeit von Urbane Künste Ruhr, sondern ebenso richtungsweisend für andere internationale Kooperationen, die sich mit der Zukunft des urbanen Lebens beschäftigen.

Obwohl Mardin, Athen, Bukarest oder auch Oberhausen ganz eigene Probleme, Möglichkeiten und Chancen aufweisen, wurde deutlich, dass bestimmte Themen für alle Städte von Bedeutung sind: soziale Ungleichheiten, teilweise prekäre Lebenssituationen und die aktuelle Bewegung geflüchteter Menschen nach und in Europa. Und doch sind die Voraussetzungen und Formen des Umgangs mit diesen Themen in den sieben Städten unterschiedlich, auf politischer Ebene ebenso wie in Form aktivistischer und künstlerischer Interventionen.

Für Oberhausen und das gesamte Ruhrgebiet ist ein Austausch, wie er im Rahmen von ACTOPOLIS stattgefunden hat, von zentraler Bedeutung. Er vermittelt einen ganz anderen Umgang mit ähnlichen Problemstellungen und liefert nicht nur einen neuen Blick auf die Strukturen unserer Städte, sondern regt dazu an, diese in einem transnationalen Prozess gemeinsam zu überdenken und in gemeinsamen Interventionen in kleinem Maßstab neu zu gestalten. Genau dies machte die Arbeit an ACTOPOLIS zu einer so wertvollen Erfahrung.

Für die enge, intensive und fruchtbare Zusammenarbeit möchten wir uns sehr herzlich bedanken bei der Projektleiterin Juliane Stegner sowie bei Angelika Fitz und Martin Fritz. Unser besonderer Dank gilt den beteiligten Kurator/innen, Künstler/innen, Aktivist/innen und Urbanist/innen, die ACTOPOLIS so vielfältig gestaltet haben.

*KATJA AßMANN, Künstlerische Leiterin,
Urbane Künste Ruhr
LUKAS CREPAZ, Geschäftsführer, Kultur Ruhr GmbH*

Foreword
Artistic Directors

What you are reading here is an interim report. The international cooperation project ACTOPOLIS | The Art of Action is still far from completion. In many cities the participants are still busy analysing the results of their projects. New material will change the exhibition as it tours, and many a study may find itself being overtaken by events just as it was about to be published. A project like ACTOPOLIS, which is devoted to contemporary strategies for action in the city, is a work in progress—just like cities themselves, in fact. Even on comparatively recent photographs of urban scenes, it is enough to pick out details like car designs, technical equipment, and advertising posters to be able to date the image. Before and after the moment recorded in a photograph, urban development goes on in a dynamic process. And our awareness of the fact that recording something can also change it means that urban life is sometimes staged specifically with a future audience in mind, thus imbuing the material with even more layers of indeterminate complexity.

Apart from accepting the dynamic nature of urban development, another given for ACTOPOLIS from the very beginning was the fact that action in the city and commitment to change are the domain of those who have steadfastly spent many years addressing the built and social living environment in their city and have thus contributed—in ways that were often unappreciated—to its development. For ACTOPOLIS, two things followed from this: first, a concept designed to take into account that any action in urban space is a communal, communicative, and long-term process and that therefore the concept itself had to be process-oriented; and second, a decision to bring on board local curators, working autonomously for the most part, whose concepts provided the basis for the activities in the participating cities. Following the initiative of Juliane Stegner and a preliminary concept put forward by Angelika Fitz, the respective local branches of the Goethe-Institut invited Ana Dana Beroš in Zagreb, Ștefan Ghenciulescu and Raluca Voinea in Bucharest, Danijela Dugandžić in Sarajevo, Elpida Karaba and Glykeria Stathopoulou in Athens, Pelin Tan in Ankara and Mardin, and Boba Mirjana Stojadinović in Belgrade to undertake this assignment; they were joined by geheimagentur in Oberhausen, which was invited by the project partner Urbane Künste Ruhr.

Armed with a concept and the people to make it happen, the ACTOPOLIS Lab in Oberhausen kicked off the project in autumn 2015, combining local action with transnational dialogue. The Lab provided a forum for all the participants to present their project proposals to the others, with a view to providing a synopsis for joint discussion at an early point in the process. It quickly became apparent that ACTOPOLIS would encompass just as many shared aspects as specific differences. As an additional frame of reference the participants also took a critical look at the two organisations sponsoring the project: the Goethe-Institut and Urbane Künste Ruhr. The question arose as to whether an "asymmetry of power" was not already inherent in such a constellation, mirroring the kind of asymmetry that also characterises or even precipitates contemporary urban conflicts. It was to the credit of the participating actors that they were able to chart productive paths through this discursively and pragmatically challenging terrain. Many of the dialogues that began in the ACTOPOLIS Lab continued during the micro-residencies, a programme of fifty brief reciprocal visits by the participants that took place throughout the project.

The curators organised ACTOPOLIS using tried and tested teams that brought a variety of experience with them. The titles of their concepts underlined the interest of the participants in influencing their respective urban societies via specific action formats: thus the research- and analysis-oriented concepts in Ankara/Mardin emphasised the need for "urban commons" in times when the provision for many inhabitants of cities does not amount to anything more than an *Invisible Belonging*, as the project title in Zagreb aptly describes it. Both Oberhausen's project *Building a New City* and Bucharest's *Build Your Own City* as well as the *ACTOPOLIS Lab Sarajevo* focused on concrete interventions in the urban space and linked this approach with installation-based strategies. Under the title *Formally Informal*, the Belgrade projects took as their theme the significance of self-organisational processes, while the Temporary Academy of Art in Athens staged a series of *Soft Power Lectures* to explore the possibilities for destabilising dominant images and narratives (that frequently brand cities as "exotic") with counter-narratives.

Understanding for differences grew, making the shared aspects stand out more strongly. All over the world, urban societies face similar challenges or, to be more precise, all over the world *those* members of urban societies seeking to preserve the city as a place of community living and shared experience in times of economic exploitation and privatisation face similar challenges.

Despite all the local, historical, and political differences, in many places we can observe alongside the global movements towards concentration and standardisation, similarly motivated, locally anchored constellations of actors trying to counter intolerable political and economic circumstances with alternative ways of living and acting. Urban activists from Bucharest, philosophers from Athens, architects from Mardin, artists from Zagreb, curators from Sarajevo, and urban researchers from Oberhausen all concur on this point, and their activities are geared towards finding enclaves in which it is still possible to shape the city and urban society.

More than two years after the project began and sixteen months after the Lab in Oberhausen, we now have an extensive collection of material from all the participating cities. More than forty-five projects were realised between April and late autumn 2016. The activities they embraced yielded such a broad repertoire of options for action that it seemed to make sense to try to identify the topics and methods that the various approaches had in common. The result of this analysis—conducted together with the participants—led to the creation of an ACTOPOLIS Glossary, in which the projects' main topics and methods were summarised. These terms and their open-ended definitions have since served as a flexible template for communicating about the projects across all the different contexts. The process of examining the projects from an observer perspective has identified several key common aspects, which can only be summarised here. For more information, please refer to the detailed reflections in the curators' texts.

Action, Intervention, Installation

Within the large variety of methods—the Glossary lists the following: Claiming, Collaborating, Collecting, Making, Playing, Recording, Researching, Sharing, and Talking—many projects work with direct interventions in space. In Hastahana Park in Sarajevo and in Bucharest-South pavilions were built as a basis for actions; in Zagreb, a temporary staircase joined various levels of the old city; in Oberhausen a new infrastructure was even created, comprising a city centre, a garden house, and a museum, while in Belgrade podium discussions and wall newspapers were taken into outdoor urban space. Here the participants often used hybrid formats, inspired both by art in public space and the practice of sculpture and installation and by architecture, activism, and sociocultural action.

Dialogue, Exchange, Education

The ACTOPOLIS Glossary lists the following as central themes: Education, Heritage, Infrastructure, Labour, Migration, Nationalism, Segregation, Self-Organisation, Social Struggle, South, Urban Geography, and Urban Warfare. In every case, the action in the urban space is a collective action. Those responsible therefore often decided to realise their projects in formats involving dialogue and exchange. It also became clear that alongside public action, "internal" self-organisation and community building were preconditions for any actions in the city. This is explained not least by the need to relearn how to act in collective formats following the neoliberal, "entrepreneurial" individualisation of recent decades. A further precondition was experience with collective education and dialogue, in which the actors communicated about key current issues in their respective urban societies. *The Soft Power Lectures* in Athens, for example, used this approach in constantly shifting settings to discuss terms such as "Energy" or "South" and the exotic qualities with which they have been associated or to look at the role of international art projects in these processes.

Research, Analysis, Documentation

Intervention, planning, and change require fundamentals. This is why the ACTOPOLIS projects also included a series of stock-taking and research processes. These served either to preserve and visualise different forms of action, as the *Bgd Art* map or *The Other Map of (South) Bucharest* projects set out to do, or they were devoted to events in recent local history that are of significance for the situation today. Examples of this include *Expiration Date* and *Druga Scena* in Belgrade. Projects like the film *The Residual*, which documented places and activities along refugee routes, or the project *Donkey Work*, which explored municipal working conditions using as an example the donkeys used for collecting refuse in Mardin, were conceived as a direct means of "writing history in the present". Research and interventions often merged into one another, as for example in *Sarajevo Album* and *Sarajevo Cloud*—digital platforms for memories and new ideas for interventions in concrete urban spaces—or in the workshop seminars *Communities of Care* and *Seminar for Walkers* in Zagreb.

Alienation, Fiction, Art

For all the sense of reality (and pragmatism) required as key qualities of those participating in ACTOPOLIS, the projects also included some intensive work on performative exaggeration and theatrical alienation as devices for arriving at new views of the city. Both fictions and reported sightings of monsters in Oberhausen and in the Savamala district of Belgrade played a not insignificant role in these strategies; other key approaches were playful set-ups such as the role play *Be a Mayor for Ten Minutes*, which was centred on local politics in Bucharest, or fictitious historical sources made up to add colour to an artist's lecture on the connotations over time of the term "South" in the *Soft Power Lectures* series. Last but not least, ACTOPOLIS used the media of art to make urban experience tangible at a super-individual level. Audio installations and performances in Oberhausen, Zagreb, and Belgrade, book projects and exhibitions in Belgrade and Athens, and films and videos from all the participating cities may serve as examples of this.

The Goethe-Institut Athens and Urbane Künste Ruhr as well as all the branches of the Goethe-Institut involved in the participating regions provided a stable and at the same time flexible framework for this project. The team from Urbane Künste Ruhr and all the staff of the Goethe-Institut therefore deserve the utmost appreciation for their valuable input. Juliane Stegner as project director and a cherished dialogue partner providing staunch support through the various phases of the project. Finally we would like to extend our sincere gratitude to Natalia Sartori, who as project coordinator mastered an enormous challenge with discretion, clarity, and a high degree of personal commitment.

ACTOPOLIS started out with the following vision: "ACTOPOLIS is a call to action and to co-author the city—across disciplines, national boundaries, and cultural differences. The ACTOPOLIS Lab sets out to hone our view of current urban questions and test strategies for action". The exhibition and this catalogue serve to return this vision to the places where it was born with numerous examples of how it has been realised. In 2017, ACTOPOLIS will be shown in a total of eleven cities—Ankara, Athens, Belgrade, Bucharest, Istanbul, Izmir, Oberhausen, Sarajevo, Thessaloniki, Vienna, and Zagreb. If the exhibition succeeds in inspiring others to follow in its footsteps at each of the venues it tours, we will have achieved a great deal. The artistic directors would like to thank all the participants in all the cities—their work has helped to create these sustainable and effective courses of action.

KATJA AßMANN, ANGELIKA FITZ, MARTIN FRITZ

Vorwort
Künstlerische Leitung

Vor ihnen liegt ein Zwischenbericht. Das internationale Kooperationsprojekt ACTOPOLIS|Die Kunst zu handeln ist noch lange nicht abgeschlossen. In vielen Städten sind die Beteiligten noch mit den Ergebnissen ihrer Projekte befasst. Neue Materialien werden die Ausstellung an ihren jeweiligen Stationen verändern, und so manche Analyse wird im Moment ihrer Veröffentlichung von aktuellen Ereignissen in den Schatten gestellt werden. Wie die Stadt ist auch ein Projekt wie ACTOPOLIS, das sich dem zeitgenössischen Handeln in der Stadt widmet, ein work in progress. Selbst auf jüngeren Aufnahmen von Städten genügen Details wie Autodesigns, technische Geräte oder Werbeplakate, um ein Bild datieren zu können. Vor und nach der Aufzeichnung findet städtische Entwicklung in einem beweglichen Prozess statt. Die Tatsache, dass auch die Aufzeichnung das Geschehene verändert und urbanes Leben bisweilen eigens für die spätere Wiedergabe inszeniert wird, überzieht das Material mit weiteren Unschärfeschichten.

Neben der Akzeptanz dieser Beweglichkeit stand für ACTOPOLIS von Beginn an außer Frage, dass das Handeln in der Stadt und das Engagement für ihre Veränderung die Domäne jener Kräfte ist, die sich kontinuierlich, jahrelang und häufig unbedankt in den jeweiligen Städten mit der gebauten und sozialen Lebensumgebung beschäftigen und damit zu deren Weiterentwicklung beitragen. Daraus folgte für ACTOPOLIS zweierlei: erstens ein Konzept, dessen Prozessorientierung dem Umstand Rechnung trägt, dass es sich beim Handeln im urbanen Raum um gemeinschaftliche, kommunikative und längerfristige Prozesse handelt, und zweitens die Einbeziehung weitgehend autonom handelnder lokaler Kurator/innen, auf deren Konzepten die Aktivitäten in den beteiligten Städten beruhten. Nach einer Initiative von Juliane Stegner und einem ersten Konzept von Angelika Fitz haben auf Einladung der jeweiligen lokalen Goethe-Institute Ana Dana Beroš in Zagreb, Ştefan Ghenciulescu und Raluca Voinea in Bukarest, Danijela Dugandžić in Sarajevo, Elpida Karaba und Glykeria Stathopoulou in Athen, Pelin Tan in Ankara und Mardin, Boba Mirjana Stojadinović in Belgrad sowie auf Einladung des Projektpartners Urbane Künste Ruhr die geheimagentur in Oberhausen diese Aufgabe übernommen.

Auf diesen Säulen aufbauend, verknüpfte sich in weiterer Folge lokales Handeln mit einem transnationalen Dialog, an dessen Beginn das ACTOPOLIS Lab im Herbst 2015 in Oberhausen stand: In ihm präsentierten alle Beteiligten ihre Projektansätze, um diese bereits zu einem frühen Zeitpunkt in einer Zusammenschau zur Diskussion zu stellen. Schnell zeigte sich, dass es innerhalb von ACTOPOLIS ebenso sehr um Gemeinsamkeiten wie um spezifische Unterschiede geht. Als zusätzlicher Bezugsrahmen wurde die Trägerschaft des Projekts durch das Goethe-Institut und Urbane Künste Ruhr einer kritischen Betrachtung unterzogen. Dabei stellte sich die Frage, ob solchen Konstellationen nicht bereits ein Teil jener „Machtasymmetrie" eingeschrieben ist, die auch die urbanen Auseinandersetzungen der Gegenwart kennzeichnet, ja hervorruft. Es war das Verdienst der Akteur/innen, produktive Pfade durch dieses diskursiv und pragmatisch herausfordernde Gelände zu legen. Weitergeführt wurden viele dieser Dialoge im Rahmen der MicroResidencies, einem projektweiten Besuchsprogramm, in dessen Rahmen über 50 wechselseitige Kurzbesuche von Projektbeteiligten erfolgten.

Die Kurator/innen gestalteten ACTOPOLIS unter Einbeziehung vielfältig erprobter Teams. Die Titel ihrer Konzepte unterstreichen das Interesse der Beteiligten, durch konkrete Aktionsformate Einfluss auf die jeweiligen Stadtgesellschaften nehmen zu wollen: So betonten die recherche- und analyseorientierten Konzepte in Ankara und Mardin die Notwendigkeit von Urban Commons in Zeiten, in denen für viele Menschen in Städten nicht mehr als ein Invisible Belonging vorgesehen ist, wie es der Projekttitel in Zagreb zutreffend beschreibt. Sowohl Building a New City in Oberhausen wie auch

*Build Your Own City in Bukarest
und das ACTOPOLIS Lab Sarajevo
stellten konkrete Interventionen im
Stadtraum in den Vordergrund und
verknüpften diesen Ansatz mit instal-
lativen Strategien. Die Projekte in
Belgrad thematisierten unter dem Titel
Formally Informal die Bedeutung
von Selbstorganisationsprozessen,
während die Temporary Academy
of Art in Athen im Rahmen der Soft
Power Lectures Möglichkeiten auslo-
tete, dominante (und häufig exotisieren-
de) Bilder und Narrative durch gegen-
läufige Erzählungen zu destabilisieren.*

*Das Verständnis für die Unter-
schiede wuchs und gerade deshalb
traten die Gemeinsamkeiten stärker
hervor. Weltweit stehen Stadtgesellschaften vor ähnlichen Herausforderungen. Genauer gesagt, stehen weltweit jene Mitglieder von Stadtgesellschaften vor ähnlichen Herausforderungen, denen es darum geht, die Stadt
in Zeiten ihrer ökonomischen Verwer-
tung und Privatisierung als Ort des
gemeinsamen Lebens und Erlebens zu
erhalten. Trotz aller lokaler, historischer
oder politischer Unterschiede ist zu
beobachten, dass sich an vielen Orten
neben den globalen Konzentrations-
und Vereinheitlichungsbewegungen
ähnlich motivierte, lokal verankerte
Akteurskonstellationen entwickeln,
die versuchen, den politischen und
ökonomischen Zumutungen alternative Lebens- und Handlungsformen
entgegenzusetzen. In diesem Punkt
treffen sich urbane Aktivist/innen aus
Bukarest, Philosoph/innen aus Athen,
Architekt/innen aus Mardin, Künstler/
innen aus Zagreb, Kurator/innen aus
Sarajevo und Stadtforscher/innen
aus Oberhausen. Ihr Handeln gilt den
Möglichkeitsräumen zur Gestaltung
von Stadt und Gesellschaft.*

*Mehr als zwei Jahre nach Projekt-
beginn und 16 Monate nach dem „Lab"*

*in Oberhausen liegt nun aus allen betei-
ligten Städten reichhaltiges Material vor.
Vom April bis in den Spätherbst 2016
wurden mehr als 45 Projekte realisiert.
Die Aktivitäten zeigten dabei ein so
reichhaltiges Repertoire an Handlungsoptionen, dass es naheliegend war, die
Ansätze auf gemeinsame Themen und
Methoden zu befragen. Das Ergebnis
dieser – gemeinsam mit den Beteiligten
vorgenommenen – Analyse mündete
im ACTOPOLIS Glossary, in dem die
grundlegenden Themen und Methoden
der Projekte zusammengefasst wurden.
Diese Begriffe und ihre offenen Defi-
nitionen dienen seither als flexibles,
kontextübergreifendes Raster für die
Vermittlung der Projekte. Dabei werden
in der beobachtenden Auseinandersetzung mit den Projekten einige zentrale
Gemeinsamkeiten deutlich, die hier nur
summarisch zusammengefasst werden
können. Auf die ausführlicheren Reflexionen in den Texten der Kurator/innen
sei verwiesen.*

Aktion, Intervention, Installation

*Innerhalb der Vielfalt der Methoden –
das Glossary nennt: Claiming, Collaborating, Collecting, Making, Playing,
Recording, Researching, Sharing und
Talking – arbeiteten viele Vorhaben
mit dem direkten räumlichen Eingriff.
Im Hastahana-Park in Sarajevo und
im Bukarester Süden wurden Pavillons
als Aktionsbasis errichtet; eine temporäre Treppe verschränkte verschiedene
Altstadtebenen in Zagreb; in Oberhausen entstand gar eine neue Infrastruktur
mit Stadtzentrum, Gartenhaus und
Museum, während in Belgrad Podiums-
diskussionen und Wandzeitungen in
den städtischen Außenraum getragen
wurden. Die Beteiligten bedienten sich
dabei häufig hybrider Formate, die sich
aus Kunst im öffentlichen Raum und*

skulptural-installativer Praxis ebenso speisten wie aus Architektur, Aktivismus und soziokulturellem Handeln.

Dialog, Austausch, Bildung

Als zentrale Themen vermerkt das ACTOPOLIS Glossary: Education, Heritage, Infrastructure, Labor, Migration, Nationalism, Segregation, Self-Organisation, Social Struggle, South, Urban Geography und Urban Warfare. Für alle Themen gilt, dass das Handeln im urbanen Raum ein gemeinsames Handeln ist. Dementsprechend häufig entschieden sich die Projektverantwortlichen dafür, ihre Vorhaben in Dialog- und Austauschformaten umzusetzen. Dabei wurde offenbar, dass neben der öffentlichen Aktion auch die „interne" Selbstorganisation und Gemeinschaftsbildung zu den Voraussetzungen des Handelns in der Stadt gehört. Dies erklärt sich nicht zuletzt aus der Notwendigkeit, im Anschluss an die neoliberal „unternehmerische" Individualisierung der letzten Jahrzehnte nun wieder kollektive Formate erlernen zu müssen. Eine weitere Voraussetzung stellten gemeinsame Bildungs- und Dialogerfahrungen dar, in denen sich die Akteur/innen über zentrale Gegenwartsfragen der jeweiligen Stadtgesellschaft verständigten. Diesen Ansatz verfolgten etwa die Soft Power Lectures in Athen, in denen – an jeweils wechselnden Schauplätzen – Begriffsbildungen wie „Energie" oder „Süden" und die damit einhergehenden Exotisierungen ebenso verhandelt wurden wie die Rolle internationaler Kunstprojekte in diesen Prozessen.

Recherche, Analyse, Dokumentation

Intervention, Planung und Veränderung benötigen Grundlagen, weswegen innerhalb der ACTOPOLIS-Projekte auch eine Reihe von Bestandsaufnahmen und Recherchen vorgenommen wurde. Diese dienten entweder der Sicherung und Sichtbarmachung von Aktionsformen, wie sie etwa die Bgd Art Karte oder das Projekt The Other Map of (South) Bucharest in Angriff nahmen, oder sie widmeten sich – wie Expiration Date und Druga Scena in Belgrad – Geschehnissen der jüngeren lokalen Geschichte, die für die heutige Situation von Bedeutung sind. Eine Form von unmittelbarer Gegenwartsgeschichtsschreibung unternahmen Projekte wie der Film The Residual, der Orte und Aktivitäten entlang von Fluchtrouten dokumentierte, oder das Projekt Donkey Work, in dem kommunale Arbeitsverhältnisse am Beispiel von den in Mardin für die Stadtreinigung eingesetzten Eseln thematisiert wurden. Recherche und Intervention gingen dabei häufig ineinander über, so etwa im Rahmen von Sarajevo Album und Sarajevo Cloud – digitalen Plattformen für Erinnerungen und neue Ideen für Eingriffe in konkrete städtische Räume – oder bei den Workshop-Seminaren Communities of Care und Seminar for Walkers in Zagreb.

Verfremdung, Fiktion, Kunst

So sehr Realitätssinn (und auch Pragmatik) zu den zentralen Qualitäten der an ACTOPOLIS Beteiligten zählen, so intensiv wurde innerhalb der Projekte daran gearbeitet, auch mit den Mitteln performativer Überhöhung und theatraler Verfremdung zu neuen Blicken auf die Stadt beizutragen. Eine nicht unwesentliche Rolle für diese Strategien spielen Fiktionen wie die Berichte von Monstern, die sowohl in Oberhausen wie auch im Belgrader Stadtteil Savamala gesichtet wurden; ebenso entscheidend sind spielerische Anordnungen wie das kommunalpolitische Rollenspiel Be a Mayor for Ten Minutes in Bukarest oder erfundene historische Quellen, mit denen im Rahmen der Soft Power Lectures ein künstlerischer Vortrag zur Begriffsgeschichte des „Südens" untermauert wurde. Nicht zuletzt wurde im Rahmen von ACTOPOLIS mit den Mitteln der Kunst daran gearbeitet, Stadterfahrung überindividuell erfahrbar zu machen. Als Beispiele dafür können Audioinstallationen und Performances in Oberhausen, Zagreb und Belgrad, Buchprojekte und Ausstellungen in Belgrad und Athen sowie Filme und Videos aus allen beteiligten Städten dienen.

Das Goethe-Institut Athen und Urbane Künste Ruhr sowie alle beteiligten Goethe-Institute in der Region schufen für diese Vorhaben einen stabilen und gleichzeitig flexiblen Rahmen. Dem Team von Urbane Künste Ruhr und allen Mitarbeiter/innen der Goethe-Institute gebührt hohe Anerkennung für ihre wertvollen Beiträge. Juliane Stegner hat uns als Projektleiterin und wertvolle Dialogpartnerin vertrauensvoll über die verschiedenen Phasen begleitet. Abschließend sei herzlich Natalia Sartori gedankt, die als Projektkoordinatorin eine enorme Herausforderung mit Umsicht, Klarheit und hohem persönlichen Einsatz gemeistert hat.

Am Beginn der Arbeit an ACTOPOLIS stand folgender Anspruch: „ACTOPOLIS ist ein Aufruf zum Handeln und Mitgestalten der Stadt – über Disziplinen, Landesgrenzen und kulturelle Unterschiede hinweg. Das ACTOPOLIS Lab schärft den Blick auf aktuelle urbane Fragestellungen und testet Handlungsstrategien." Die Ausstellung und der vorliegende Katalog dienen nunmehr dazu, diesen Anspruch mit zahlreichen Beispielen an die Orte ihres Entstehens zurückzubringen. Im Jahr 2017 wird ACTOPOLIS in insgesamt elf Städten – Ankara, Athen, Belgrad, Bukarest, Istanbul, Izmir, Oberhausen, Sarajevo, Thessaloniki, Wien und Zagreb – zu sehen sein. Wenn es der Ausstellung gelingt, an jeder ihrer Stationen Nachahmer/innen zu motivieren, wäre viel erreicht. Der Dank der künstlerischen Leitung gilt allen Beteiligten in allen Städten, deren Arbeit diese nachhaltig wirksamen Handlungsoptionen geschaffen haben.

KATJA AßMANN, ANGELIKA FITZ, MARTIN FRITZ

The ACTOPOLIS Lab in Oberhausen kicked off the project in autumn 2015. The Lab provided a forum for all the participants to present their project proposals to one another, with a view to providing a synopsis for joint discussion at an early point in the process. The work-in-progress was documented in drawings by María García.

Am Beginn stand das ACTOPOLIS Lab im Herbst 2015 in Oberhausen: In ihm präsentierten alle Beteiligten ihre Projektansätze, um diese bereits zu einem frühen Zeitpunkt in einer Zusammenschau zur Diskussion zu stellen. Die Arbeitsprozesse wurden von der Zeichnerin María García dokumentiert.

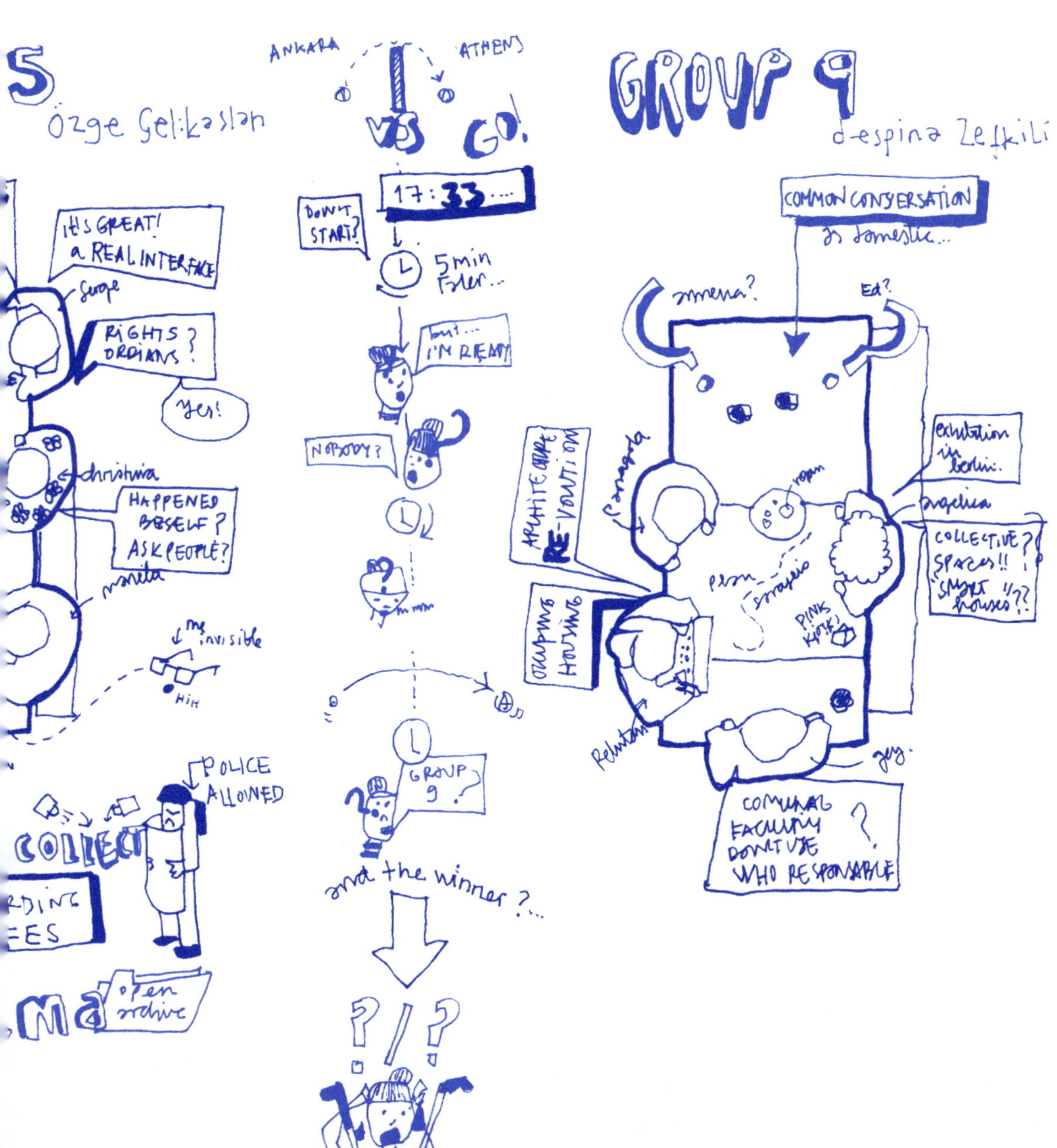

doing an EXPERIMENT
ROUND RUN RUN ... 2 tables!
J sound
PORTABLE
ANKARA   ATHENS
VS   GO!
GROUP 9
Özge Celikaslan
despina zefkili
COMMON CONVERSATION
as domestic...
DON'T START?
17:33...
5min later...
but... I'M READY
NOBODY?
It's GREAT! a REAL INTERFACE
Surge
RIGHTS? ORDINS?
Yes!
christina
HAPPENED BESELF? ASK PEOPLE?
marita
ms invisible
Him
POLICE ALLOWED
COLLECT
RDING EES
open archive
Ma
GROUP 9?
and the winner?...
?/?
mrena?
Ed?
exhibition in berlin.
angelica
COLLECTIVE? SPACES!! SMART houses!/??
rajen
ARCHITECTURE RE-VOLUTION
OCCUPING HAUSING
PINK KIOK
Relentam
jey.
COMUNAL FACILITY DON'T USE WHO RESPONSABLE

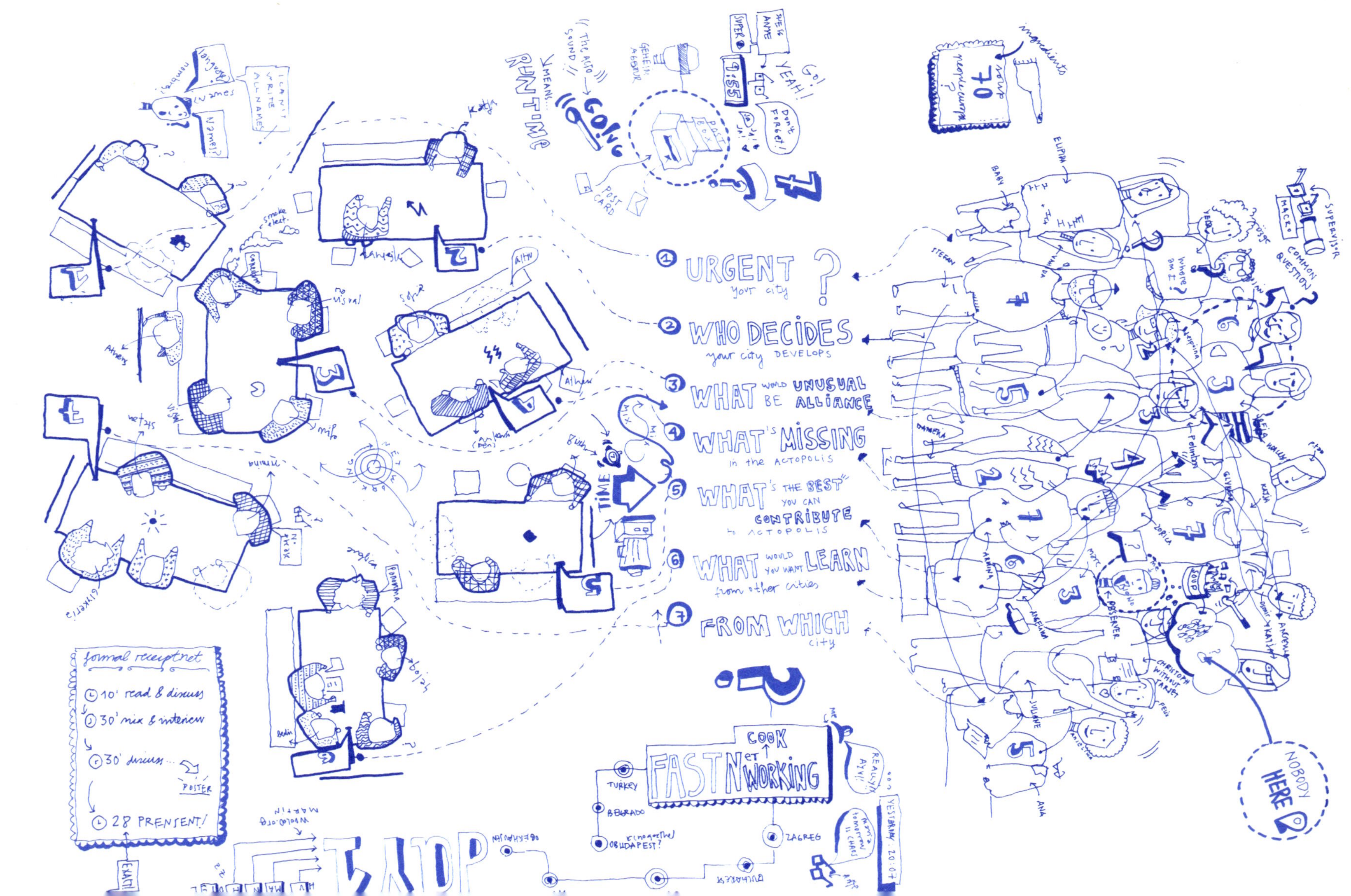

1 URGENT ? your city
2 WHO DECIDES your city DEVELOPS
3 WHAT WOULD UNUSUAL BE ALLIANCE
4 WHAT'S MISSING in the ACTOPOLIS
5 WHAT'S THE BEST you can CONTRIBUTE to ACTOPOLIS
6 WHAT WOULD YOU WANT LEARN from other cities
7 FROM WHICH city
RUNTIME
MEANS...
The ACTO SOUND!!
GO!NG
GEHEIM AGENTUR
POST BOX
POST CARD
SUPER
SHE IS ANYE
9:55
GO! YEAH!
Don't FORGET!
ingredients
soup
70
people europa?
I CAN'T WRITE ALL NAMES
Names!?
Name!?
smoke elect.
Athens
TIME
MIX
journal receptnet
10' read & discuss
30' mix & interview
30' discuss
POSTER
28 PRESENT!
FASTNETWORKING
COOK
TURKEY
BELGRADO
OBUDAPEST?
ZAGREG
YESTERDAY. 20:07
REALLY AYV!!
tomorrow is CHAOS
STOP
MARTIN
Wrodo.org
EXACT
COMMON QUESTION
SUPERVISOR
MACRO
Where am I?
BABY
ELIPIDA
STEFAN
OBSERVER
CHRISTOPH WITHOUT PLANET
JULIANE
ANA
NOBODY HERE
SOUP

TACTIC
sarajevo
presents...
daniela dugandžic
feminist activist
IMAGINE
INVISIBLE
EMOTIONAL
urban mobility
CITYLOGY
urban governance
uses Public Space
development
URBAN COMMONS
memory
Ways to RELATE
feelings
stories
OPEN CALL
"nobody ask who sarajevo"
suggestions
Components
urban TERMINOLOGY
ONLINE Maps
collective WALKS
city
city
"images city"
BUILD COMMONS
GOAL!
THE RIGHT OF THE CITY
professionals
citizens
NEW local TERMINOLOGY
Sharing local NEWS!
simple modification
prACTica
GROUP 3
presents
the informal table & peanuts
we missed one person two
MUTE
Where are we?
coffee!
TABLE
JUST 3 PERSON
THE CLOUD
ASMIR MUTEVELIC by
SARAJEVO
no participation
opinions
dispersion
conversation instalation
PUBLIC INTEREST
GOAL!
cloud with legs
SYMBOL CONNECTIVITY
TRAVEL
collection OPINIONS
HOW design
ONE DIRECTION NOT SO MUCH ASK....
INFRASTRUCTUR VS CONTENT
you've to OFFER
WHO DECIDES TOPICS
IT'S A PLATFORM?
reasons being there
Control...?
FORM DEFINE ALREADY
VINCENTO
CHRISTOPH NOTES
live more 2nd cities?!
description sarajevo
WHO DECIDES
HOW MANY PEOPLE
christoph
Felix
gummi
DEFENSE BARRIER
...
DISCUSSION
ASMIR
CHAOS
the peanuts
ideas
SHARING TABLES
HOW GET PEOPLE there
TO MOVE OVER THE PROBLEM
PING PONG
me
WHY NOT COMMERCIAL?
citizen
computer
Marc
HOW CONNECT
I'm no sure the materiality
MANY WORDS!!
I've doubts
FOR WHOM HOW
GARANTIE QUANTY ANSWER
What's meaning?
BLA BLA BLA
MAIN TRAFFIC download illegal?
EXPANSIVE set up and down
start point
max city
people are serious
WHAT'S DEAL working with cooperation
HOW DECIDE site
connect SPONSOR telefon COMPANIES
DECIDE
WHOW
DIRECTION
CONNECTIONS

TACTIC
Athens
urator
ELPIDA KARABA
POLITICAL THEORY
DOCUMENTARY
ACTIVIST
?
HOW ART related SITUATION
Regimen CRYSIS CRASH!
DE-ORGANISATION
KNOWLEDGE EDUCATION
EXPERIMENTAL
ART education
transformation
NEW MODELS
NO
RE-THINKING
Zel volution
SELF ORGANISATED PROJECT
power
new vocabulary
create dynamics
EXCHANGE
NEED SPACE
SOURCES MATERIAL KNOWLEDGE
collect material
city
migration
what means
SYMPOSIUM
PERFORMANCE LECTURE
PRACTICA
GROUP 1
by
Sofia Dona
ATHENS building
stones
JOURNALIST ARQUITECTURE
BUILD SITUATION
MIGRATION
School cooking
VISA
POLITICAL RELIGION
apotothical church
SERBIA
NIGERIA
correct form
Exhive an Ending!!
BOARDING HOUSE
RENT
migrants
SAT/SUM
DAVOFF
IN/OUT
other country labours
work
vacation
CREATE COMMONS SPACES
LINKS in 3
ACADAMY + SPACES
sonka
Performative lectures
esther
Sofia
apartament TRY CONNECTION with ARCHITECT
Karolina
women table
WITH ACADEMY? how materialy ideas?
FORMAL VS INFORMAL
DIFERENT ALADAMY
informal academy?
define ACADEMY?
TOOL KIT OPEN SOURCE
Karolina with CONNECTION
HOW TURN IT PEDAGRICAL FORM?
drawings? MAPS?
stories + maps

PERFECT ACTOPOLIS
day 2
29.9. NOBODY HAS
why?
instructions
5' FIND your team
5' CHOSE a delegate
60' CREATE "perfect ACTOPOLIS"
4' PRESENT "your PAP"
29.9
webs?
RAINER
We're part of struggle!
economic cities "citismarketing"
NO STAR
1
What about 2014?
2
?
MANY UMLAUT
COMMUNITY AREA/CITY?
collective FARM!
conversation table
6
smoke
CITIES HAS MONSTER
monster table
3
urban transport
LIKE HERE!
OBERHAUSEN NEEDS A MONSTER
GASOMONSTER!!
what's political function
MONUMENT NEIGHBORHOOD ≠ NATIONAL
BABEL oo BUBBLETOWER
FIGHTS FROM EUROPE
virtual + real?
DON'T TOUCH!
CONFLICT
7
mmm... I ... I ... have no answer...
public origami
geheim
static projects puddles...
5
LEVELS?
Personalisation menu
SHOULD ANALISE THESE POINTS
physical meeting political
BUS train station
FUN
Julian
JA ja
4
comic
DAY 1 myths
over MULTIPLE LEVELS
conflict
OK!!!
TIME
ACT
KAKATHON
SUPER PERFORMANCE
Katja
Find other QUESTIONS
MINIMUM LEVEL COLLECTIVITY
COLLECTIVE BANK?
LIMITS POTENTIAL COLLECTIVE
collective FARM
collectivity has LIMITATION
Angelika
BUBBLETOWER BABEL
common places cities
kiosk
ey! it's my project!
ANTI-monument
What's mean TRANSITIONAL?
MAX. PUBLIC EXPOSURE
multi le ve ls
we didn't design public space
impossible with site
LOCAL LEVEL
FOLLOW einfach!
WITHOUT ABER NO WORKING
WE NEED MORE TIME
Katja
Time bank - APP
Refugees
EXCHANGE SOCIAL CULTURAL
HUMANHOTEL
interesting PUBLIC SPACES PHYSICALLY VIRTUAL
I think it's the perfect project
Angelika
1. The TransNational
2. Urgent PROBLEM
ALLIANCE
3. MAXIMUM
4. direct INVOLVMENT the critical distance
5. max PUBLIC exposure
6. max COLLECTIVE WORK
7. MAX capacity FRANCHISING
confusion
CURATOR VS ARTISTS
ATTA agency travel
ACTOBUS
NEXT STATION
More time together
ACTO. NO LIKE A CARAVAN PROJECT
conditions of work?
I don't feel connected with nobody
complicated question & complicated discussion
many factors
FREE Seats
workshops on BUS + Performances
NEW COLLECTIVE FARM + BUS COLL.
WE SHOULD DO IT!!
Katja
Lars

ANK
ARA
MAR
DIN

Urban Commons:
Surplus of Collective Action

"What is our commons and how should it be renewed, sustained, enlarged, drawn down, and/or extended to others?"

J. K. GIBSON-GRAHAM

"The creation of instituting society, as instituted society, is each time a common world (*kosmos koinos*): the positing of individuals, of their types, relations and activities; but also the positing of things, their types, relations and signification—all of which are caught up each time in receptacles and frames of reference instituted as common, which make them exist together."

CORNELIUS CASTORIADIS

In the wake of the Gezi Park resistance, there has been a profound transformation in the creation of modalities—especially within the neighbouring territories and cities—within the context of "commons" practices. The key terms that we defined under commons in connection with the ACTOPOLIS project are "state of emergency/policy", "surplus/labour", "refugees/borders", and "solidarity/ modalities". Spatial practices in conflicted urban spaces have prompted society to invent a new collective dictionary not only to cater to the constrained environment of the recent sociopolitical and economic crisis but also to rebuild a collective consciousness that can relate to our communal coexistence.

Commons is not what we own or share or produce in terms of property but rather the building of collective social relations that are closely connected to everyday life. According to Massimo De Angelis, "commons are a means of establishing a new political discourse that builds on and helps to articulate the many existing, often minor struggles and recognizes their power to overcome capitalist society" ("On the Commons", *e-flux journal* 17, June 2010). He defines three notions (pooled resources, community, and communing), not simply as a means to explain the commons in terms of the resources that we share but also to delineate a way of commoning—that is, a social process of "being common": the way in which resources are pooled and made available to a group of individuals, who then build or rediscover a sense of community. This is also about how solidarity movements should act in solidarity with other movements. The concept of commons holds a sensitive position within any given community or public, especially in contested territories or cities subject to the threat of a neoliberal destruction of their built environment. Negotiation and the resolution of conflicting values are key to such commoning practices. As Stavros Stavrides argues, more than the act or fact of sharing, it is the existence of a common ground for negotiation that is most important. Conceptualising commons with reference to the public does not focus so much on similarities or commonalities but on exploring the differences between people on a purposefully instituted common ground. We need to establish grounds for negotiation rather than grounds for affirming that which is shared.

The project sets out to look at the trans-local level of practices in Mardin, Ankara, and other nearby cities, focusing on spatial practices and social issues. Artist Ahmet Öğüt is working on the demolished neighbourhood of Sur in the historical city of Diyarbakır, which is also his home town. Sur was completely destroyed by urban warfare this year—not only was its historical memory obliterated but its indigent population of Kurdish residents was also forced to migrate elsewhere. As a student of the art academy, Öğüt worked on constructing a model of the Sur neighbourhood in a theme park project for the Istanbul municipality, which led him to combine the memories of a demolished social environment with the site of a recently created tabula rasa. His video work *Foucault's Typewriter* is an attempt to show representations of this demolished neighbourhood.

In his work *Urban Defenders*, Seçkin Aydın seeks to create narratives and track patterns of migration in the Sur neighbourhood: he conducted several ethnographic interviews with different generations in which they explored their sense of belonging to this neighbourhood during and after the state of curfew. In his project *Territorial Islands* Yelta Köm brings his architectural background to bear in focusing on spatial interventions and a security-related analysis of the recent urban warfare and curfews in Turkey. As a historical city, Mardin, which is a tourist attraction and a frequent subject of negotiation with UNESCO, also has a conflicted public space including mixed ethnic communities. With its Kurdish mayors under arrest, the city faces a political conflict that affects everyday life, which is characterised by a high degree of surveillance and control. Mardin's ambiguous identity presents different cases for research and possible artistic intervention.

Önder Özengi questions the distinction between human labour and animal labour by following the donkeys that officially work for the municipality collecting rubbish. In his ethnographic video research project *Donkey Work* Özengi conducts a series of interviews with local mayors, municipality workers, and citizens. In *Commanding Heights* Sevgi Ortaç takes ancient Mardin Castle as her material, a site for her core forensic research, which aims to reveal surveillance strategies and the problematisation of heritage. The work questions the archaeological artefact as speculative forensic material.

Turkey is confronted with a huge number of refugees as an outcome of the war in Syria. Mardin, which is located thirty minutes from the Syrian border, receives a large number of refugees and is surrounded by refugee camps. In *Spaces of Exodus*, architect Eda Soyal maps the domestic and everyday life of refugees inside the city and analyses how public space is reformed. Finally, *The Residual*— a research project conducted by the Artıkişler Collective (Alper Şen, Özge Çelikaslan, and Pelin Tan)—tracks and follows refugees on their journey from Syria and Iraq to Europe via Turkey and Greece in order to understand the refugees' sense of solidarity and survival strategies and to use video research and written records to examine how urban spaces are affected and public space is co-created. The residual videograms follow and reveal the paths of human movement under the shadow of the negotiations between the EU and Turkey, in which migrants and refugees are seen as residuals by hegemonic powers.

Political pressure, censorship, geopolitical conflict, insecurity, and social fear are acute problems in Turkey's contemporary society and urban spaces. As a result, since its inception, ACTOPOLIS has experienced some unexpected realities, which are also reflected in the research and projects undertaken by the artists. Seçkin Aydın was detained while

conducting his research; Önder Özengi
and Sevgi Ortaç witnessed the arrest
of the Mardin mayor; Eda Soyal and
Pelin Tan continued with their research
and pedagogical activities inside the war
zone operating under a state of emergency. Ankara suffered bomb attacks
that endangered participants. One workshop in Mardin was cancelled because
of security risks. The trans-local conditions within ACTOPOLIS meant that
members were able to continue the discourse and share experiences in order
to maintain solidarity and the belief
that artistic research/action can make
a difference in our society.

PELIN TAN

Urbane Gemeingüter: ein Überschuss an kollektivem Handeln

*„Was sind unsere Gemeingüter und wie
sollen sie erneuert, erhalten, vermehrt,
in Anspruch genommen und/oder auf
andere ausgedehnt werden?"*

J.K. GIBSON-GRAHAM

*„Die Schöpfung der instituierenden
Gesellschaft – die instituierte Gesellschaft – ist jeweils die Schaffung einer
gemeinsamen Welt (kosmos koinos):
Setzung von Individuen und deren
Typen, Beziehungen und Tätigkeiten;
aber auch Setzung von Dingen, von
deren Typen, Beziehungen und Bedeutungen. Dinge wie Individuen werden
dabei in Behältern und Bezugs-
systemen als gemeinsame instituiert,
die sie erst zusammen sein lassen."*

CORNELIUS CASTORIADIS

*Nach den Protesten im Gezi Park
hat es im Zusammenhang mit Praktiken
der Gemeingüter besonders in den
benachbarten Gebieten und Städten tief
greifende Veränderungen der Gestal-
tungsmodalitäten gegeben. Die Schlüs-
selbegriffe, die wir im Zusammenhang mit dem ACTOPOLIS-Projekt
unter der Rubrik Gemeingüter geprägt
haben, sind „Ausnahmezustand/Politik",
„Überschuss/Arbeit", „Geflüchtete/
Grenzen" und „Solidarität/Modalitäten".
Räumliche Praktiken in konfliktbelade-
nen urbanen Räumen waren Anlass für
die Gesellschaft, ein neues kollektives
Vokabular zu erfinden, das nicht nur
auf das begrenzte Umfeld der jüngsten
soziopolitischen und ökonomischen
Krise eingeht, sondern auch ein kollektives Bewusstsein erneuern soll, welches
einen Bezug zu unserem kommunalen
Zusammenleben herstellt.*

*Commons oder Gemeingüter
sind nicht das, was wir in Form von
Eigentum besitzen, teilen oder produzieren, sondern vielmehr der Aufbau
kollektiver sozialer Beziehungen, die
eng mit dem täglichen Leben verknüpft
sind. Massimo de Angelis zufolge
sind „Commons ein Mittel zur Etablie-
rung eines neuen politischen Diskurses,
der an die vielen bestehenden, oft
kleinen Kämpfe anknüpft, diese artiku-
liert und ihre Bedeutung zur Überwindung der kapitalistischen Gesellschaft
anerkennt." („On the Commons",
e-flux journal 17, Juni 2010) Er prägt
drei Begriffe (Ressourcenbündelung,
Gemeinschaft und In-Beziehung-Treten),
die Gemeingüter nicht nur hinsichtlich
der von uns geteilten Ressourcen
definieren, sondern auch eine Form
des commoning beschreiben, eines
gesellschaftlichen Prozesses des
„Gemeinsam-Seins". Er meint die Art
und Weise, wie Ressourcen gebündelt
und einer Gruppe von Individuen
zugänglich gemacht werden, die daraus*

ein Gemeinschaftsgefühl ableitet oder wiederentdeckt. Hierbei geht es auch darum, wie Solidaritätsbewegungen in Solidarität mit anderen Bewegungen agieren sollten. Das Konzept der Gemeingüter nimmt in jeder Gemeinschaft oder Öffentlichkeit eine heikle Position ein, besonders in umstrittenen Gebieten oder Städten, in denen der Neoliberalismus die gebaute Umwelt zu zerstören droht. Verhandlung und Annäherung widerstreitender Werte sind für solche gemeinschaftlichen Praktiken des commoning essentiell. So argumentiert Stavros Stavrides, dass eine gemeinsame Verhandlungsgrundlage wichtiger sei als der Akt oder die Tatsache des Teilens. Die Konzeptualisierung von Gemeingütern in Bezug auf die Öffentlichkeit stellt weniger die Ähnlichkeiten oder Gemeinsamkeiten in den Mittelpunkt als vielmehr die Unterschiede zwischen Menschen auf einer eigens hierfür geschaffenen gemeinsamen Basis. Wir müssen eher Verhandlungsgrundlagen schaffen als Grundlagen, die Gemeinsamkeiten bestätigen.

Das Projekt befasst sich mit der translokalen Ebene von Praktiken in Mardin, Ankara und anderen nahe gelegenen Städten und nimmt dabei räumliche Praktiken und gesellschaftliche Aspekte in den Blick. Der Künstler Ahmet Öğüt beschäftigt sich mit dem zerstörten Sur-Viertel in der historischen Altstadt von Diyarbakır, seiner Heimatstadt. Sur ist dieses Jahr durch Straßenkämpfe vollkommen zerstört worden; dabei wurde nicht nur das historische Gedächtnis ausgelöscht, sondern auch die notleidende kurdische Bevölkerung zur Abwanderung gezwungen. Als Student an der Kunstakademie arbeitete Öğüt im Rahmen eines Themenparkprojekts der Stadt Istanbul an einem Modell des Sur-Viertels, wobei er die Erinnerung an ein zerstörtes soziales Umfeld mit dem Ort verknüpfte,

an dem gerade Tabula rasa gemacht wurde. Seine Videoarbeit Foucault's Typewriter *ist der Versuch, dieses zerstörte Viertel darzustellen.*

In seiner Arbeit Urban Defenders *hält Seçkin Aydın Narrative und Spuren der Migration im Sur-Viertel fest: Er führt ethnografische Interviews mit Vertretern unterschiedlicher Generationen, in denen er die Teilnehmer zu ihrem Gefühl der Zugehörigkeit zu diesem Viertel während und nach der verhängten Ausgangssperre befragt. In dem Projekt* Territorial Islands *fokussiert sich Yelta Köm auf räumliche Interventionen und eine Analyse der Sicherheitsfragen im Zusammenhang mit den jüngsten Straßenkämpfen und Ausgangssperren in der Türkei und bringt so seinen Hintergrund als Architekt ein. Als historische Stadt ist Mardin nicht nur eine Touristenattraktion und wiederkehrendes Verhandlungsthema der UNESCO, sondern auch ein von Widersprüchen und gemischten ethnischen Gruppen geprägter öffentlicher Raum. Da die kurdischen Bürgermeister in Haft sind, sieht sich die Stadt mit politischen Konflikten konfrontiert, die das alltägliche Leben beeinträchtigen und ein hohes Maß an Überwachung und Kontrolle mit sich bringen. Mardins schwer fassbare Identität lässt Situationen entstehen, die sich für Untersuchungen und mögliche künstlerische Interventionen anbieten.*

Önder Özengi folgt den Eseln, die für die städtische Müllabfuhr im Einsatz sind, und hinterfragt so die Unterscheidung zwischen der von Menschen bzw. Tieren geleisteten Arbeit. In seiner ethnografischen Videorecherche Donkey Work *führt Özengi eine Reihe von Interviews mit Bürgermeistern, Mitarbeitern der Stadtverwaltung und Bürgern. In* Commanding Heights *dient die Burg von Mardin der Künstlerin Sevgi Ortaçals als Material für ihre forensische Studie,*

die auf die Enthüllung von Überwachungsstrategien und die Problematisierung von Kulturerbe abzielt. Die Arbeit stellt das archäologische Artefakt als spekulatives forensisches Material infrage.

Die Türkei sieht sich mit einer ungeheuren Zahl von Geflüchteten aus den Kriegsgebieten in Syrien konfrontiert. Mardin, nur 30 Minuten von der syrischen Grenze entfernt, nimmt eine große Zahl von Flüchtlingen auf und ist von Flüchtlingslagern umgeben. In Spaces of Exodus zeichnet die Architektin Eda Soyal das häusliche und alltägliche Leben der Geflüchteten in der Stadt auf und analysiert die Umgestaltung des öffentlichen Raums. Schließlich folgt das Forschungsprojekt The Residual des Artıkişler Collective (Alper Şen, Özge Çelikaslan und Pelin Tan) Flüchtlingen auf ihrer Reise von Syrien und aus dem Irak über die Türkei und Griechenland bis nach Europa, um das Gefühl der Solidarität und die Überlebensstrategien der Flüchtlinge zu verstehen. Dabei nutzt das Künstlerkollektiv Videoaufnahmen und schriftliche Protokolle, um den Einfluss der Geflüchteten auf urbane Räume und die gemeinsame Gestaltung des öffentlichen Raums zu untersuchen. Die Videogramme dieser Arbeit verfolgen und verdeutlichen Wege menschlicher Wanderungsbewegungen, werden jedoch überschattet von den Verhandlungen zwischen der EU und der Türkei, in denen Migrant/innen und Flüchtlinge von den Hegemonialmächten lediglich als Überreste betrachtet werden.

Politischer Druck, Zensur, geopolitische Konflikte, Unsicherheit und soziale Ängste sind in der aktuellen türkischen Gesellschaft und ihren urbanen Räumen akute Probleme. Daher wurde ACTOPOLIS seit Projektbeginn Zeuge einiger unerwarteter Geschehnisse, die sich auch in den künstlerischen Untersuchungen und Projekten widerspiegeln. Seçkin Aydın wurde während seiner Untersuchungen inhaftiert; Önder Özengi und Sevgi Ortaç wurden mit der Festnahme des Bürgermeisters von Mardin konfrontiert; Eda Soyal und Pelin Tan setzten ihre Untersuchungen und pädagogischen Aktivitäten im Kriegsgebiet unter Bedingungen des Ausnahmezustands fort. Die Teilnehmer/innen in Ankara standen unter dem Eindruck von Bombenattentaten. Ein Workshop in Mardin musste aufgrund von Sicherheitsrisiken abgesagt werden. Dank der translokalen Bedingungen von ACTOPOLIS waren die Teilnehmer/ innen dennoch in der Lage, den Diskurs fortzusetzen und Erfahrungen zu teilen, um die Solidarität und den Glauben daran zu erhalten, dass künstlerische Recherchen und künstlerisches Handeln in unserer Gesellschaft Wirkung entfalten können.

PELIN TAN

Commanding Heights

The publication brings together debates, controversies, and ideas focused on Mardin Castle and exploring the issues of "cultural heritage", the "militarisation of public space", and the possibilities of creating additional urban value.

Die Publikation thematisiert die sich überlagernden Vorstellungen zur Rekonstruktion des historischen Erbes und die Militarisierung des öffentlichen Raums. Am Beispiel der Burg von Mardin wird gezeigt, wie im städtischen Kontext symbolischer Mehrwert entstehen kann.

The project, which researches territorial disputes, archaeology, and the militarisation of public land, focuses on the ancient castle of Mardin, which stands on the heights overlooking the old city. The castle has been closed to the public for decades and, because of its advantageous location, it has been used for military surveillance purposes to monitor the surrounding border regions. The restoration of the castle and the archaeological excavations of the site were controversial, as the local authorities requested the closure of the military facilities including the NATO radar station situated there that had been left over from the Cold War era. The publication aims to explore collective knowledge, conflicts, and the possibility of local, ethically-based alliances forged through the production of heritage and space by combining military terms, archaeological concepts, and geographical features with local narratives from Mardin.

Project: Sevgi Ortaç → Format: research, artist's book → Dates: May–October 2016 → Venue: Mardin → Participants: Mardin Museum, local authorities, people of Mardin

Das Projekt beschäftigt sich mit dem Konflikt um die archäologische Erforschung und die Militarisierung der alten Burg von Mardin. Die Festungsanlage, von der aus sich die gesamte Stadt überblicken lässt, wurde vor Jahrzehnten zum militärischen Sperrgebiet erklärt und dient der Überwachung des Grenzgebietes. Die umstrittene Restaurierung und die archäologische Untersuchung des Geländes gingen mit der Forderung der Stadtverwaltung einher, die militärischen Einrichtungen an diesem Ort, darunter eine NATO-Radarstation aus dem Kalten Krieg, zu schließen. Die Publikation soll Debatten, Kontroversen und Vorstellungen zusammenbringen, die sich am Beispiel der Burg von Mardin mit den Themen „kulturelles Erbe" und „Militarisierung des öffentlichen Raums" beschäftigen, und Möglichkeiten der Schaffung urbanen Mehrwerts erörtern.

Ankara/Mardin—Urban Commons

Un
ÜNEY UN

Donkey Work

The research focuses on the donkeys used by the Mardin municipality for collecting refuse, especially in the narrow streets of the district of Old Mardin.

Im Mittelpunkt des Projekts stehen die Lastesel, die in den engen Gassen der Altstadt von Mardin von der Stadtverwaltung zur Straßenreinigung eingesetzt werden.

The research project focuses on the use of animals as workers in Mardin. Since 2009 the municipality has been using donkeys to collect and carry garbage in certain streets in the old city that large vehicles cannot pass through. During the research, Özengi interviewed the main actors, from the municipality to the owners and workers who take care of the donkeys, while at the same time filming the donkeys' living and working conditions. Treating the animals as workers, this research project seeks to look at the relationship between human institutions and animals from the perspective of labour.

Das Projekt beschäftigt sich mit der Verwendung der Arbeitskraft von Eseln in Mardin. Seit 2009 setzt die öffentliche Stadtreinigung von Mardin in für den Autoverkehr unzugänglichen Straßen Esel ein. Im Rahmen unseres Projekts sollen die Hauptbeteiligten – von den Beamt/innen der Stadtverwaltung bis zu den Eselhalter/innen und -pfleger/innen – befragt und der Tageslauf und die Arbeitsbedingungen der Esel filmisch dokumentiert werden. Wir betrachten die Esel als Arbeiter und wollen das Verhältnis Mensch – Tier aus dem Blickwinkel der Arbeitswelt thematisieren.

     Project: Önder Özengi → Format: video, research → Venue: Mardin

Foucault's Typewriter

This project focuses on the double damage that has been wreaked, affecting both reality and the representation of that reality.

Dieses Projekt richtet den Blick auf den doppelten Schaden, den nicht nur die Realität, sondern auch die Darstellung dieser Realität davonträgt.

This project is inspired by a complete scale model of the historic Sur district of Diyarbakır made by a car mechanic, Fesih Gündoğar, and assembled by hand piece by piece. Using a detailed aerial photo, Fesih Gündoğar examined the area and individually numbered each house and its location. He then completed the ramparts, bastions, and the earth-roofed houses one by one over a period of twenty-one years. More than 1,500 of Sur's over 500-year-old buildings have been listed as historic. UNESCO named the forty-foot-high stone fortifications that encircle Sur a World Heritage Site. After a long period of repeated round-the-clock curfews, a large part of the Sur district has been completely destroyed. Fesih Gündoğar's model, which was hosted at a municipality building, was also damaged during the conflict, with bullets hitting the walls and the Ulucami (Great Mosque).

Anstoß zu diesem Projekt gab ein maßstabsgetreues Modell des historischen Stadtteils Sur in Diyarbakır, das der Automechaniker Fesih Gündoğar Stück für Stück von Hand zusammenfügte. Fesih Gündoğar untersuchte das Gebiet anhand einer detaillierten Luftaufnahme und versah jedes einzelne Haus und seinen Standort mit einer Nummer. Über einen Zeitraum von 21 Jahren fügte er jede Schutzmauer, jeden Turm und jedes erdgedeckte Haus hinzu. Mehr als 1500 der über 500 Jahre alten Gebäude in Sur sind denkmalgeschützt. Die UNESCO hat die gut zwölf Meter hohe historische Stadtmauer um Sur zum Weltkulturerbe erklärt. Nach einer langen Phase wiederholter ganztägiger Ausgangssperren liegt ein großer Teil von Sur inzwischen in Schutt und Asche. Das Modell von Fesih Gündoğar, das in einem städtischen Gebäude untergebracht war, wurde während des Konflikts ebenfalls beschädigt, da Kugeln die Mauern und die Ulucami (Große Moschee) trafen.

Spaces of Exodus

The project focuses on the rapid transformation of the residential forms and social patterns of Mardin since the city was designated a reception point for Syrian refugees.

Das Projekt untersucht den Wandel von Wohnformen und sozialen Mustern in Mardin, seitdem die Stadt als Zwischenstation für syrische Flüchtlinge dient.

Syrian refugees live outside camps in cities across Turkey, most of them unregistered and with no passport. These non-camp refugees are beginning a makeshift new life while they wait for the war to end so that they can go back to their homeland. The project aims to investigate the conflicts arising in the local area and reveal the interim dwellings occupied by the refugees. The project sets out to visualise the intricate condition of Mardin, and the problems posed by spatial transformations and speculation at the local level. The mapping and visual observations act as triggers to promote an understanding of the presence of refugees —as workers, political actors, and sometimes as relatives—and the life they share with the people of Mardin in the kaleidoscopic conditions of the city's current circumstances.

Syrische Flüchtlinge, die in vielen Städten der Türkei außerhalb von Lagern leben – meistens ohne Pass und ohne Registrierung –, führen ein provisorisches Leben auf Zeit, während sie auf das Ende des Krieges und eine Rückkehr in ihre Heimat warten. Unser Projekt beschäftigt sich mit den vor Ort entstehenden Konflikten und dokumentiert die Interimswohnformen der Flüchtenden. Dabei versuchen wir, die durch Transformation und Spekulation entstehenden Probleme für die Stadt Mardin sichtbar zu machen. Gesammelte Kartierungen und Bilder liefern Anstoß, die Anwesenheit und das Zusammenleben der Flüchtlinge mit Menschen aus Mardin als Arbeiter, politisch Handelnde und teils auch als Verwandte unter den facettenreichen Bedingungen der aktuellen Lage der Stadt zu verstehen.

Project: Eda Soyal → Format: research → Dates: June–September 2016 → Venue: Mardin →
Participants: refugee inhabitants

Territorial Islands

A series of architectural drawings thematising territorial and urban warfare in which traditional architectural methods are questioned and new forms of expression are put to the test for isolated territories in a state of emergency

Territoriale Konflikte und moderner Häuserkampf thematisiert in Form von Architekturzeichnungen, in denen herkömmliche architektonische Methoden hinterfragt und neue Ausdrucksformen für isolierte Territorien im Ausnahmezustand erprobt werden

A research project on combat zones, focused on creating a collective memory of people and action. This project focuses on research by investigating historical maps, territorial powers, and the architecture of security and resistance. Conventional architectural methodologies always observe from a distance, but conventional representation methods could also be used to create lateral drawings and mental mappings. Over a period of time, through site visits, interviews, and workshops, the project has established a base on the site, and all the drawings and media have been produced with this local knowledge. The drawings also merge with geographical and cartographical information.

Project: Yelta Köm → Format: research, drawings → Dates: 2015–ongoing → Venues: Mardin, Diyarbakır, Ankara

Im Mittelpunkt des Projekts steht die Darstellung von Kampfzonen, für die neue Formen des kollektiven Bewusstseins und Engagements gesucht werden. Der Fokus liegt auf der Arbeit mit historischem Kartenmaterial und der Auseinandersetzung mit Erscheinungsformen territorialer Macht sowie Formen von Sicherheits- und Widerstandsarchitektur. Während der herkömmliche architektonische Blick auf Distanz bleibt, geht es hier um die Erstellung von begleitenden Zeichnungen und kognitiven Karten mit konventionellen Darstellungsmitteln. Besuche vor Ort, Interviews und Workshops bilden die Grundlage des Projekts. Das vor Ort erworbene Wissen fließt unmittelbar in die Zeichnungen ein. Ergänzend wird mit geografischem und kartografischem Material gearbeitet.

The Residual

The video research project seeks the traces of Syrian refugees who have journeyed on from Mardin to construct a new life and investigates new forms of struggle for the commons in the cities they have left behind.

Die Videorecherche geht den Spuren syrischer Flüchtlinge nach, die von Mardin aus weitergereist sind, um sich ein neues Leben aufzubauen. Sie untersucht neue Formen des Ringens um die gemeinschaftliche Nutzung von Ressourcen (commoning) in Städten, die Zwischenstation für Geflüchtete waren.

Our multimedia research project *The Residual* has two goals. First, it attempts to narrate the tragic story underlying the traces left behind by the flow of refugees in the various Turkish cities they have passed through in their escape from the Syrian conflict, before boarding boats bound for the Greek islands. Second, it reflects the strong sense of excitement around the creation of new "commoning" experiences in the towns and cities from which migrants have fled, like those in the Rojava region of Syrian Kurdistan. *The Residual* recounts the narratives of refugees and migrants both in new, state-run refugee camps and in housing initiatives started by migrant solidarity movements throughout the south-eastern region of Turkey. The city of Mardin is near the border crossing where the Turkish government deports refugees back to Syria. It is also home to a migration department that monitors the legal situation of migrants.

Unsere multimediale Forschungsarbeit konzentriert sich auf zwei Kernaspekte: Zunächst soll die tragische Geschichte hinter den Spuren erzählt werden, die syrische Flüchtlinge in zahlreichen türkischen Städten hinterließen, bevor sie auf eines der Boote mit Kurs auf die griechischen Inseln stiegen. Außerdem beschäftigen wir uns mit der großen Euphorie über neue Formen des commoning, die auch nach dem Abzug der Geflüchteten beispielsweise in den Städten Westkurdistans zu spüren sind. Zudem untersucht das Projekt, wie sich die Situation der Geflüchteten in neuen staatlichen Aufnahmelagern von der in Unterkünften der Solidaritätsbewegung in der Südosttürkei unterscheidet. Nahe der Grenze gelegen, ist Mardin Sitz der Migrationsbehörde, die für die Überwachung und Abschiebung von Flüchtlingen zuständig ist.

Project: Artıkişler Collective → Format: video, research → Dates: May–October 2016 → Venues: Rojava, Mardin, Ankara, Thessaloniki, Athens, Berlin, Zagreb → Participants: Artıkişler Collective (Özge Çelikaslan, Alper Şen, Pelin Tan)

OPEN ALL
BORDERS

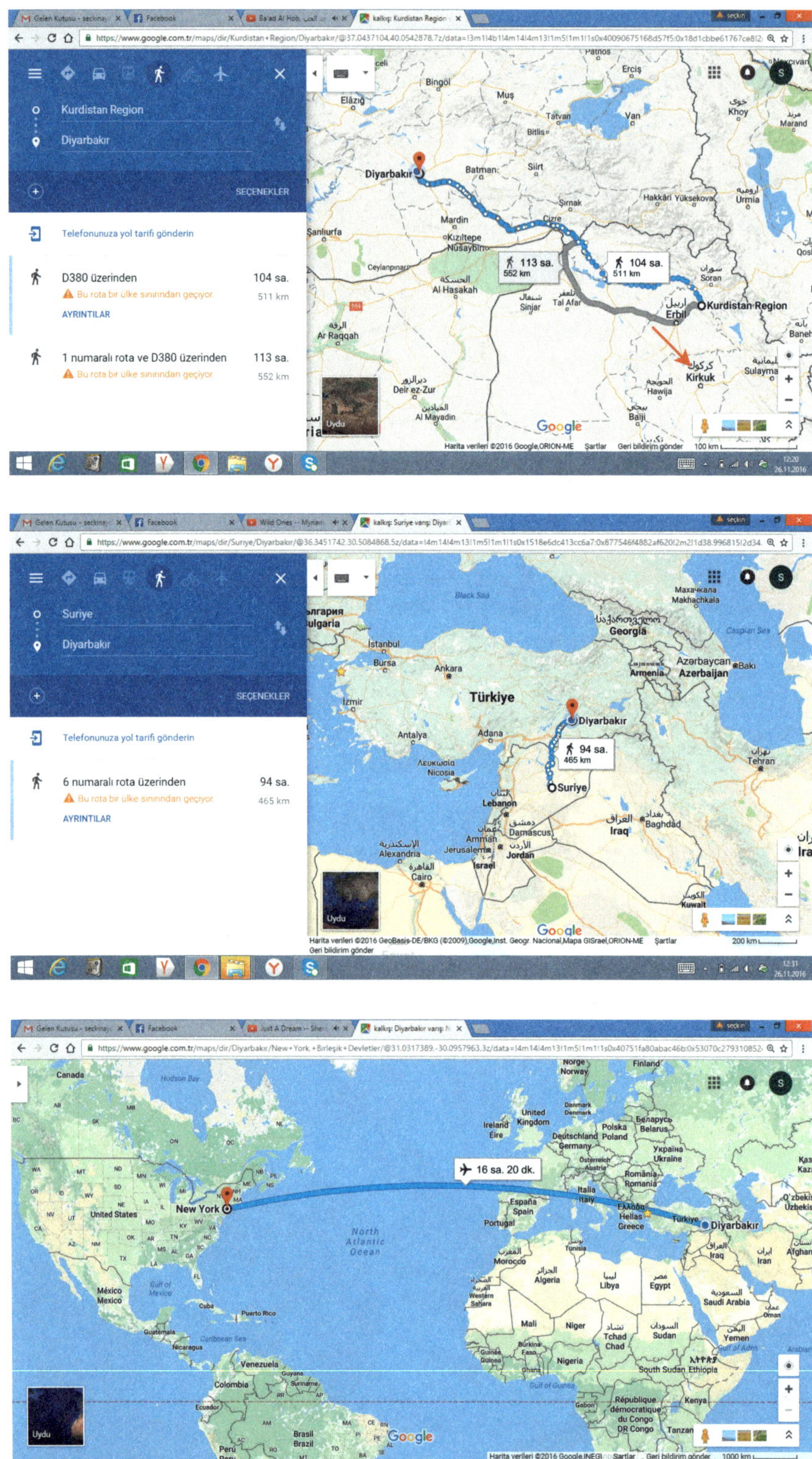

Ankara/Mardin—Urban Commons

Urban Defenders

Visual narratives of urban resistance

Visuelle Narrative des urbanen Widerstands

This project focuses on the visual narratives of two generations that experienced urban conflicts at the beginning of 2000 and from 2015 on. The project also presents me as a subject. I lie in between these two generations that experienced eviction from our village, became nomadic, and escaped to the city in order to survive. The nineties' generation, who faced the regional conflict and were evicted in a state of fear, prefer to live in peace in the cities, although they are still under political pressure. The second generation is the children born to the evicted families who moved to the cities from the villages. This generation is not able to establish a connection with urban life because of their lack of cultural, economic, and social capital. Moreover, they are frustrated by the sociopolitical pressure. This younger generation sees the urban space as a space of resistance.

Schwerpunkt dieses Projekts sind die visuellen Narrative zweier Generationen, die urbane Konflikte zu Beginn des Jahres 2000 und seit 2015 erlebt haben. Daneben präsentiert das Projekt auch mich selbst als Subjekt. Ich stehe zwischen den beiden Generationen, die aus unserem Dorf ausgewiesen wurden, wurde Nomade und floh in die Stadt, um zu überleben. Die Generation der 90er-Jahre, die sich dem Konflikt stellte und in Angst ausgewiesen wurde, steht noch immer politisch unter Druck, lebt heute jedoch vorzugsweise friedlich in den Städten. Die zweite Generation sind die Kinder der vertriebenen Familien, die aus den Dörfern in die Stadt gezogen sind. Diese Generation ist aufgrund ihres mangelnden kulturellen, ökonomischen und Sozialkapitals außerstande, eine Verbindung zum Leben in der Stadt herzustellen. Außerdem frustriert sie der gesellschaftspolitische Druck. Diese jüngere Generation sieht den städtischen Raum als Raum des Widerstands.

Project: Seçkin Aydın → Format: interview, observation → Dates: April–October 2016 → Venue: Mardin (Diyarbakır) → Participants: Local people from Sur

Claiming

Claiming is an active right or a title to a place, condition, or an environment (be it political, social, or natural). We can claim a right to the city, public space, running water, a clean environment, or living as decent human beings. Claiming involves taking an active role as an individual or a group to remind decision-makers and those in power of the public interest and commons.

> *Ein Anspruch ist ein aktives Recht auf einen Ort, einen Zustand oder ein Umfeld (sei es politisch, sozial oder natürlich). Wir können ein Recht auf die Stadt, den öffentlichen Raum, auf fließendes Wasser, eine saubere Umwelt oder ein menschenwürdiges Leben geltend machen. Dazu muss man als Einzelperson oder als Gruppe aktiv werden, um politische Entscheidungsträger und Machthabende an öffentliche Interessen und Gemeingüter zu erinnern.*

Danijela Dugandžić

Collaborating

When different individuals engage in a process of working together to achieve common goals we call it collaboration. We can collaborate in real space or online, we can do it in the same office or work on just one initiative, we can work locally and transnationally, with hierarchy or without, but if we want a successful collaboration, we have to work in a motivating, open, and synchronised environment that enables knowledge-sharing and allows us to focus on the same goal. Collaborations are never easy and if we wish to build a collective it requires time, energy, mediation, and constant reflection. Most of the time it also requires friendship and support as well as a great deal of determination from everyone involved. Nevertheless, the experience shows that the results of a collective practice can lead to

the most rewarding processes, from which everyone gains
more and produces results that could never have been
achieved individually.

> *Wenn sich verschiedene Einzelpersonen in einem gemein-
> samen Arbeitsprozess engagieren, um gemeinsame Ziele
> zu erreichen, nennen wir das Zusammenarbeit. Wir können
> in einem realen Raum oder online zusammenarbeiten;
> wir können im selben Büro oder am selben Projekt arbeiten;
> wir können lokal und transnational arbeiten, hierarchisch
> oder auf einer Ebene. Aber wenn wir eine erfolgreiche
> Zusammenarbeit wollen, müssen wir in einer motivierenden,
> offenen und aufeinander abgestimmten Umgebung arbeiten,
> die es uns ermöglicht, Wissen zu teilen und uns auf das-
> selbe Ziel zu konzentrieren. Zusammenarbeit ist nie einfach,
> und wenn wir ein Kollektiv aufbauen möchten, braucht
> das Zeit, Energie, Vermittlung und ständige Reflexion. Meis-
> tens erfordert es auch Freundschaft und Unterstützung
> sowie ein großes Maß an Entschlossenheit bei allen Betei-
> ligten. Die Erfahrung zeigt jedoch, dass kollektives Handeln
> zu den lohnendsten Entwicklungen führen kann, bei denen
> alle gewinnen und Ergebnisse erzielt werden, die man
> allein nicht hätte erreichen können.*

Danijela Dugandžić

Collecting

Urban Collectors is a platform for graffiti and street art in Bucharest. Collecting, unlike hoarding (an obsession many Romanians manifested post-1989 when confronted with a limitless number of products to consume), comes from the need to appropriate and to make sense of things. A need to confront and contest existing categories. Artists may collect litter from the streets and press it between the pages of a book (Daniel Knorr); writers may collect oral histories and legends (constantly validating or redefining places in the city and their reputation); mayors may collect citizens' wishes and ideas.

Urban Collectors ist eine Plattform für Graffiti und Straßenkunst in Bukarest. Im Gegensatz zum Horten (einer Obsession, der in Rumänien nach 1989 viele Menschen erlagen, als sie sich plötzlich einer unendlichen Fülle an Konsumprodukten gegenübersahen) ist das Sammeln dem Bedürfnis zuzuschreiben, sich Dinge anzueignen und zu verstehen. Einem Bedürfnis, sich mit bestehenden Kategorien auseinanderzusetzen und sie infrage zu stellen. Künstler/innen sammeln vielleicht Weggeworfenes von den Straßen auf und pressen es zwischen Buchseiten (Daniel Knorr); Schriftsteller/innen sammeln manchmal mündlich überlieferte Geschichten und Legenden (wobei sie ständig Orte in der Stadt und deren Ruf bestätigen oder neu definieren); Bürgermeister/innen sammeln möglicherweise die Wünsche und Ideen ihrer Bürger/innen.

Raluca Voinea

The Soft Power Lectures

For some years now, Greece and its capital Athens have been at the centre of attention, labelled as a paradigmatic case of failure and survival, on the one hand stretched and stripped of resources and, on the other, charged with the artistic expectation that comes with being on the edge. And indeed, at this point in time the energy of the city seems to be very high. A youngish left-wing government is claiming a paradigm shift for Europe, while at the same time various systemic breakdowns are catapulting this energy sky-high. As a side benefit, various powerful art institutions, such as the New Museum in New York, the relocated documenta 14, and others, see Athens and Athenians as case studies of particular interest. Athens is viewed as a focal point of resistance that can educate, suggest strategies of survival, and find novel ways to make art without money, through alternative economies and communitarian practices. In light of this interest, the local art scene seems to have generated expectations and a sense of anticipation as well as an awareness of the exoticisation of the city and its subjects. In any case, the scene has already changed: foreign visitors, official and unofficial, stroll in the galleries, trendy hangouts, and occupied spaces of the city. Airbnb property investors calculate that Athens will be the place to be, the focus of an alternative exotic tourism of catastrophe and survival.

As happens in places caught in the eye of the storm, this attention, as well as the development of a certain accompanying discourse, is expected. The spectacle is welcome—from the episode of the removal of the artistic director of the Athens and Epidaurus Festival to the controversial interventions of Ai Weiwei in the refugee camps in Lesbos and Idomeni, amongst others—indicating that there is little alternative other than to re-address issues of power and institutions in order to understand who is talking on behalf of whom and what it really means to be institutional, extra-institutional, or para-institutional. At the moment we are part of a New South experiment, as a paradigm of "creative sustainability". This New South, though, is based on power relations and stereotypes that are repeated, that re-localise and re-regionalise the world and its subjects in order to maintain a minimum of the existing status quo. Athens is swinging back and forth in its bipolar identity, poised between economic catastrophe, refugee asphyxiation, and exemplary creative energy. Power relations and institutions were of interest for practitioners living and working in Athens well before the crisis, since, as professionals working in Athens, we perpetually oscillate between amateurism and professionalism, between "giving" for contemporary art and eking out a badly paid livelihood doing jobs that, frequently, have little to do with our professional specificity. The dilemmas we confront every day, questions of survival and acquiescence, are bound to the larger, tough reality of labour and the complex relationship between menial and immaterial, voluntary and remunerated work.

As part of a decision to work within or on the side of the institutions, in 2013 Elpida Karaba initiated a structure called the Temporary Academy of the Arts (PAT), an educational and artistic project in which different educational modes and forms and alternative pedagogical methods and programmes are tried and implemented as curatorial practice. Understanding the institution as processual (the process of instituting) and critically subverting the term "academy" into a self-instituted practice, PAT, through its projects, tests self-instituted forms of culture and politics and explores the diverse methodological articulations and nuances existing between the institution and the self-instituted. PAT is developing a para-institutional action: in other words, it is part of the cultural machinery and does not proscribe institutions altogether but rather attempts to participate in the construction of new institutions.

The theorisations of the institution and the institutional critique that currently dominate the discourse tend to highlight the process of instituting and emphasise a politics of autonomy. The practices that are often associated with this theorisation are self-organised, activist, and propositional. PAT critically explores the possible implications of this, connecting it with issues and problematics around the new organisation of labour in view of the broader European landscape of precarity, the processes of neo-institutionalism and post-institutional critique, and the way various (art) institutions can be analysed in the larger sociopolitical and economic systemic structures and frameworks. In every project PAT invites colleagues to design and perform its programme.

Within the framework of the ACTOPOLIS project, PAT designed and performed a series of performative lectures, called the *Soft Power Lectures* (SPL). ACTOPOLIS is an ambitious project, initiated by the Goethe-Institut, which has expanded across South-East Europe and to the Ruhr region in Germany, with the aim of addressing the pressing issues confronting the contemporary city and the critical repercussions of a rapidly changing metropolis facing the predicament of (in many cases, forced) mobility and economic and institutional instability. The idea of connecting, initially at the regional level, a large area with so much diversity—in terms of its economic, social, working, and political realities—has been a methodological challenge. The network and exchange practice which was encouraged and supported by the project gave us the opportunity to meet and communicate our ideas and resources and to address our common issues and problematics as well as the differences between the subjectivities and conditions involved in each project. "South" has been adopted as a quasi-empty signifier in order to reconnect the local, the transnational, and the global.

The SPL were co-curated by the writers, Elpida Karaba and Glykeria Stathopoulou, together with Panos Sklavenitis, Sofia Dona, Despina Zefkili, Constantinos Hadzinikolaou, and invited artists.[1] Soft Power, a kind of power derived from diplomacy, is the exercise of power that aligns subjects to one's own perspective using persuasion, example, seduction, and myth. We know from Foucault's analytics of power, that power is "omnipresent", pervasive in every "background condition" underlying all social relations. It represents an all-encompassing undercurrent of norms, values, ideas, and knowledge that inspires the very processes of socialisation at the most general levels of human interaction. In that sense, the SPL aimed to explore how a city and an academy can exercise soft power in order to hegemonise the discourse around itself and everything surrounding it, asking if it is possible to take advantage of the exoticisation of the crisis and to produce a "beneficial branding"—to utilise the "germ" of creativity and enjoy the benefits of this "applied imagination"—for the city and the subjects that are involved in it.

The SPL focused on the topics of the South and its precarious, creative, and sustainable subjects, revisiting some central, though open questions that have re-emerged, such as what the relation is between centres and margins, art and labour—namely an investigation of what the economic and labour conditions are for artists and cultural workers in Greece at the moment and the exotic gaze drawn to the crisis.

In the *Soft Power Lectures*, as well as in the *Soft Power Lectures Show* (a presentation on a basketball court that took the format of a performative exhibition of works as apparatus and archival material), we activated mechanisms of power relations. The material produced and put on display functioned literally and symbolically, in explicit and implicit ways, its aim being to claim our subjecthood, as the issues of power raised by Foucault still seem to be very persistent and by no means resolved. The methodological—or strategic—function of the term *dispositif*, for example, allowed us to bind together heterogeneous elements and to look at how their interplay results in a specific formation producing both power structures and knowledge.

Soft Power was appropriated as a method for activating public space, not merely as a physical space but as a condensed space of "(re-)claiming". The issue of public space as an antagonistic space has been the focus of art practice and theory for the last decades. More particularly, the democratisation of public space has been top of the agenda for cultural institutions and events, a position followed by the ACTOPOLIS project as well. Hence, for the SPL we didn't focus on public demonstrations or constructions of large kiosks or installations in squares or on practices of squatting or occupation of any kind but rather on "formations" of public space and public claim. We wanted to examine the potential of public speech acts, archives, and works of art to serve as public domains where one can lay claim to history, identity, and the re-designing of institutions. If subjects are also constructed in language, the constitution of a lecture, a public speech act, or an archive primarily attempts to produce a conceptual space that enables identities, concepts, and groups to detach themselves from specific, naturalised ideological images —allowing crucial categories for the subjects and society to emerge and get revised, emptied, and reformulated. These acts create a space where claims connected to symbolic struggles and new interpretative framings are supported in the public realm.[2]

If we understand the term "public" as something that ought to concern all of us and "public space" as a place where such public affairs can be expressed, made known, and brought into general awareness, archives and speech acts can also be public spaces. The SPL were intended as public claims in both legitimate and temporarily designed public spaces (i.e. in places that were perceived performatively as public spaces).

For example, PAT has activated the mechanics of "discursive opportunities" like visibility, resonance, and legitimacy. Within the scope of the "Performative Interviews" event orchestrated by PAT, we confronted the interviewees with straightforward and blunt questions about their professional situation. In response to our question as to whether art is a profession, most of the answers were negative, putting art in a sphere somewhere between a vocation and some indefinable other. As for the question of whether Southern women, transgender, or other subjects are paid differently, the answer was mostly no, as if it had been forgotten that the South is paid less for the same services; we tend to disregard that it is somehow legitimate for people in the former Eastern Bloc to be paid substantially smaller salaries than those working in central or northern Europe; we ignore the fact that in big international cultural events one will rarely find subjects from exotic Athens in top influential positions in an art world that, strange to say, also capitalises on cultural difference. From such responses one can assume a lot about how precarious cultural professionals in our field have internalised the fallacy of unpaid cultural work and how difficult it is for them to eradicate this and claim different labour conditions for themselves. The Western world intensifies the mechanisms of assigning different rates of pay according to gender, colour, and origin, and this question was a public statement expressed on PAT's behalf.

Gestures and apparatuses create an effect, a means to understand the content of the lectures and orient the reactions of the audience. PAT relies on critical reflection, claiming an educational dimension for itself. Some gestures in SPL provocatively targeted preconceptions and reactionary attitudes that are either obvious or latent in our society. We presented Panos Sklavenitis's *South*, where a controversial persona narrates the South in a provocative way, developing ideas around a European geography of top and bottom, challenging constructions of national pride and inferiority and superiority complexes. Another example would be the video lecture *The Champions of Pleasure*, where another persona proposes a gay reading of Greek history from ancient to modern times. Further gestures, such as the work *Aspa* by Constantinos Hadzinikolaou, were based in much

more subtle movements of looking into our recent history and cultural tradition to understand our past and, more acutely, our current condition and interpretations of our identity— as women, cultural workers, or subjects of a certain time and locality. These gestures offer framing combined with political subjectivity. They comment on the framing of the process of collective action, which performs a transformative function in the sense of altering the meaning of the object(s) or reconfiguring aspects of one's biography.

Organising material, such as lectures, archives, works of art, and texts on the crisis and its subjects— as per the SPL Archive and performing speech acts on the South and its social, economic, and private subjects—raises questions of power and identity, as well as firing the will to create new structures. These are instituent practices aiming to shatter naturalised categories and promote new meanings of public space and public claims. The production of such speech acts and archives is an action that deliberately or inadvertently produces stories. It produces outer (physical) and inner (psychic) space in the same natural way in which construction is understood to produce tangible objects. We cannot unconditionally perform the articulation of different militant or precarious and subaltern subjects as an a priori positive development, but we should appreciate the decisive role of their public appearance through a speech act or an archive, i.e. through a discursive, condensed public space, where the publishing, alignment, and dispersion of their demands and their conditions of existence take place.

The Temporary Academy of Arts, through the programme of the *Soft Power Lectures*, set out to examine and specify the modes of action required to generate critical practices within institutions, while also interrogating established modes of knowledge production and subjectification. Reflecting on the institution in relation to critical practices and debates in the art field since the 1990s, such as the "institution as a process"[3] and, more specifically, the notion that instituting also takes place within subjects and social formations, the *Soft Power Lectures* adopted the standpoint of power rather than retreating to a moralising, accessory role. The South claimed a voice relative to its geopolitical and bio-political location. But South is not a notion that claims locality either as an autonomist, separatist unity or—opposing itself to a global "threat"—as a resistance to North or any other locality. South is a provocation challenging the idea that claims are a neutral cosmopolitan notion, the principal risk here being that cosmopolitanism can be used merely to designate a flexible subject with the right documents—a travelling elite. On the contrary, South is a pretence that underlines that these claims happen within the economic, working, and social contexts in which we are operating.

ELPIDA KARABA, GLYKERIA STATHOPOULOU

1. We would like to express our special appreciation and thanks to Anastasia Douka, Nikos Alexopoulos, Angelos Krallis, Yiannis Papadopoulos, Thalia Raftopoulou, and Kostis Velonis, who created works and apparatuses for the *Soft Power Lectures*. Their input enriched the lectures in more ways than one.
2. Terms relating to the public claim are examined in Nikos Stasinopoulos, "The Subject and the Object of the Claim: Towards a Lacanian Discourse Theoretic Approach", part of a forthcoming volume of essays (Athens: Papazisis Publishers), http://www.academia.edu/28988568/The_Subject_and_the_Object_of_the_Claim._Towards_a_Lacanian_discourse_theoretic_approach.
3. For more information on the institution as a process, see Gerald Raunig and Gene Ray, *Art and Contemporary Critical Practice: Reinventing Institutional Critique* (London: MayFly Books, 2009).

The Soft Power Lectures

Seit einigen Jahren stehen Griechenland und seine Hauptstadt Athen nun schon im Mittelpunkt der Aufmerksamkeit und gelten als Paradebeispiel für Versagen und Überlebenskampf. In der aufgrund finanzieller Engpässe bzw. völliger Mittellosigkeit am Abgrund stehenden Stadt steigen automatisch die Erwartungen an die Kunst. Und tatsächlich scheint Athen derzeit sehr energiegeladen zu sein. Eine relativ junge linksgerichtete Regierung fordert einen Paradigmenwechsel für Europa, während gleichzeitig verschiedene systemische Zusammenbrüche das Energielevel immer weiter in die Höhe schnellen lassen. Ein zusätzlicher positiver Nebeneffekt ist, dass mehrere mächtige Kunstinstitutionen, wie beispielsweise das New Yorker New Museum oder die nach Athen verlegte documenta 14, Athen und die Athener/innen als besonders interessante Fallstudien ansehen. Athen gilt als Brennpunkt des Widerstands, von dem man lernen kann. Hier werden Überlebensstrategien entwickelt und neue Wege erforscht, wie man durch alternatives Wirtschaften und kommunitaristische Initiativen Kunst ohne Geld machen kann. Vor diesem Hintergrund scheinen sich in der lokalen Kunstszene nicht nur Erwartungen und eine gewisse Vorfreude breitzumachen, sondern es scheint sich auch ein Bewusstsein für die Exotisierung der Stadt und ihrer Bürger/innen einzustellen. Auf jeden Fall hat sich die Szene bereits verändert: Galerien, angesagte Orte und besetzte Räume der Stadt haben reichlich offiziellen und privaten Besuch zu verzeichnen. Die über Airbnb tätigen Immobilieninvestoren rechnen damit, dass Athen zu einem begehrten Reiseziel werden wird – zu einem Schwerpunkt eines alternativen exotischen Katastrophen- und Überlebenstourismus.

Wie häufig bei krisengeschüttelten Orten kommt diese Aufmerksamkeit nicht unerwartet und geht mit bestimmten Begleitdiskursen einher. Das Spektakel ist willkommen – vom Rücktritt des künstlerischen Leiters des Theaterfestivals Athen und Epidaurus bis hin zu Ai Weiweis umstrittenen Interventionen in den Flüchtlingslagern auf Lesbos und in Idomeni. Man kommt offensichtlich nicht darum herum, die Fragen von Macht und Institutionen wieder aufzugreifen, um zu verstehen, wer in wessen Auftrag spricht und was es wirklich bedeutet, institutionell, außerinstitutionell oder parainstitutionell zu handeln. Momentan sind wir als Musterbeispiel für „kreative Nachhaltigkeit" Teil des Experiments „Neuer Süden". Dieser Neue Süden basiert jedoch auf alten Machtverhältnissen und Stereotypen, die die Welt und ihre Subjekte erneut lokal und regional eingrenzen, um den Status quo zumindest in Ansätzen aufrechtzuerhalten. Athen schwankt in seiner bipolaren Identität hin und her und balanciert zwischen Wirtschaftskatastrophe, lähmendem Flüchtlingszustrom und beispielhafter kreativer Energie. Schon lange vor der Krise hatten Machtbeziehungen und Institutionen eine große Bedeutung für uns in Athen lebende Kunstschaffende, denn als solche pendeln wir seit jeher zwischen zwei Welten: unserem Wunsch, substanziell etwas zur zeitgenössischen Kunst beizutragen, und der Realität, uns mit schlecht bezahlten Jobs, die häufig wenig mit unserer Kunst zu tun haben, durchs Leben schlagen zu müssen. Das Dilemma, vor dem wir täglich stehen, die Frage von Überleben und Aushalten, ist verknüpft mit der übergeordneten harschen Realität der Arbeit und der komplexen Beziehung zwischen niederer und ideeller, ehrenamtlicher und bezahlter Arbeit.

Vor der Entscheidung stehend, innerhalb oder außerhalb von Institutionen zu arbeiten, gründete Elpida Karaba 2013 die Temporäre Kunstakademie (PAT), ein Bildungs- und Kunstprojekt, in dem verschiedene Bildungsmethoden und alternative pädagogische Ansätze und Programme erprobt und als kuratorische Praktiken umgesetzt werden. Mit ihrem Verständnis von Institution als prozesshaft (als im Prozess des Institutionalisierens befindlich) und ihrer kritisch-subversiven Umdeutung des Begriffs „Akademie" zu einer selbstinstitutionalisierten Praktik testet die PAT in ihren Projekten nicht nur von ihr selbst etablierte Kunst- und Politikformen, sondern untersucht auch die verschiedenen methodischen Ausdrucksweisen und Nuancen zwischen der Institution und dem Selbsteingerichteten. Die PAT entwickelt parainstitutionelle Formen des Handelns. Mit anderen Worten: Sie begreift sich als Teil eines Kulturapparats und ächtet Institutionen nicht völlig, sondern ist vielmehr bemüht, sich am Aufbau neuer Institutionen zu beteiligen.

Die derzeit den Diskurs beherrschende Theoretisierung der Institution und die Institutionskritik heben häufig den Prozess des Institutionalisierens hervor und setzen den Akzent auf eine Politik der Autonomie. Die oft mit dieser Theoretisierung in Verbindung gebrachten Praktiken sind selbst organisiert, aktivistisch und propositional. Die PAT nimmt die möglichen Auswirkungen dieses Phänomens kritisch unter die Lupe und verbindet es mit Fragen und Problemen rund um die Arbeit, die angesichts der in Europa immer weiter verbreiteten Prekarisierung, der Prozesse des Neoinstitutionalismus und der postinstitutionellen Kritik neu organisiert wird. Sie beschäftigt sich auch damit, wie verschiedene (Kunst-) Institutionen unter weiter gefassten soziopolitischen und ökonomischen systemischen Struktur- und Rahmenbedingungen analysiert werden können. Zu jedem Projekt lädt die PAT Kolleg/innen ein, die Veranstaltungen der Akademie zu gestalten und durchzuführen.

Im Rahmen von ACTOPOLIS konzipierte und veranstaltete die PAT mit den sogenannten Soft Power Lectures (SPL) eine Reihe performativer Lesungen. ACTOPOLIS ist ein vom Goethe-Institut initiiertes ambitioniertes Projekt, das sich über Südosteuropa erstreckt, aber auch das deutsche Ruhrgebiet mit einschließt. Es zielt darauf ab, die drängenden Fragen anzugehen, mit denen sich moderne Städte heute konfrontiert sehen, und die wesentlichen Auswirkungen der sich rasant verändernden Metropolen anzusprechen, die vor dem Dilemma einer (in vielen Fällen erzwungenen) Mobilität sowie wirtschaftlicher und institutioneller Instabilität stehen. Die Idee, eine so große Region zu verbinden, die im Hinblick auf ihre wirtschaftliche, soziale und politische Realität sowie die in den einzelnen Ländern vorherrschenden Arbeitsbedingungen überaus unterschiedlich ist, stellte eine methodische Herausforderung dar. Die vom Projekt geförderte und unterstützte Praxis der Vernetzung und des Austauschs eröffnete uns die Gelegenheit, uns zu treffen, um nicht nur über Ideen und Ressourcen und unsere gemeinsamen Fragestellungen und Problematiken zu sprechen, sondern auch, um die Unterschiede zwischen den Subjektivitäten und Bedingungen der einzelnen Projekte zu erörtern. Der Begriff „Süden" wurde als quasi leerer Bedeutungsträger übernommen, um wieder eine Verbindung zwischen dem Lokalen, Transnationalen und Globalen herzustellen.

Die SPL wurden von den Autorinnen Elpida Karaba und Glykeria Stathopoulou kuratiert und zusammen mit Panos Sklavenitis, Sofia Dona, Despina Zefkili, Constantinos Hadzinikolaou und weiteren geladenen Künstler/innen durchgeführt.[1] Soft Power, also die sanfte Macht der Diplomatie, ist eine Form der Machtausübung, bei der man andere Personen durch Überzeugung, Vorbilder, Verführung und Mythen dazu bringt, sich der eigenen Sichtweise anzuschließen. Dank Foucaults Machtanalysen wissen wir, dass Macht „allgegenwärtig" ist, sämtliche „Hintergrundbedingungen" durchdringt und die Grundlage aller gesellschaftlichen Beziehungen ist. Sie stellt eine allumfassende Unterströmung aus Normen, Werten, Ideen und Wissen dar, die wiederum den Sozialisationsprozess auf der allgemeinsten Ebene menschlicher Interaktion prägt. In diesem Sinne sollten die SPL erforschen, wie eine Stadt und eine Akademie sanfte Macht ausüben können, um den Diskurs um die Stadt selbst und ihre Umgebung in den Vordergrund zu rücken. Dabei wurde auch hinterfragt, ob es möglich ist, dass die Stadt und ihre Bewohner/innen von der Exotisierung der Krise profitieren und ein „nützliches Markenzeichen" erzeugen können – ob also der „Keim" der Kreativität und die Vorteile dieser „angewandten Vorstellungskraft" genutzt werden können.

Im Fokus der SPL standen die Themen des Südens mit seinen prekären Lebensbedingungen, seiner Kreativität und Nachhaltigkeit, wobei einige zentrale, aber unbeantwortete Fragen wieder auftauchten und aufgegriffen wurden, wie etwa die Frage zur Beziehung zwischen Stadtzentrum und Stadtrand sowie zwischen Kunst und Arbeit – und zwar anhand einer Untersuchung zu den derzeit in Griechenland für Kunst- und Kulturschaffende *herrschenden Wirtschafts- und Arbeitsbedingungen und zu dem auf die Krise gerichteten exotischen Blick.*

In den Soft Power Lectures *und auch in der* Soft Power Lectures Show *(einer Präsentation auf einem Basketballfeld in Form einer performativen Ausstellung von Werken, die als Apparate und Archivmaterial dienen) setzten wir Mechanismen von Machtbeziehungen in Gang. Das entstandene und ausgestellte Material hatte eine sowohl explizit als auch implizit zum Ausdruck kommende buchstäbliche und symbolische Funktion, mit der wir unser Subjektsein geltend machen wollten, da die von Foucault angesprochenen Fragen zur Macht noch immer nachhallen und keineswegs beantwortet sind. Die methodische – bzw. strategische – Funktion des Begriffs* Dispositiv *gestattet uns beispielsweise, zwei heterogene Elemente miteinander zu verbinden und zu erkunden, inwieweit ihr Zusammenspiel zur Herausbildung von bestimmten Machtstrukturen und Wissen führt.*

Die Soft Power *wurde als Methode zur Belebung des öffentlichen Raums eingesetzt, und zwar nicht nur des physischen Raums, sondern auch des verdichteten Raums der „(Wieder-)Inanspruchnahme". In den letzten Jahrzehnten stand das Thema des öffentlichen Raums als antagonistischer Raum im Mittelpunkt der Kunstpraxis und -theorie. Für Kulturinstitutionen und bei kulturellen Veranstaltungen stand vor allem die Demokratisierung des öffentlichen Raums ganz oben auf der Tagesordnung. Das gilt auch für ACTOPOLIS. Deshalb konzentrierten wir uns bei den SPL nicht auf öffentliche Präsentationen oder den Aufbau großer Informationsstände bzw. Installationen auf Plätzen oder auf irgendeine Art von Besetzung öffentlicher Gebäude oder Räume, sondern auf die „Aus-*

formungen" des öffentlichen Raums und seiner öffentlichen Inanspruchnahme. Wir wollten erkunden, inwieweit öffentliche Sprechakte, Archive und Kunstwerke als Gemeingüter dienen können, bei denen man Anspruch auf die Geschichte, die Identität und die Umgestaltung von Institutionen erheben kann. Wenn Sujets auch Teil der Sprache sind, versucht der Aufbau einer Lesung, eines öffentlichen Sprechakts oder eines Archivs vor allem, einen begrifflichen Raum zu schaffen, der es Identitäten, Konzepten und Gruppen ermöglicht, sich von bestimmten naturalisierten ideologischen Bildern zu lösen – wodurch sich für die Subjekte und die Gesellschaft möglicherweise maßgebliche Kategorien herausbilden, die überarbeitet, geleert und umformuliert werden können. Diese Akte schaffen einen Raum, in dem Forderungen im Zusammenhang mit symbolischen Kämpfen und neuen Deutungsrahmen im öffentlichen Bereich unterstützt werden.[2]

Wenn wir den Begriff „öffentlich" als etwas verstehen, das uns alle betreffen sollte, und „öffentlichen Raum" als einen Ort begreifen, an dem öffentliche Belange zum Ausdruck, zur Kenntnis und ins allgemeine Bewusstsein gebracht werden können, dann sind auch Archive und Sprechakte öffentliche Räume. Die SPL waren als öffentliche Forderungen sowohl in realen als auch in vorübergehend konzipierten öffentlichen Räumen gedacht (das heißt an Orten, die performativ als öffentliche Räume betrachtet wurden).

Die PAT hat beispielsweise die Mechanismen „diskursiver Gelegenheiten" wie Sichtbarkeit, Resonanz und Legitimität aktiviert. Im Rahmen der von der PAT durchgeführten Veranstaltung „Performative Interviews" konfrontierten wir die Gesprächspartner/innen mit direkten und unverblümten Fragen über ihre berufliche Situation. Unsere Frage, ob Kunst ein Beruf sei, verneinten die meisten und verorteten die Kunst in einer Sphäre irgendwo zwischen Berufung und einigen anderen undefinierbaren Dingen. Auch die Frage, ob Frauen, Transgender oder andere Menschen im Süden anders bezahlt werden, verneinten die meisten, so als ob sie vergessen hätten, dass es im Süden generell weniger Lohn für die gleichen Dienstleistungen gibt. Wir lassen häufig außer Acht, dass es im ehemaligen Ostblock irgendwie legitim zu sein scheint, den Menschen weit niedrigere Löhne und Gehälter zu zahlen als in Mittel- oder Nordeuropa. Wir ignorieren die Tatsache, dass bei großen internationalen Kulturveranstaltungen nur selten Persönlichkeiten aus dem exotischen Athen in einflussreichen Spitzenpositionen zu finden sind – und das in einer Kunstszene, die, so seltsam es klingen mag, auch vom kulturellen Unterschied profitiert. Diese Antworten machen deutlich, wie sehr prekär arbeitende Kulturschaffende auf unserem Gebiet den Irrweg unbezahlter kultureller Arbeit internalisiert haben und wie schwierig es für sie ist, dies zu überwinden und andere Arbeitsbedingungen für sich zu fordern. Die westliche Welt verschärft die Mechanismen unterschiedlicher Bezahlung nach Geschlecht, Hautfarbe und Herkunft, weshalb diese Fragestellung ein öffentliches Statement im Namen der PAT war.

Gesten und Apparate erzielen eine Wirkung; sie sind ein Mittel zum Verständnis des Inhalts der Lesungen und zur Einordnung der Reaktionen des Publikums. Die PAT setzt auf kritische Reflexion und will ihre pädagogische Dimension zur Geltung bringen. Einige Gesten in den SPL zielten provokativ auf Vorurteile und reaktionäre Einstellungen ab, die in unserer Gesellschaft entweder offensichtlich oder unterschwellig vorhanden sind. Wir präsentierten Panos Sklavenitis' Videoinstallation South, in der eine umstrittene Persönlichkeit in provokanter Weise über den Süden spricht. Dabei entwickelt sie Ideen rund um eine europäische Geografie von oben und unten, die Konstrukte wie Nationalstolz sowie Minderwertigkeits- und Überlegenheitskomplexe hinterfragt. Ein weiteres Beispiel ist der Videovortrag The Champions of Pleasure, bei dem eine weitere Persönlichkeit eine schwul-lesbische Lesart der griechischen Geschichte von der Antike bis zur Neuzeit vorschlägt. Weitere Gesten wie das Werk Aspa von Constantinos Hadzinikolaou blickten in subtilerer Art und Weise auf unsere jüngere Geschichte und kulturelle Tradition, um unsere Vergangenheit und vor allem unsere gegenwärtige Lage zu verstehen, aber auch die Deutungen unserer Identität als Frauen, Kulturschaffende oder einfach nur als Bürger/innen in einer bestimmten Zeit und an einem bestimmten Ort. Diese Gesten bieten einen Rahmen, der mit politischer Subjektivität einhergeht. Sie kommentieren den Prozess des kollektiven Handelns, der im Sinne einer Veränderung der Bedeutung von Gegenständen bzw. von Aspekten unserer Biografie eine transformative Funktion übernimmt.

Die Zusammenstellung von Lesungen, Archiven, Kunstwerken und Texten zur Krise und ihren Themen – wie das SPL-Archiv und die Performance von Sprechakten über den Süden und seine sozialen, wirtschaftlichen und privaten Themen – wirft Fragen zu Macht und Identität auf und bestärkt den Willen, neue Strukturen zu schaffen. Dies sind instituierende Praktiken mit dem Ziel, naturalisierte Kategorien aufzubrechen und neue Bedeutungen für öffentliche Räume und öffentliche Ansprüche zu fördern. Die Erzeugung

*solcher Sprechakte und Archive
ist eine Aktion, die bewusst oder unbe-
absichtigt Geschichten produziert.
Äußerer (physischer) und innerer
(psychischer) Raum werden dabei auf
die gleiche natürliche Weise erzeugt,
in der wir die Erschaffung greifbarer
Objekte verstehen. Wir können in
unseren Performances nicht vorbe-
haltlos die Äußerungen verschiedener
militanter oder prekärer und unterge-
ordneter Individuen als eine a priori
positive Entwicklung darstellen, sollten jedoch die entscheidende Rolle
würdigen, die ihrem öffentlichen Auf-
treten durch einen Sprechakt oder ein
Archiv zukommt, das heißt durch einen
diskursiven, verdichteten öffentlichen
Raum, in dem die Veröffentlichung,
Abstimmung und Verbreitung ihrer
Forderungen und Existenzbedingun-
gen stattfindet.*

Mit den Soft Power Lectures
*setzte sich die Temporäre Kunstaka-
demie das Ziel, die Wirkmechanismen
zu untersuchen, die nötig sind, um
innerhalb von Institutionen kritische
Praktiken in Gang zu setzen. Gleichzeitig hinterfragte sie etablierte Methoden der Wissenserzeugung und Sub-
jektivierung. Mit der Reflexion über
die Institution im Verhältnis zu kritischen Praktiken und über die seit den
1990er-Jahren geführten Debatten im
Kunstbereich wie über die „Institution
als Prozess"[3] und spezifischer über
den Gedanken, dass Instituierung
auch innerhalb von Einzelpersonen
und sozialen Gefügen stattfindet,
agierten die* Soft Power Lectures *von
der Position der Macht aus, statt sich
auf eine moralisierende Nebenrolle
zurückzuziehen. Der Süden bean-
spruchte eine Stimme, die seiner geo-
und biopolitischen Lage entsprach.
Allerdings ist Süden kein Konzept, das
eine Verortung als eine autonome,
separate Einheit verlangt oder sich –*

*der globalen „Bedrohung" widersetzend
– als Widerstand gegen den Norden
oder irgendeine andere Region definiert.
„Süden" stellt den Gedanken infrage,
dass Forderungen eine neutrale kosmo-
politische Vorstellung sind, wobei das
Hauptrisiko darin besteht, dass Kosmo-
politismus ausschließlich zur Bezeich-
nung flexibler Menschen mit den richtigen Papieren – einer reisenden Elite
– verwendet werden kann. Im Gegenteil:
Die Verwendung des Begriffs Süden ist
ein Vorwand, der unterstreicht, dass
diese Forderungen innerhalb der Kon-
texte von Wirtschaft, Arbeit und Gesellschaft erhoben werden, in denen wir
uns bewegen.*

ELPIDA KARABA, GLYKERIA STATHOPOULOU

1. *Unser besonderer Dank gilt Anastasia Douka, Nikos
   Alexopoulos, Angelos Krallis, Yiannis Papadopoulos,
   Thalia Raftopoulou und Kostis Velonis, die Werke
   und Apparate für die* Soft Power Lectures *schufen.
   Ihr Beitrag bereicherte die Lesungen in mehr als
   einer Hinsicht.*
2. *Begriffe im Zusammenhang mit öffentlichen Forde-
   rungen untersucht Nikos Stasinopoulos in seinem
   Beitrag „The Subject and the Object of the Claim:
   Towards a Lacanian Discourse Theoretic Approach"
   für einen in Kürze erscheinenden Essayband (Athen,
   Papazisis Publishers), http://www.academia.edu
   /28988568/The_Subject_and_the_Object_of_the
   _Claim._Towards_a_Lacanian_discourse_theoretic
   _approach.*
3. *Näheres über Institutionen als Prozess findet sich bei
   Gerald Raunig und Gene Ray,* Art and Contemporary
   Critical Practice: Reinventing Institutional Critique
   (London, MayFly Books, 2009).

Athens–Oberhausen: The Energy of Two Cities

Where does the assumption that the crisis produces creative subjects and "creative cities" come from?

Wie ist die Annahme entstanden, dass die Krise kreative Subjekte und „kreative Städte" erzeugt?

The *Soft Power Lectures* performative series begins with the visit of the Temporary Academy of Arts (PAT) to the ex-industrial city of Oberhausen in Germany. PAT attempts to think out loud about the conditions governing programmes of urban development in six Balkan cities. The Academy is invited to bring art into play in matters relating to the city, immigration, and labour. Utilising lectures as one tool amongst a number of other media, PAT attempts to highlight the contradictions, hidden agendas, and its own controversial role as an artistic/educational programme with regard to contemporary methods of gentrification and compliance affecting cities and their subjects. Where does the assumption that the crisis produces creative subjects and "creative cities" come from? How are narratives of contemporary urban centres as "energies" constructed? How can these energies be symbolically capitalised in market terms? In what way are they made to conform to regulative art and urban projects.

Die Veranstaltungsreihe The Soft Power Lectures *beginnt mit der Reise der Temporären Kunstakademie (PAT) in die ehemalige Industriestadt Oberhausen. Die PAT versucht, laut über die Bedingungen für die Durchführung von Stadtentwicklungsprogrammen in sechs Balkanstädten nachzudenken. Die PAT ist aufgefordert, die Kunst in Bezug auf die Gegenstandsbereiche Stadt, Migration und Arbeit ins Spiel zu bringen. Vorlesungen sind eines von mehreren Medien, mit denen die PAT versucht, Widersprüche, heimliche Absichten und ihre eigene kontroverse Rolle als Kunst-/Bildungsprojekt gegenüber den gegenwärtigen Erscheinungsformen der Gentrifizierung und der Willfährigkeit zu beleuchten, von denen Städte und ihre Bürger/innen betroffen sind. Wie kam es zu der Annahme, die Krise erzeuge kreative Subjekte und „kreative Städte"? Wie sind die Narrative über moderne urbane Zentren als „Energien" aufgebaut? Wie kann man von diesen Energien unter Marktbedingungen symbolisch profitieren? Wie werden sie an regulierende Kunst und urbane Projekte angepasst?*

Project: Temporary Academy of Arts (PAT) → Format: lecture, performance, installation, video → Date: 27 February 2016 → Venue: State of Concept, Tousa Botsari 19, Athens → Participants: Elpida Karaba (lecture); Panos Sklavenitis, Constantinos Hadzinikolaou, Anastasia Douka (artworks)

ACTOPOLIS

Interviews

Currently the energy of the city seems to be very high. A "youthful" left-wing government is laying claim to a paradigm shift for Europe, while at the same time various events are catapulting this energy sky high.

Zurzeit scheint die Stadt voller Energie zu sein. Eine „junge" linke Regierung fordert einen Paradigmenwechsel für Europa, während gleichzeitig verschiedene Veranstaltungen diese Energie in schwindelerregende Höhen treiben.

In anticipation of documenta 14, the local art scene seems to be alert and full of expectations, experiencing not only euphoria but also a heightened awareness of the exoticisation of the city and its subjects. In any case, the scene has already changed: foreign visitors, official and unofficial, stroll in the galleries, trendy hangouts, and occupied spaces of the city. At the same time, the Athens Biennale is taking place, aptly reflecting upon its own role as an institution that is in a critical bottleneck both at a local and international level. While in the occupied space of Green Park, artists and politicians, intellectuals and non-intellectuals contemplate the issues of anti-/meta-/institutionalism. PAT is organising a series of performative interviews, inviting various "creative" subjects who take the city as their topic, who narrate the city, along with artists and activist groups who occupy the city, who occupy active or inactive joints, who are participating in the Biennale or working for documenta as well as those who are not taking part in either of these events.

Im Vorfeld der documenta 14 herrschen in der Kunstszene Euphorie und eine erhöhte Erwartungshaltung; es besteht aber auch die Befürchtung, dass die Stadt und ihre Einwohner/innen exotisiert werden könnten. Auf jeden Fall hat sich die Szenerie bereits verändert, offizielle und inoffizielle Besucher/innen aus dem Ausland schlendern durch Galerien, Trendläden und besetzte Räume der Stadt. Die PAT veranstaltet eine Reihe performativer Interviews, zu denen sie „Kreative" einlädt, die die Stadt zu ihrem Thema gemacht haben und zu ihrem Narrativ beitragen. Des Weiteren werden Künstler/innen und politische Gruppen angesprochen, die die Stadt besetzen, sich an aktiven oder inaktiven Nahtstellen befinden, an der Biennale oder der documenta mitwirken oder aber auch nicht an diesen Veranstaltungen teilnehmen.

Project: Temporary Academy of Arts (PAT) → Format: lecture, interviews → Date: 18 March 2016 → Venue: Café Bar, Socratous 42, Athens → Participants: Sepake Angiama, Ana Dana Beroš, Constantinos Giannaris, Xenia Kalpaktsoglou & Poka Yio, Fanis Kafantaris, Yelta Köm, Petros Moris, Vassilis Noulas, Constantina Theodorou, Mirjana Utvić, Danijela Dugandžić, 3137, Despina Zefkili, Panos Sklavenitis, Elpida Karaba, Glykeria Stathopoulou

How much I enjoy listening to people in the elevator speaking Romanian

Creating networks and exchanging knowledge

Netzwerke schaffen und Kenntnisse austauschen

In an attempt to examine the practical and pragmatic aspects of the narratives of the crisis and creative resilient cities, the Temporary Academy of Arts (PAT) is organising parallel lectures, inviting partners from Balkan countries that are participating in the ACTOPOLIS programme in order to create a network and exchange knowledge about the ways one can deal with the instrumentalisation of symbolic artistic capital as it relates to the normalisation of contemporary cities and the survival of workers in the art field.

Um die praktischen und pragmatischen Aspekte von Krisennarrativen und Narrativen kreativer, unverwüstlicher Städte zu erkunden, veranstaltet die Temporäre Kunstakademie (PAT) Parallelvorlesungen, zu denen die Partner aus den an ACTOPOLIS teilnehmenden Balkanländern eingeladen sind. Dabei sollen auch ein Netzwerk aufgebaut und Kenntnisse darüber ausgetauscht werden, wie man mit der Instrumentalisierung von symbolischem künstlerischen Kapital umgehen kann, damit es zur Normalisierung moderner Städte und zum Überleben der Kunstschaffenden beiträgt.

Project: Temporary Academy of Arts (PAT) → Format: lectures, talks → Dates: 19 March 2016 →
Venue: Circuits and Currents, Project Space of the Athens School of Fine Arts, Notara 13 & Tositsa,
Exarcheia, Athens → Participants: Ana Dana Beroš, Yelta Köm, Mirjana Utvić, Danijela Dugandžić
(speakers); Elpida Karaba (moderator)

Where will you go after this?

The lecture aims to explore the exotic view of Athens as a Southern experiment of creative sustainability in times of crisis.

Der Vortrag untersucht den exotischen Blick auf Athen als südliches Experiment kreativer Nachhaltigkeit in Krisenzeiten.

Can we problematise the emphasis that is placed exclusively on the positive aspects of characteristics such as flexibility, sustainability, performativity, resourcefulness, creativity, informality, etc., which have lately become fixed points of reference for both institutions and the art scene? Athens is delineated as a focal point of resistance that can educate and suggest strategies of survival and novel ways to make art without money, through alternative economies and communitarian practices. What problems does this image create, viewed through the lens of a European landscape of precarity, of cuts in funding for cultural programmes and the humanities, and the establishment of art as an unpaid hobby?

68 Project: Temporary Academy of Arts (PAT) → Format: lecture → Date: 31 March 2016 →
Venue: Athens School of Fine Arts, Piraeus Street, Athens → Participants: Despina Zefkili (lecture)

Können wir die ausschließlich positiven Vorzeichen von Eigenschaften wie Flexibilität, Nachhaltigkeit, Performativität, Einfallsreichtum, Kreativität, Informalität usw., die in letzter Zeit feste Bezugspunkte nicht nur für große Institutionen, sondern auch für den Athener Kulturbetrieb sind, kritisch hinterfragen? Athen wird als Zentrum des Widerstands dargestellt, das Überlebensstrategien erlernen und vorschlagen sowie neue Wege finden kann, wie Kunst ohne finanzielle Mittel mithilfe alternativer wirtschaftlicher und kommunitaristischer Praktiken machbar ist. Wie problematisch ist dieses Bild in einem prekären Europa, wo Mittel für Kultur und Geisteswissenschaften gekürzt werden und Kunst nur noch als unbezahltes Hobby gilt?

Soft Power Screenings:
The Gaze

An assemblage of cinematographic
views of the cities of the crisis,
on their subjects and their physical
being

*Eine Montage aus kinematografi-
schen Blicken auf Städte der Krise,
ihre Subjekte und ihr physisches
Befinden*

A series of *Soft Power* projections
in Munich. Munich meets Athens—
not Munich or Athens themselves
but rather cities representing the
centre and the periphery, West and
East, Germany and the Balkans/
Greece—and the two exchange
awkward, guilty, sullen, innocent,
and aggressive glances. The common variables include students
of architecture, urban planning,
art, and other media, citizens, and
passers-by.

Eine Reihe von Soft Power-*Film-
vorführungen in München. München
trifft Athen – nicht München oder
Athen selbst, sondern vielmehr
Städte, die Zentrum und Peripherie
versinnbildlichen, West und
Ost, Deutschland und den Balkan/
Griechenland – und beide wech-
seln verlegene, schuldbewusste,
finstere, unschuldige und aggressive
Blicke. Zu den üblichen Variablen
zählen Studierende von Architektur
und Städtebau, Kunst und anderen
Medien sowie Bürger/innen und
Passanten.*

Project: Sofia Dona → Format: screenings → Films: *Oi voskoi* (1967), directed by Nikos Papatakis;
The Idlers of the Fertile Valley (1978), directed by Nikos Panayotopoulos; *Girls in the Sun* (1968),
directed by Vasilis Georgiadis—performed with simultaneous translation; *Katzelmacher* (1969),
directed by Rainer Werner Fassbinder—performed in Athens with simultaneous translation →
Dates: April/May 2016 → Venues: Oskar von Miller Forum, Munich; Das Kreativquartier, Munich →
Participants: students of architecture, art, and film, invited artists, and architects

Athens—The Soft Power Lectures

From Sunset to Sunrise

"I have a sunset and a sunrise, but what do I show in between? Everything is that bastard Buñuel's fault who sliced the eye of the dog, taming cinema. If he had left it intact, now maybe we might have had some courage to see our own images, but look how we ended up! Finding pleasure and retreat in the hooey of exoticism." Starting with the opening scene of *India Song* by Marguerite Duras, Constantinos Hadzinikolaou attempts to connect the films he has chosen with the permanent collection of the Folk Art Museum of Acharnes, where the evening starts with a tour.

„Ich habe einen Sonnenuntergang und einen Sonnenaufgang, aber was zeige ich dazwischen? Das alles ist die Schuld von diesem Mistkerl Buñuel, der dem Hund das Auge aufschlitzte und damit das Kino zähmte. Hätte er es intakt gelassen, dann hätten wir jetzt vielleicht den Mut, unsere eigenen Bilder anzusehen, aber seht nur, wo wir gelandet sind! Vergnügen und Zuflucht in exotischem Blödsinn zu finden." Ausgehend von der Eingangsszene des Films India Song *von Marguerite Duras, versucht Constantinos Hadzinikolaou, die von ihm ausgewählten Filme mit der Dauerausstellung des Volkskundemuseums von Archarnes zu verbinden, in dem der Abend mit einer Führung beginnt.*

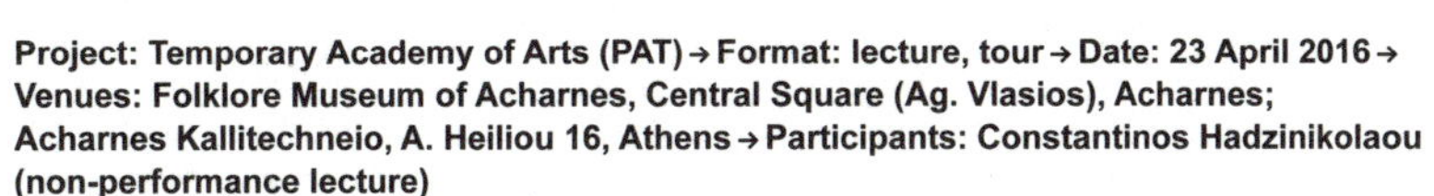

Project: Temporary Academy of Arts (PAT) → Format: lecture, tour → Date: 23 April 2016 → Venues: Folklore Museum of Acharnes, Central Square (Ag. Vlasios), Acharnes; Acharnes Kallitechneio, A. Heiliou 16, Athens → Participants: Constantinos Hadzinikolaou (non-performance lecture)

South: Ideas around a European Geography of Top and Bottom

Maps—the way we read them: the North at the top and the South at the bottom. OK. Now let's think about what that might mean.

Landkarten, so wie wir sie sehen: Der Norden ist oben und der Süden unten. Na gut. Und was bedeutet das?

If we try to locate the connotations of the "top" and the "bottom", it is easy to see that the top is equated exclusively with a plus sign and the bottom with a minus. The North is indeed naturally and inevitably higher than the South on all levels. It enjoys an undeniable economic, social, cultural, and political supremacy, and even though that supremacy was fairly won, at the same time it has also been bestowed on it. In any case, this natural superiority of the North has a geopolitical aspect. When we finally stop sucking on the candy of the elevated geopolitical importance supposedly enjoyed by Greece due to its geographical location, we may be able to see the obvious. Consider the famous Dorian invasion or the headlong manner in which Indo-Europeans surged from North to South, and now try to think of any great historical route that has witnessed such a movement in the opposite direction. Right, there aren't any.

Wenn wir versuchen, die Konnotationen von „oben" und „unten" einzuordnen, stellen wir sehr schnell fest, dass „oben" ausschließlich mit positiven und „unten" mit negativen Vorzeichen behaftet sind. Der Norden ist sogar naturgemäß und zwangsläufig auf allen Ebenen dem Süden voraus. Er nimmt eine klare wirtschaftliche, soziale, kulturelle und politische Vormachtstellung ein, die er sich zwar erkämpft hat, die ihm aber gleichzeitig auch geschenkt wurde. Diese natürliche Vormacht des Nordens hat allerdings auch einen geopolitischen Aspekt. Wenn wir endlich aufhören, uns an der erhöhten geopolitischen Bedeutung zu ergötzen, die Griechenland aufgrund seiner geografischen Lage angeblich genießt, können wir vielleicht das Offensichtliche erkennen. Denken Sie nur an die berühmte Dorische Wanderung oder an den massiven Vorstoß der Indoeuropäer vom Norden in den Süden und versuchen Sie, sich an eine historisch gesehen ebenso bedeutsame Wanderbewegung in entgegengesetzter Richtung zu erinnern. Ganz genau, es gibt sie nicht.

Project: Temporary Academy of Arts (PAT) → Format: lecture → Date: 12 May 2016 → Venue: Panteion University, Department of Anthropology → Participants: Panos Sklavenitis (lecture)

South.
Ideas around a European geography of the top and the bottom

The Soft Power Lectures Show

In its sixth and final edition, the *Soft Power Lectures* culminated in a polyphonic event on a basketball court at Panteion University.

Mit ihrer sechsten und letzten Vorlesung erreichte die Reihe der Soft Power Lectures *in einer vielstimmigen Veranstaltung auf einem Basketballfeld der Panteion-Universität ihren Höhepunkt.*

At the *Soft Power Lectures Show,* various materials were presented, such as artist's books, videos, lectures, artworks, and apparatuses produced within the context of the *Soft Power Lectures* presented by the Temporary Academy of Arts (PAT). This discursive and variable material forms a particular narrative around the South and its subjects that runs counter to its stereotypical depiction. Some of the recurring themes in the *Soft Power Lectures* series have been reflections on our institutional surroundings, precarity, and labour issues as well as the mechanisms of the art field. For the final show, PAT invited international artists and ACTOPOLIS participants from Hamburg and Bucharest to reflect on the material and the artworks presented and freely respond to the *Soft Power Lectures* through their own practices.

In dieser Soft Power Lectures Show wurden verschiedene Materialien präsentiert, von Kunstbüchern und Videos über Vorlesungen und Kunstwerke bis hin zu Geräten, die im Rahmen der von der Temporären Kunstakademie (PAT) präsentierten Soft Power Lectures entstanden sind. Dieses diskursive und unterschiedliche Material bildet ein besonderes Narrativ rund um „den Süden" und seine Bewohner/innen, das der üblichen stereotypen Beschreibung zuwiderläuft. Wiederkehrende Themen in der Lecture-Reihe waren Betrachtungen über unsere institutionelle Umgebung, Prekarität sowie Fragen zur Arbeit und den Mechanismen des Kunstbereichs. Zu dieser Abschlussveranstaltung lud die PAT internationale Künstler/innen und ACTOPOLIS-Teilnehmer/innen aus Hamburg und Bukarest ein, um über die präsentierten Materialien und Kunstwerke zu reflektieren und mit ihren eigenen Praktiken frei auf die Soft Power Lectures zu reagieren.

Project: Temporary Academy of Arts (PAT) → Format: exhibition → Date: 31 May 2016 →
Venue: Basketball Court, Panteion University, Ipponaktos Street, Neos Kosmos, Athens →
Participants: Temporary Academy of Arts (PAT) (Elpida Karaba, Glykeria Stathopoulou, Sofia Dona, Constantinos Hadzinikolaou, Panos Sklavenitis, Despina Zefkili); Stefania Ablianiti & Stavroula Morakea, Angelos Krallis, Yannis Papadopoulos, Thalia Raftopoulou, Kostis Velonis (invited artists)

Making

This dubious hope of changing things on a material level: of doing something real, something immediate, maybe even using your hands—like the hand on the big Hornbach billboard that we saw displayed across five storeys on this building in Bucharest. Would it help if people knew how much time artists spend in DIY stores?

Nevertheless. We still want to make things, make things happen, make things real. It is about the things we imagine actually manifesting physically, about sharing time and space with something that before was only an idea.

Diese zweifelhafte Hoffnung, Dinge auf materieller Ebene zu verändern: etwas Reales, etwas Unmittelbares zu tun, vielleicht sogar mit den Händen – wie die Hand auf der riesigen Reklametafel von Hornbach, die sich an einem Gebäude in Bukarest über fünf Stockwerke erstreckt. Würde es helfen, wenn die Leute wüssten, wie viel Zeit Künstler/innen in Baumärkten verbringen?

Trotzdem. Wir wollen immer noch Dinge tun, Dinge in Gang setzen, Dinge real werden lassen. Es geht darum, die Dinge, die wir uns vorstellen, tatsächlich physisch umzusetzen, und darum, Zeit und Raum mit etwas zu teilen, das zuvor nur eine Idee war.

geheimagentur

Playing

Two things related to playing that we like:
1. Having fun.
2. Pretending, acting "as if"—"as if" another world was possible, as if we could build a new city, etc.—the "as if" of any manifesto: as if this was realistic, as if we were in a position to do something. And then see how real it becomes. Realism is the problem, not reality.

Playing: entering into a long-distance relationship with reality; sometimes, meeting each other halfway.

Am Spielen gefallen uns zwei Dinge:
1. Spaß haben
2. Etwas vorspielen, so tun, „als ob" – „als ob" eine andere Welt möglich wäre, als ob wir eine neue Stadt bauen könnten usw. – das „Als-ob" eines jeden Manifests: als ob das realistisch wäre, als ob wir etwas tun könnten. Und dann sehen, wie real es wird. Der Realismus ist das Problem, nicht die Realität.

Spielen heißt, eine Fernbeziehung mit der Realität einzugehen und sich manchmal auf halbem Weg zu treffen.

geheimagentur

Recording

Recording visually is a bodily experience. Although subjectivity is the main protagonist, the image regime is dependent on the action and layers of research, which leads to a shift in the role of the subject (who is recording). Visual and sound recording in research are also related to forensics, in which recording serves as an image-based act of forensic evidence.

> *Visuelles Aufnehmen ist eine körperliche Erfahrung. Obwohl die Subjektivität die Hauptakteurin ist, hängt das Bildregime vom Handeln und den Erkundungsebenen ab, was zu einer Verschiebung in der Rolle der (aufnehmenden) Person führt. Im Rahmen der Erforschung stehen Bild- und Tonaufnahmen auch mit der Forensik in Zusammenhang, bei der Aufnahmen als bildbasierte forensische Beweise dienen.*

Pelin Tan

BELGRADE

Social Disorganisation and Self-Organised Cultural Production in Belgrade

The Belgrade edition of ACTOPOLIS, titled *Formally Informal: Belgrade Self-Organised Cultural Production*,[1] is oriented towards questioning the circumstances in which we find ourselves today, looking deeply into the practices of cultural professionals and their mutual differences and achievements, and trying to avoid imagining we are a unified group and understandable to one another. Because we are not. Moreover, the more particular and specific each of us is, the more challenging and vital cultural production becomes.

The urban cultural sphere in Serbia, particularly in Belgrade, has drastically altered over the past twenty-five years. The internal and external circumstances of the country's statehood have changed due to the demise of SFR Yugoslavia (whose capital was Belgrade), civil wars, full international sanctions,[2] monetary inflation, huge demographic changes, civil protests, bombing, the decay of one political regime and its replacement with another—and another and yet another—territorial fragmentation, a decrease in living standards, economic instability, etc. In the meantime, the contexts throughout the European continent have themselves been engulfed in turbulent processes.

In the former Yugoslavia, time is usually referred to as "before" or "after" the 1990s. The 1990s tested all aspects of civilisation, and everyone failed.

Since 2000 many state institutions have been closed down in Serbia—some permanently, some temporarily—including the National Museum, the Museum of Contemporary Art, and the annual October Salon; one can observe the development of an events industry and the festivalisation of cultural production with an emphasis on amateur and folkloric productions, and hence a lack of support for process-based professional productions. The official cultural policies express a preference for "cultural institutions" over cultural professionals who are not employed in state institutions, creating an atmosphere of polarisation—even though everyone is, in fact, underfunded.

Outlining the general circumstances of cultural production not only in Serbia and Belgrade but also on a much wider scale, reveals what one might call "social disorganisation": "a state of society characterized by the breakdown of effective social control resulting in a lack of functional integration between groups, conflicting social attitudes, and personal maladjustment."[3] In an attempt to keep up with the tendencies of Western society, particularly since 2000, most of the social and political concepts in Serbia seem to have been imported as ready-to-use, critically unchecked, and locally uncalibrated, with an uncanny feeling of a "collective failure of imagination".[4] The question we are going to tackle here is, what kind of urban culture survived this chicanery, and what substance and significance does it retain today?

The Belgrade edition of the ACTOPOLIS project lands in this particular urban (art) context. It is focused on the specificities of relevant non-institutional cultural production manifested in performative research. The programme brings together fourteen artists, art groups, activists, and cultural practitioners of very different orientations, whose practices resonate with the questions of what, how, and for whom critical urban culture is produced in times of ongoing crisis, refracted through self-organised methodologies. What characterises the economy of cultural independence in Serbia fifteen years after the beginning of the century and twenty-five years after the country's social meltdown? What is the critical potential of self-organisation in cultural practices? To what extent can self-organisation secure the autonomy of thought and action in the arts? To what extent is self-organisation an alternative to non-functional institutions and what role does neo-liberalism play in this?

The Goethe-Institut Belgrade, as the co-producer of ACTOPOLIS, came up with two lines of production: on the one hand, *City Guerilla* (Gradska Gerila)/ *Goethe Guerilla* (GG) and *Urban Incubator* (UI)—both masterfully coordinated by Zorica Milisavljević—and on the other, a selection that I curated and coordinated.

The participation of GG and UI in *Formally Informal* was focused on an exploration of what they had achieved so far and the outlook for future productions. They also used the ACTOPOLIS temporary venue to test their practices in a new environment, other than Savamala, and did a number of performances, talks, and presentations during the first two weeks of May.

In selecting my projects, I invited artists or cultural practitioners who were intentionally chosen to express a high degree of diversity and to bring the different micro-politics of cultural production within the scope of the project, shedding light on Belgrade's heterogeneous cultural practices and their impact on current economic, social, and political conditions: Will it ever be possible to attain an overview of the current cultural climate and its production, or will it remain just a vague and fragmented image of another turbulent era, as lasting and trying as this one? How does the lack of state policy in culture and the social (or otherwise) position of the arts reflect in contemporary urban culture?

Before the programme was publicly presented, the participants and I went through an internal process of negotiating our individual positions. Over several months we fostered unlikely alliances—the intentional temporality of the project's spatial format reflected the temporality of the group.

Instead of using the existing venues or spaces for culture that bear a distinct aura of their founders, managers, artists, and audiences, a conscious decision was made to stage *Formally Informal* primarily in a rented ground-floor apartment space in the historical urban neighbourhood of Dorćol—which is currently going through a process of gentrification—throughout May 2016, when the majority of the programmes happened.

The apartment itself is part of a post–World War I house. Though a hybrid space, it had never before been used for culture and most likely never would be again. It was a neutral ground for everyone, where a unique bunch of project participants and audiences intersected with each other. We were experimenting with the possibility of communicating while occupying this temporary space together.[5] It was curious that all the exhibits, performances, and discussions were carefully layered and amalgamated one with the other, day after day—not least on the physical level, within the space.[6]

A few programmes happened outside the apartment, in public squares, in alternative underground cultural centres like Matrijaršija, or even in a private house in the outer suburbs of Belgrade. The other Belgrade independent venues that directly relate to the project—Magacin u Kraljevića Marka (MKM8), Remont Gallery, Art Space U10,

Oktobar, Kvaka 22, Cultural Centre Grad, and the Centre for Cultural Decontamination—are scattered all over the city.

The response the individual artists and activists gave to the overall theme of *Formally Informal* was very different, in keeping with the initial idea. Some of the participants tried to pinpoint the agency we use in facing the discontinuation of culture as we know it (Ristić, Radić, Cvetković, Sekulić/Đorđević, and Nikolić), others performed their practices (Vučetić, Radoš/Karić, U10, and Cvetić), while a third group used activist means to address relationships established on the outer limits of the cultural field (Milikić/Kurepa, KURS, and Ramujkić/Treister).

Irena Ristić questioned the essence of the notion of "self-organisation" framing the *Formally Informal* project through which she examined the potential of contemporary cultural practices of collectivity, togetherness, and commons versus individual endeavours. Nikola Radić Lucati and Marijana Cvetković questioned the conditions that allowed the appearance of practices that we today call "self-organised", spanning the period from the beginning of the 1990s to the mid-2000s. Aleksandra Sekulić/Ivica Đorđević elucidated one of the curious phenomena coming out of these circumstances, while Aleksandar Nikolić produced a current map of Belgrade's visual arts venues and their programmes, where there is no distinction made between those founded by a government body (be it local, state, or foreign) and the alternative, marginal, and experimental ones. Anica Vučetić, Marija Radoš/Miroslav Karić, the U10 Art Collective, and Mariela Cvetić performed the artistic positions and practices of different generations in a variety of ways. Nebojša Milikić/Tadej Kurepa, KURS, and Vahida Ramujkić/Noa Treister each negotiated particular social issues from their artist-activist position. As it happened, all of them claimed group authorship. In addition, Sandra Stojanović, one of the younger generation of Belgrade's visual artists, produced a series of critical blogs about the ACTOPOLIS Belgrade programme.

Throughout the project, revealing contradictions emerged—leftist artists arguing for unequal payment; precarious workers advocating the corporate system of production; public discussions that faced away from the interested audience; a critique of a self-(un)reflexivity that excludes one's own position… Then again, some of the ambiguities in the project were brought out intentionally as a means to question the boundaries of the field being researched, like inhabiting a private apartment space in an area that is currently undergoing gentrification or producing a project on self-organisation in the context of a large-scale national institution such as the Goethe-Institut.

Formally Informal was an attempt by non-institutional individuals—most often cultural professionals and activists who are not satisfied with the system (and systemic framework) they find themselves part of [7]—to articulate a sense of urgency to communicate through forms of culture and art that are oriented towards the public, from the bottom up. One could say that on a day-to-day basis these relations produce a non-commercial cultural climate of self-empowerment.

Within the project, the notion of self-organisation itself was highly stimulating and left no one indifferent: greeted with scorn, opposition, and denial at the outset, over time it became more comprehensible but also tended towards the more or less uncritical assimilation of the concept of self-organisation. The outcomes of the project's highly intentional openness were often treated as incidental. In this way, some of the participants in turn censored the framework that hosted their works and projects—similar to the censorship their independent/self-organised cultural production had been subjected to in the past by the bodies in power, who overlooked the significant contribution they made to the cultural scene. Having said that, invaluable support in understanding the topic came from the most unexpected quarters.[8]

One of the biggest crossroads we encountered in trying to reach an understanding of the practice of self-organisation was the question of whether self-organising empowers one to be artistically proactive or whether it can also denote the inner power to face adverse circumstances with schemes that are less pretentious and project-like. Self-organisation is definitely not a recipe for a self-sufficient system. Rather, it offers a certain distrust of options offered to us by the state or the corporations (of late, it is ever more difficult to separate these)—a drop of our own cynicism as an antidote to the growing cynicism and mistrust that surround us at every possible level, including disseminated mass self-organisation, which, it would appear, is precariously self-exploitative.

The term "self-organisation" is often identified as a neo-liberal term of alienation from the welfare state and a path of brutish one-way commercialisation of the arts. Yet, could it be reconceived as a daily practice for individuals (or, even better, a "multitude of singularities"[9]) resisting ongoing processes of monopolisation in the arts and culture? Could self-organisation in such a case become a means of autonomy, opposed to the loss of the individual voice through its concealment in/by the crowd? The dilemma we face should definitely not be this: Should I exploit myself or should somebody else do it? In this way, self-organised cultural production is forced into a particular methodology as a means to resist circumstances.

Formally Informal was not developed as some kind of consolidation plan for contemporary cultural production in Serbia—and even less as a plan of action. Essentially, *Formally Informal* opened up a space of reflection that is otherwise difficult to find. The project examined ways in which artistic and activist agency deals with newly found circumstances questioning the overall frame that subdues or appears highly unfavourable to the slowly developing (which is not necessarily a bad thing) cultural production of an essentially modernist heritage. What is today's economy of creative, critical, and intellectual needs, and what are its conditions of production?

MIRJANA BOBA STOJADINOVIĆ

1   Even though the term "self-organisation" is ambiguous, it is used here to retain consistency in the language of a three-year project, applying to a specific spectrum of meanings, some affirmative, some critical. If at some point after the completion of the project we find a better term to describe what we currently understand as "self-organised", the term should definitely be changed.
2   These applied to, among other things, sport, culture, education, and medical supplies.
3   See http://www.merriam-webster.com/dictionary/social%20disorganization.
4   Martha Rosler, "Culture Class: Art, Creativity, Urbanism, Part II", e-*flux journal* 23 (March 2011).
5   See Hito Steyerl, "Art as Occupation: Claims for an Autonomy of Life", e-*flux journal* 30 (December 2011), http://www.e-flux.com/journal/art-as-occupation-claims-for-an-autonomy-of-life-12/.
6   Recordings of all the discussions (*in Serbian) can be listened to here: https://www.mixcloud.com/actopolis2016/.
7   Pinning down "the system" is indeed a treacherous task, but one could say that it is precisely this diffuseness and inconsistency that today's system is based on.
8   Not least from artists and curators Renée Turner, Simon Kentgens, and Jason E. Bowman, and journalist Snežana Stamenković. I regret in the end not having been able to host writers and curators Jan Verwoert and Federica Bueti in the project, whose contributions would have been vital in the general discussion.

9 These ideas draw inspiration from, among other
   things, the conceptual practices of the "artist in the
   first person" from the 1970s, which convey the
   vulnerability and exposure experienced by singularities—rather like Agamben's "whatever singularities".

Further resources:
Blagojević, Jelisaveta, *Politike nemislivog: Uvod
   u ne-fašistički život* (Belgrade: Centar za medije
   i komunikacije, FMK, Univerzitet Singidunum, 2014).
Boym, Svetlana, *The Future of Nostalgia* (New York:
   Basic Books, 2001).
Ćurčić, Branka, "Autonomous Spaces of Deregulation
   and Critique: Is a Cooperation with Neoliberal Art
   Institutions Possible?", in "Progressive Institutions",
   Transversal (June 2007), http://eipcp.net
   /transversal/0407/curcic/en. See also Boris Buden's
   commentary.
Denegri, Ješa, *Opstanak umetnosti u vremenu krize*
   (Belgrade: Cicero, 2004).
Hebert, Stine and Anne Szefer Karlsen (eds.),
   Self-Organised (London/Bergen: Open editions/
   Hordaland Kunstsenter, 2013).
Hubeli, Ernst, "City-culture versus City of Culture?", in *M
   City: European Cityscapes* (Graz: Kunsthaus Graz, 2006).
Jakšić, Jasna, et al., *From Consideration to Commitment:
   Art in Critical Confrontation to Society (Belgrade,
   Ljubljana, Skopje, Zagreb: 1990–2010)*, e-book
   produced as part of the LTCA project implemented by
   SEEcult.org (Belgrade, Serbia), in collaboration with
   Artservis.org (Ljubljana, Slovenia), Forum Skopje
   (Skopje, Macedonia [FYROM]), and Kulturpunkt.hr
   (Zagreb, Croatia), http://inseecp.blogspot.gr/2011
   /04/e-book-art-in-critical-confrontation-to.html.
Karić, Miroslav, and Marija Radoš, "Actopolis Belgrade/
   Studija individualnog slučaja", *Supervizuelna:
   Magazine for Contemporary Art* (blog; 21 September
   2016), http://www.supervizuelna.com/actopolis
   -belgrade-studija-individualnog-slucaja/.
Mickov, Biljana, *Kulturna transformacija grada* (Novi Sad:
   Zavod za kulturu Vojvodine 2015).
Milosavljević, Vesna, *ACTOPOLIS | The Art of Action,
   Belgrade—Formally Informal: Belgrade Self-Organized
   Cultural Production*, YouTube video, 21:39 (longer
   version), 7 September 2016, https://www.youtube.com
   /watch?v=edRm1UYAnx4; 6:57 (shorter version),
   7 September 2016, https://www.youtube.com
   /watch?v=2YO6H-xdre0.
Montman, Nina (ed.), *Art and Its Institutions: Current
   Conflicts, Critique and Collaborations* (London: Black
   Dog Publishing, 2006).
Phelan, Peggy, *Unmarked: The Politics of Performance*
   (London/New York: Routledge, 1996).
Ristić, Irena, "Ka novim vidovima samoorganizacije:
   superstrukcija i modelovanje lokalne kulturne scene"
   (forthcoming).
Rosler, Martha, "Culture Class: Art, Creativity, Urbanism
   (Part I, Part II, Part III)", *e-flux journal* 21 (December
   2010), 23 (March 2011), and 25 (May 2011).
Stamenković, Snežana, "Actopolis Beograd",
   Supervizuelna: Magazine for Contemporary Art (blog;
   26 October 2016), http://www.supervizuelna.com
   /actopolis-beograd-3/.
Stanković, Maja, *Fluidni kontekst: Kontekstualne prakse
   u savremenoj umetnosti* (Belgrade: FMK, Univerzitet
   Singidunum, 2015).

Steyerl, Hito, "Art as Occupation: Claims for an
   Autonomy of Life", *e-flux journal* 30 (December 2011).
——, "Freedom from Everything: Freelancers and
   Mercenaries", *e-flux journal* 41 (January 2013).

Gesellschaftliche Desorganisation und selbst organisiertes kulturelles Schaffen in Belgrad

Die Belgrader Ausgabe von ACTOPOLIS mit dem Titel „Formally Informal: Belgrade Self-Organised Cultural Production"[1] hinterfragt die Bedingungen, unter denen wir heute leben, und beschäftigt sich eingehend mit den unterschiedlichen Praktiken von Kulturschaffenden und ihren Ergebnissen. Dabei lösen wir uns von der Vorstellung, wir seien eine einheitliche Gruppe und könnten uns gegenseitig verstehen. Das sind wir nicht und das können wir nicht. Und je eigenartiger und spezieller jede/r von uns ist, desto fordernder und lebendiger das kulturelle Schaffen.

Der urbane Kulturbereich in Serbien, insbesondere in Belgrad, hat sich in den letzten 25 Jahren zusammen mit den inneren und äußeren Umständen der Staatlichkeit des Landes grundlegend gewandelt. Gründe dafür waren die Auflösung der SFR Jugoslawien (mit ihrer Hauptstadt Belgrad), Bürgerkriege, umfangreiche internationale Sanktionen,[2] Inflation, ein tief greifender demografischer Wandel, Bürgerproteste, Bombardierungen, der Zerfall eines politischen Regimes und seine Ablösung durch ein anderes – und noch ein anderes und noch eines –, territoriale Zersplitterung und gesunkene Lebensstandards, wirtschaftliche Instabilität usw. Gleichzeitig wurde der gesamte europäische Kontinent von turbulenten Entwicklungen erschüttert.

Im ehemaligen Jugoslawien wird die Zeit unterteilt in „vor" und „nach" den 1990er-Jahren. In den 1990ern wurden alle Aspekte der Zivilisation auf den Prüfstand gestellt und keiner von ihnen hielt der Prüfung stand.

Seit 2000 wurden viele staatliche Institutionen in Serbien – einige vorübergehend, andere dauerhaft – geschlossen, darunter das Nationalmuseum, das Museum für Zeitgenössische Kunst und der alljährlich stattfindende Oktobersalon. An ihre Stelle trat eine Eventindustrie und die „Festivalisierung" des kulturellen Schaffens mit Schwerpunkt auf Laien- und folkloristischen Produktionen, was zu mangelnder Unterstützung für prozessorientierte professionelle Arbeiten führte. Die offizielle Kulturpolitik zeigt eher eine Vorliebe für „kulturelle Institutionen" als für Kulturschaffende, die nicht in staatlichen Institutionen beschäftigt sind. Dadurch entstand eine Atmosphäre der Polarisierung, auch wenn in Wirklichkeit alle unterfinanziert sind.

Fasst man die allgemeinen Bedingungen kulturellen Schaffens nicht nur in Serbien und Belgrad, sondern in größerem Rahmen zusammen, dann ergibt sich eine Art „gesellschaftliche Desorganisation", ein gesellschaftlicher Zustand, der vom Zusammenbruch wirksamer gesellschaftlicher Kontrolle geprägt ist und zu fehlender funktionaler Integration von Gruppen, zu widerstreitenden gesellschaftlichen Einstellungen und zu mangelnder persönlicher Sozialisation geführt hat.[3] Bei dem Versuch, mit den Entwicklungen in westlichen Gesellschaften Schritt zu halten, wurden insbesondere seit dem Jahr 2000 die meisten gesellschaftlichen und politischen Konzepte in Serbien ohne kritische Prüfung und ohne Anpassung an die lokalen Verhältnisse gebrauchsfertig übernommen, begleitet von einem gewissen Unbehagen angesichts des „kollektiven Versagens der Vorstellungskraft".[4] Die Frage, mit der wir uns hier beschäftigen, lautet: Welche Formen von urbaner Kultur haben diese Art der Missachtung des Eigenen überlebt und welche inhaltliche Substanz, welche Bedeutung hat urbane Kultur heute?

In diesem speziellen urbanen (Kunst-)Kontext etabliert sich die Belgrader Ausgabe von ACTOPOLIS. Ihr Schwerpunkt liegt auf den Besonderheiten relevanten nicht-institutionellen kulturellen Schaffens, das in performativen Untersuchungen zum Ausdruck kommt. Das Programm bringt 14 Künstler/innen, Künstlergruppen, Aktivist/innen und Kulturschaffende mit sehr unterschiedlichen Ausrichtungen zusammen. Ihre Arbeiten stehen im Einklang mit Fragen, wie und für wen kritische urbane Kultur welcher Art in Zeiten der andauernden Krise, gebrochen durch Methoden der Selbstorganisation, produziert wird. Was kennzeichnet die Ökonomie kultureller Unabhängigkeit in Serbien 15 Jahre nach Beginn des neuen Jahrhunderts und 25 Jahre nach dem gesellschaftlichen Zusammenbruch des Landes? Worin liegt das kritische Potenzial der Selbstorganisation von Kulturschaffenden? Inwieweit kann Selbstorganisation eigenständiges Denken und Handeln im Bereich der Kultur sichern? Inwieweit ist Selbstorganisation eine Alternative zu nichtfunktionalen Institutionen und welche Rolle spielt dabei der Neoliberalismus?

Als Koproduzent von ACTOPOLIS entwickelte das Goethe-Institut Belgrad zwei Projektbereiche: zum einen City Guerilla (Gradska Gerila)/Goethe Guerilla (GG) und Urban Incubator (UI) – beide hervorragend koordiniert durch Zorica Milisavljević – und zum anderen eine von mir kuratierte und koordinierte Auswahl.

Der Schwerpunkt der Arbeiten von GG und UI innerhalb von Formally

Informal lag auf der Untersuchung des bislang Erreichten und auf dem Ausblick auf künftige Produktionen. Außerdem nutzten sie den temporären Veranstaltungsort von ACTOPOLIS, um ihre Praxis in einem anderen Umfeld als Savamala zu testen. In den beiden ersten Maiwochen produzierten sie Performances und veranstalteten Gespräche und Präsentationen.

Bei der Zusammenstellung meiner Projekte lud ich bewusst eine große Vielfalt an Künstler/innen und Kulturschaffenden ein, um die verschiedenen mikropolitischen Bedingungen kulturellen Schaffens einzubeziehen und damit die heterogenen kulturellen Praktiken Belgrads und ihre Auswirkungen auf aktuelle wirtschaftliche, gesellschaftliche und politische Bedingungen zu beleuchten. Ist es überhaupt möglich, sich einen Überblick über das aktuelle kulturelle Klima und das entsprechende Kulturschaffen zu verschaffen, oder bleibt es bei dem vagen, fragmentierten Bild einer turbulenten Phase, die so anhaltend und aufreibend ist wie unsere? Wie spiegelt die zeitgenössische Stadtkultur den Mangel an staatlicher Kulturpolitik und die gesellschaftliche (oder anderweitige) Rolle von Kultur wider?

Vor der öffentlichen Präsentation des Programms verhandelten die Künstler/innen und ich intern unsere jeweiligen Positionen. Im Laufe mehrerer Monate gingen wir Allianzen ein, die zuvor unwahrscheinlich erschienen wären; die absichtliche Begrenzung des räumlichen Projektformats korrespondierte dabei mit der zeitlich befristeten Existenz der Gruppe.

Wir entschieden uns bewusst, nicht die bestehenden Räumlichkeiten für Kultur mit ihrer Prägung durch Gründer/innen, Manager/innen, Künstler/innen und Zuschauer/innen zu nutzen, sondern den Großteil des Formally Informal-Programms im Mai 2016 hauptsächlich in einer gemieteten Parterrewohnung stattfinden zu lassen.

Die Wohnung befindet sich in einem nach dem Ersten Weltkrieg gebauten Haus im historischen Stadtteil Dorćol, der derzeit einen Prozess der Gentrifizierung erlebt. Die Räume sind zwar für verschiedene Funktionen ausgelegt, wurden jedoch zum ersten und höchstwahrscheinlich auch letzten Mal für kulturelle Zwecke genutzt. Sie boten allen einen neutralen Boden, auf dem sich die Wege der unterschiedlichen Projektbeteiligten mit denen der Zuschauer kreuzten. Bei der Besetzung dieses temporären Raums experimentierten wir mit Möglichkeiten der Kommunikation.[5] Es war bemerkenswert, dass alle Ausstellungen, Performances und Gespräche tagtäglich sorgfältig geschichtet und miteinander vermischt wurden, und dies nicht zuletzt auf der konkreten physischen Ebene im Raum.[6]

Ein Teil des Programms fand außerhalb der Wohnung an öffentlichen Plätzen, in alternativen Kulturzentren wie dem Matrijaršija oder auch in privaten Räumlichkeiten in einem entfernteren Vorort von Belgrad statt. Die anderen unabhängigen Orte mit direktem Projektbezug – Magacin u Kraljevića Marka (MKM8), Remont Gallery, Art Space U10, Oktobar, Kvaka 22, Cultural Centre Grad und das Centre for Cultural Decontamination – liegen über die Stadt verstreut.

Die Reaktionen der einzelnen Künstler/innen und Aktivist/innen auf das Gesamtthema von Formally Informal fielen gemäß dem ursprünglichen Konzept sehr unterschiedlich aus. Einige Teilnehmer – Ristić, Radić, Cvetković, Sekulić/Đorđević und Nikolić – versuchten, sich der Diskontinuität der Kultur, wie wir sie kennen, zu stellen, andere führten ihre Praxis vor (Vučetić, Radoš/ Karić, U10 und Cvetić) und eine dritte Gruppe thematisierte die Beziehungen an den Außengrenzen des Kulturbereichs mit Mitteln des Aktivismus (Milikić/Kurepa, KURS und Ramujkić/Treister).

Irena Ristić hinterfragte das Konzept der „Selbstorganistion", das den Rahmen von Formally Informal bildet, indem sie das Potenzial zeitgenössischer kultureller Praktiken von Kollektivität, Miteinander und Allgemeingütern in Abgrenzung zu individuellen Bemühungen untersuchte. Nikola Radić Lucati und Marijana Cvetković beschäftigten sich mit den Bedingungen, die von den 1990er-Jahren bis zum Beginn des 21. Jahrhunderts Praktiken hervorbrachten, welche wir heute als „selbst organisiert" bezeichnen. Aleksandra Sekulić/Ivica Đorđević stellten eines der seltsamen Phänomene heraus, das sich aus diesen Bedingungen ergab. Aleksandar Nikolić erstellte eine aktuelle Karte der Belgrader Ausstellungsorte für bildende Kunst, in die er sowohl die von der öffentlichen Hand (einer lokalen, staatlichen oder auch ausländischen Stelle) finanzierten als auch die alternativen, marginalen und experimentellen Einrichtungen der freien Szene aufnahm. Anica Vučetić, Marija Radoš/Miroslav Karić, das U10 Kunstkollektiv und Mariela Cvetić boten vielfältige Performances der künstlerischen Positionen und Praktiken verschiedener Generationen. Nebojša Milikić/Tadej Kurepa, KURS und Vahida Ramujkić/Noa Treister behandelten konkrete gesellschaftliche Themen aus ihrer künstlerisch-aktivistischen Perspektive. Zufälligerweise beanspruchten alle diese Künstler/innen kollektive Urheberschaft. Außerdem verfasste Sandra Stojanović, eine bildende Künstlerin der jüngeren Generation aus Belgrad, einige kritische Blogbeiträge zum Belgrader ACTOPOLIS-Programm.

Während des gesamten Projekts ergaben sich aufschlussreiche Widersprüche – politisch linke Künstler/innen sprachen sich für ungleiche Bezahlung aus, Teilnehmer/innen in prekären Beschäftigungsverhältnissen für kommerzielle Produktion; in öffentlichen Gesprächen wandte man sich vom interessierten Publikum ab; eine selbstreflexive (oder eben nicht selbstreflexive) Kritik schloss die eigene Position aus usw. Andererseits wurden einige Widersprüchlichkeiten des Projekts bewusst herausgestellt, um so die Grenzen des Untersuchungsgebiets infrage zu stellen. Ein Thema war etwa das Wohnen in einer Eigentumswohnung, deren Umgebung sich gerade gentrifiziert, oder aber die Umsetzung eines Projekts zur Selbstorganisation im Kontext eines großen nationalen Instituts wie des Goethe-Instituts.

Formally Informal war der Versuch von nicht institutionell gebundenen Künstler/innen – die meisten von ihnen sind professionelle Kulturschaffende und im Kulturbereich arbeitende Aktivist/innen, die „ihrem" System und Systemrahmen[7] kritisch gegenüberstehen –, ein Gefühl zu vermitteln, wie dringlich das Kommunizieren durch Formen von Kunst und Kultur ist, die sich an der breiten Basis und der Öffentlichkeit ausrichten. Diese Beziehungen, so könnte man sagen, schaffen tagtäglich ein nicht-kommerzielles kulturelles Klima der Selbstermächtigung.

Bei der Projektarbeit war das Konzept der Selbstorganisation sehr anregend und ließ niemanden unberührt. Wurde es anfangs mit Spott, Widerstand und Ablehnung aufgenommen, so entwickelte sich im Laufe der Zeit größeres Verständnis bis hin zu einer mehr oder weniger unkritischen Übernahme. Die Ergebnisse des bewusst offenen Projekts galten häufig als nebensächlich. Auf diese Weise zensierten einige Teilnehmer/innen den Rahmen ihrer Arbeiten und Projekte, ähnlich

wie ihr unabhängiges/selbstorganisier-
tes kulturelles Schaffen in der Vergan-
genheit von den maßgebenden Stellen
zensiert worden war, die die Bedeutung
ihrer Beiträge zur Kulturszene verkann-
ten. Aus völlig unerwarteten Richtungen
kam jedoch auch wertvolle Unterstüt-
zung für das Thema.⁸

Einer der wichtigsten Scheide-
punkte bei unserer Verständigung über
die Praxis der Selbstorganisation war
die Frage, ob Selbstorganisation Künst-
ler/innen zur Eigeninitiative befähigt
oder ob sie auch die innere Kraft be-
zeichnen kann, widrigen Umständen mit
weniger prätentiösen und eher projekt-
basierten Konzepten zu begegnen.
Selbstorganisation ist entschieden kein
Rezept für ein autarkes System. Sie
begegnet den Optionen von staatlicher
oder privatwirtschaftlicher Seite – in
letzter Zeit wird die Abgrenzung zwi-
schen beiden zunehmend schwierig
– mit einem gewissen Misstrauen. So ist
der eigene Zynismus auch ein Gegengift
für den zunehmenden Zynismus und
das wachsende Misstrauen, die uns auf
jeder erdenklichen Ebene begegnen,
einschließlich der verbreiteten massen-
haften Selbstorganisation, die anschei-
nend eine prekäre Form der Selbstaus-
beutung ist.

Mit dem Begriff „Selbstorgani-
sation" ist häufig auch die Entfremdung
vom Wohlfahrtstaat in Zeiten des
Neoliberalismus und die brutale, einsei-
tige Kommerzialisierung von Kultur
gemeint. Ließe sich der Begriff neu
fassen als tägliche Praxis von Individu-
en (oder besser noch von einer „irredu-
ziblen Vielzahl von Singularitäten"⁹),
die der fortlaufenden Monopolisierung
in Kunst und Kultur widerstehen?
Könnte Selbstorganisation in diesem
Fall ein Mittel zur Unabhängigkeit und
eben nicht der Verlust der einzelnen
Stimme in und durch die Massen
werden? Unsere Alternativen sollten

definitiv nicht lauten: Soll ich mich selbst
ausbeuten oder soll dies eine andere
Person tun? Denn dies würde selbst
organisiertem kulturellem Schaffen eine
bestimmte Methodik auferlegen, um
sich den Verhältnissen zu widersetzen.

Formally Informal wurde nicht
als eine Art Konsolidierungsplan,
geschweige denn als Aktionsplan für
das aktuelle kulturelle Schaffen in
Serbien entwickelt. Vielmehr bot es vor
allem einen ansonsten schwer zu
findenden Raum für Reflexionen. Das
Projekt untersuchte Wege, wie Künstler/
innen und Aktivist/innen sich mit neuen
Bedingungen beschäftigen und den
allgemeinen Rahmen infrage stellen
können, der das sich langsam entwi-
ckelnde kulturelle Schaffen eines im
Grunde modernistischen Erbes über-
wältigt oder ihm zumindest sehr entge-
gensteht (wobei die Langsamkeit
nicht notwendigerweise schlecht ist).
Wie sehen die kreativen, kritischen und
intellektuellen Bedürfnisse und ihre
Produktionsbedingungen heute aus?

MIRJANA BOBA STOJADINOVIĆ

1 Der Begriff „Selbstorganisation" ist mehrdeutig.
Hier deckt er mal affirmativ, mal kritisch ein konkretes
Bedeutungsspektrum ab und wahrt sprachliche
Stringenz bei einem auf drei Jahre angelegten Projekt.
Falls wir nach Projektabschluss einen besseren
Begriff für das finden, was wir derzeit mit
„Selbstorganisation" bezeichnen, sollte der Begriff
definitiv geändert werden.
2 Diese betrafen unter anderem Sport, Kultur, Bildung
und medizinische Versorgung.
3 Siehe http://www.merriam-webster.com/dictionary
/social%20disorganization
4 Martha Rosler, „Culture Class: Art, Creativity,
Urbanism", Part II, e-flux journal 23 (März 2011).
5 Siehe Hito Steyerl, „Art as Occupation: Claims for an
Autonomy of Life", e-flux journal 30 (Dezember 2011),
http://www.e-flux.com/journal/art-as-occupation
-claims-for-an-autonomy-of-life-12/.
6 Die Aufzeichnungen aller Gespräche können
nachgehört werden unter: https://www.mixcloud.com
/actopolis2016/ (in serbischer Sprache).
7 „Das System" festlegen zu wollen ist sicherlich eine
tückische Aufgabe. Andererseits ließe sich auch
sagen, dass das System heutzutage auf eben jenen
diffusen und widersprüchlichen Aspekten beruht.
8 Nicht zuletzt von den Künstler/innen und
Kurator/innen Renée Turner, Simon Kentgens und

Jason E. Bowman sowie der Journalistin Snežana Stamenković. Ich bedaure, dass ich die Schriftsteller/innen und Kurator/innen Jan Verwoert und Federica Bueti letztlich nicht zur Teilnahme am Projekt einladen konnte. Ihre Beiträge wären von großem Wert für die allgemeine Diskussion gewesen.

9 *Diese Ideen sind unter anderem von den konzeptuellen Praktiken des „Künstlers in der Ich-Form" der 1970er-Jahre inspiriert; sie vermitteln die Verletzlichkeit und Ausgesetztheit von Singularitäten, die im Gegensatz zu den „beliebigen Singularitäten" Agambens stehen.*

Weitere Quellen:

Blagojević, Jelisaveta, Politike nemislivog: Uvod u ne-fašistički život, *Belgrad: Centar za medije i komunikacije, FMK, Univerzitet Singidunum, 2014.*

Boym, Svetlana, The Future of Nostalgia, *New York: Basic Books, 2001.*

Ćurčić, Branka, „Autonomous Spaces of Deregulation and Critique: Is a Cooperation with Neoliberal Art Institutions Possible?", in: Progressive Institutions, Transversal, *Juni 2007, http://eipcp.net /transversal/0407/curcic/en. Siehe auch die Anmerkungen von Boris Buden.*

Denegri, Ješa, Opstanak umetnosti u vremenu krize, *Belgrad: Cicero, 2004.*

Hebert, Stine und Karlsen, Anne Szefer (Hrsg.), Self-Organised, *London/Bergen: Open editions/ Hordaland Kunstsenter, 2013.*

Hubeli, Ernst, „City-culture versus City of Culture?", in M City: European Cityscapes, *Graz: Kunsthaus Graz, 2006.*

Jakšić, Jasna u. a., From Consideration to Commitment: Art in Critical Confrontation to Society, *Belgrad, Ljubljana, Skopje, Zagreb: 1990–2010, eBook im Rahmen des von SEEcult.org (Belgrad, Serbien) umgesetzten LTCA-Projekts, in Zusammenarbeit mit Artservis.org (Ljubljana, Slowenien), Forum Skopje (Skopje, Mazedonien [FYROM]) und Kulturpunkt.hr (Zagreb, Kroatien), http://inseecp.blogspot.gr/2011 /04/e-book-art-in-critical-confrontation-to.html.*

Karić, Miroslav und Radoš, Marija, „Actopolis Belgrade/ Studija individualnog sluČaja", in Supervizuelna: Magazine for Contemporary Art, *Blog, 21. September 2016, http://www.supervizuelna.com/actopolis -belgrade-studija-individualnog-slucaja/.*

Mickov, Biljana, Kulturna transformacija grada, *Novi Sad: Zavod za kulturu Vojvodine 2015.*

Milosavljević, Vesna, ACTOPOLIS | The Art of Action, Belgrade – Formally Informal: Belgrade Self-Organized Cultural Production, *YouTube-Video, 21:39 (Langfassung), 7. September 2016, https://www .youtube.com/watch?v=edRm1UYAnx4; 6:57 (Kurzfassung), 7. September 2016, https://www.youtube.com/watch?v=2YO6H-xdre0.*

Montman, Nina (Hrsg.), Art and Its Institutions: Current Conflicts, Critique and Collaborations, *London: Black Dog Publishing, 2006.*

Phelan, Peggy, Unmarked: The Politics of Performance, *London/New York: Routledge, 1996.*

Ristić, Irena, „Ka novim vidovima samoorganizacije: superstrukcija i modelovanje lokalne kulturne scene", im Erscheinen.

Rosler, Martha, „Culture Class: Art, Creativity, Urbanism" (Part I, Part II, Part III), e-flux journal 21 (Dezember 2010), 23 (März 2011) und 25 (Mai 2011).

Stamenković, Snežana, „Actopolis Beograd", Supervizuelna: Magazine for Contemporary Art, *Blog, 26. Oktober 2016, http://www.supervizuelna.com /actopolis-beograd-3/.*

Stanković, Maja, Fluidni kontekst: Kontekstualne prakse u savremenoj umetnosti, *Belgrad: FMK, Univerzitet Singidunum, 2015.*

Steyerl, Hito, „Art as Occupation: Claims for an Autonomy of Life", e-flux journal 30 (Dezember 2011).

---, „Freedom from Everything: Freelancers and Mercenaries", e-flux journal 41 (Januar 2013).

Bgd Art
A Map of Belgrade's
Visual Arts Venues

A bimonthly, bilingual printed map with an up-to-date programme of Belgrade's art spaces

Ein alle zwei Monate in zwei Sprachen erscheinender Stadtplan mit dem aktuellen Programm der Belgrader Kunsträume

In accordance with contemporary trends and promotional possibilities, the project *Bgd Art* map acts as a mediator for over ninety Belgrade art galleries and their audience—the regular one, the non-audience, and the potential audience from the local community and wider. With the aim of creating new contents in the city and connecting different sectors and resources, *Bgd Art* map offers audiences up-to-date information on all current and permanent shows as well as other additional programmes, opens exhibition spaces for new audiences, and contextualises the art scene. The result is a much-needed but as yet non-existent, bimonthly, bilingual printed map showing the Belgrade art space programme, accompanied by a website containing additional information.

Den aktuellen Trends und Werbemöglichkeiten folgend tritt das Projekt Bgd Art map als Vermittler für über 90 Belgrader Kunstgalerien und ihr Publikum auf – für das Stammpublikum, das Nichtpublikum und das potenzielle Publikum aus Belgrad und der Region. Ziel von Bgd Art map ist es, neue Inhalte in der Stadt zu schaffen und verschiedene Sektoren und Ressourcen miteinander zu verknüpfen; das Projekt bietet Interessierten daher aktuelle Informationen über alle laufenden und dauerhaften Ausstellungen und über weitere Programmangebote; es verschafft Ausstellungsräumen ein neues Publikum und stellt die Kunstszene in einen größeren Zusammenhang. So entstand ein dringend benötigter, bislang allerdings nicht existierender zweisprachiger Stadtplan, der alle zwei Monate das Programm der Belgrader Kunsträume vorstellt. Eine begleitende Internetseite liefert zusätzliche Informationen.

Project: Aleksandar Nikolić → Format: publication → Dates: May–December 2016 → Venues: over 50 galleries, museums, and art/project spaces around Belgrade → Participants: Mirjana Stojadinović, Marija Radoš, Virdžinija Đeković, Darka Radosavljević, Mane Radmanović, Đorđe Stanojević, Miroslav Karić, Andrija Stojanović, Luka Knežević-Strika

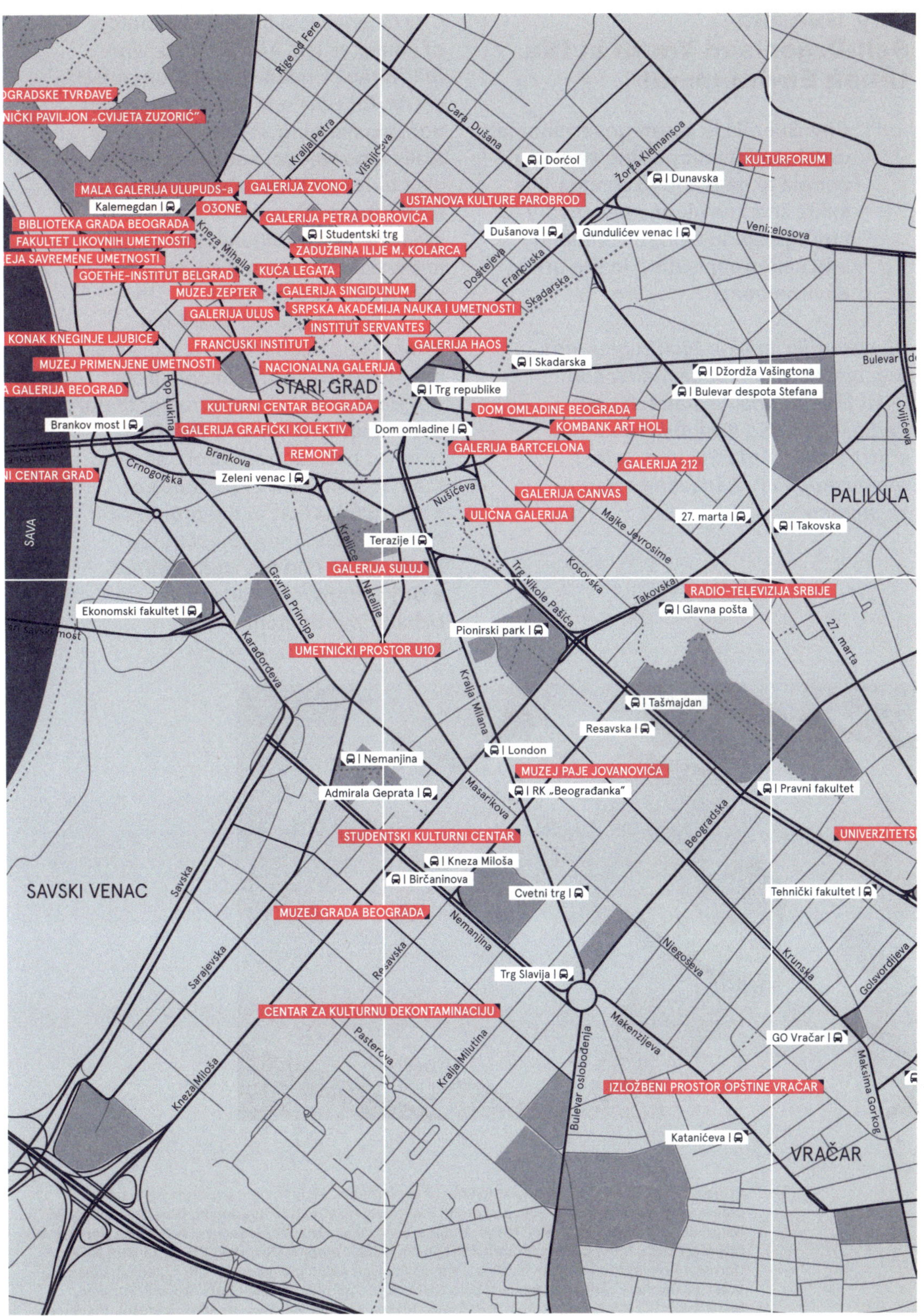

Rige od Fere
OGRADSKE TVRĐAVE
NIČKI PAVILJON „CVIJETA ZUZORIĆ"
Cara Dušana
Žorža Klemansoa
Dorćol
KULTURFORUM
Dunavska
MALA GALERIJA ULUPUDS-a
GALERIJA ZVONO
USTANOVA KULTURE PAROBROD
Kalemegdan
OЗONE
GALERIJA PETRA DOBROVIĆA
Venizelosova
BIBLIOTEKA GRADA BEOGRADA
Studentski trg
Dušanova
Gundulićev venac
FAKULTET LIKOVNIH UMETNOSTI
ZADUŽBINA ILIJE M. KOLARCA
Kralja Petra
Višnjićeva
EJA SAVREMENE UMETNOSTI
KUĆA LEGATA
GOETHE-INSTITUT BELGRAD
Dositejeva
Francuska
MUZEJ ZEPTER
GALERIJA SINGIDUNUM
Skadarska
GALERIJA ULUS
SRPSKA AKADEMIJA NAUKA I UMETNOSTI
Kneza Mihaila
INSTITUT SERVANTES
KONAK KNEGINJE LJUBICE
FRANCUSKI INSTITUT
GALERIJA HAOS
Bulevar de
MUZEJ PRIMENJENE UMETNOSTI
Skadarska
Džordža Vašingtona
A GALERIJA BEOGRAD
NACIONALNA GALERIJA
Bulevar despota Stefana
STARI GRAD
Trg republike
Cvijićeva
KULTURNI CENTAR BEOGRADA
DOM OMLADINE BEOGRADA
Pop Lukina
Brankov most
GALERIJA GRAFIČKI KOLEKTIV
Dom omladine
KOMBANK ART HOL
REMONT
GALERIJA BARTCELONA
Brankova
GALERIJA 212
NI CENTAR GRAD
Crnogorska
Zeleni venac
Nušićeva
GALERIJA CANVAS
PALILULA
Majke Jevrosime
SAVA
ULIČNA GALERIJA
27. marta
Takovska
Kraljice Natalije
Terazije
Kosovska
27. marta
GALERIJA SULUJ
Trg Nikole Pašića
Takovska
RADIO-TELEVIZIJA SRBIJE
Gavrila Principa
Ekonomski fakultet
Glavna pošta
ari savski most
Pionirski park
Karađorđeva
UMETNIČKI PROSTOR U10
Kralja Milana
Tašmajdan
Resavska
Nemanjina
London
MUZEJ PAJE JOVANOVIĆA
Pravni fakultet
Admirala Geprata
Masarikova
RK „Beograđanka"
Beogradska
UNIVERZITETS
STUDENTSKI KULTURNI CENTAR
SAVSKI VENAC
Kneza Miloša
Savska
Birčaninova
Cvetni trg
Tehnički fakultet
Njegoševa
MUZEJ GRADA BEOGRADA
Nemanjina
Krunska
Sarajevska
Resavska
Golsvordijeva
Trg Slavija
Kneza Miloša
CENTAR ZA KULTURNU DEKONTAMINACIJU
Makenzijeva
GO Vračar
Pasterova
Kralja Milutina
Maksima Gorkog
Bulevar oslobođenja
IZLOŽBENI PROSTOR OPŠTINE VRAČAR
Katanićeva
VRAČAR

City Guerilla
Self-Organised Youth in the Urban Environment

City Guerilla is a non-governmental organisation supporting young people to gain and exchange the skills and knowledge necessary for strengthening self-sustainability and self-organisation in the urban environment.

City Guerilla ist eine Nichtregierungsorganisation, die junge Menschen beim Erwerb und Austausch von Fertigkeiten und Kenntnissen unterstützt, um so Autarkie und Selbstorganisation im städtischen Raum zu stärken.

City Guerilla is a creative laboratory of young artists and activists who follow the principles of self-organised youth, for peer and alternative education, exchanging a wide range of skills, knowledge, and ideas. Synergies between these diverse factors foster the production of specific creative spaces where various ideas in the fields of art and social activism can be put into practice.

During the six years the project has been running, more than one hundred young people from Belgrade took the opportunity to put their ideas into action. The City Guerilla project framework allowed them to gain new experience of self-organisation in the process of implementing the projects they themselves had devised: *Right to a City: Improving Your Own Urban Environment.*

Project: City Guerilla → Format: exhibitions, interventions, happenings, performances, talks, online archive → Dates: May–December 2016 → Venue: ACTOPOLIS apartment, Despota Stefana 36, Belgrade → Participants: Simon Marić, Mirjana Utvić, Milica Nikolić, Arsenije Savić, Milan Stanimirović, Stanislav Drča, Irena Ostojić, Katarina Kragović, Ivana Andrejić, Olivera Petrović, Tamara Miletić, Doroteja Roković, Marija Brđović, Olga Jorgačević, Ivan Avdić (members of City Guerilla); Jelena Vojvodić (archive workshop leader); Lara Calić, Tina Oparnica, Aleksej Nutz, Bojana Vojnović, Vanja Žikić, Iva Milojković, Stefan Malešević, Jovana Stevanović, Teodora Jelena Stošić, Vladimir Ilić, Nemanja Stojanović (happening, Open Library performance, and photo-walk); Dragana Krtinić (designer); Zorica Milisavljević, Goethe-Institut Belgrade (City Guerilla Project coordinator) → Acknowledgements: Andreja Rondović, Faculty of Technical Science, University of Novi Sad (DA:SEIN happening); Jovan Stamatović-Karić, Theatre NK Studio (GG Dialogues)

City Guerilla ist ein Kreativlabor für junge Künstler/innen und Aktivist/innen. Gemäß den Prinzipien selbst organisierter Jugendlicher strebt sie die Bildung durch Gleichgestellte bzw. eine alternative Bildung an, bei der zahlreiche Fertigkeiten, Kenntnisse und Ideen ausgetauscht werden. Synergien zwischen diesen verschiedenen Faktoren fördern die Entstehung von konkreten Kreativräumen, in denen Ideen auf dem Gebiet der Kunst und des gesellschaftlichen Engagements in die Praxis umgesetzt werden können.

Während der sechsjährigen Projektlaufzeit haben über 100 junge Belgrader/innen die Gelegenheit genutzt und ihre Ideen in die Tat umgesetzt. Der Projektrahmen von City Guerilla bot ihnen die Möglichkeit, bei der Umsetzung der von ihnen konzipierten Projekte neue Erfahrungen in der Selbstorganisation zu sammeln: Right to a City: Improving Your Own Urban Environment.

Druga Scena / Other Scene
Belgrade Self-Organised Scene

A research project exploring the background to the effacement of Druga Scena from public memory

Ein Forschungsprojekt, das die Gründe für die Auslöschung von Druga Scena aus dem öffentlichen Gedächtnis untersucht

Druga Scena/Other Scene was among the first self-organised networks of organisations and individuals who were active in the field of contemporary arts. Its creation came as a response to the cultural policies articulated at the time by the first post-Milošević governments with their clear liberal orientation. Druga Scena, based in Belgrade, was gathered around regular critical discussions on current policies and processes, claiming the space for the independent scene. This research sets out to uncover reasons for the deletion of Druga Scena from public memory and founds its arguments on the ideological shift in Serbia in the early 2000s.

Druga Scena war eines der ersten selbst organisierten Netzwerke diverser individueller Akteur/innen und Organisationen, die sich auf dem Gebiet der zeitgenössischen Kunst engagierten. Ihre Gründung war eine Reaktion auf die ersten kulturpolitischen Ansätze in der eindeutig neoliberal ausgerichteten Post-Milošević-Ära. Zu jener Zeit versammelten sich die Mitglieder/innen von Druga Scena regelmäßig in Belgrad, um kritische Debatten über aktuelle politische Entscheidungen und Vorgänge zu führen und sich für die Schaffung von Freiräumen für die unabhängige Kunst- und Kulturszene einzusetzen. Dieses Forschungsprojekt sucht nach Gründen, warum Druga Scena aus dem öffentlichen Gedächtnis gelöscht wurde. Die Ursachen, so die These, sind in der ideologischen Wende in Serbien zu Beginn des 21. Jahrhunderts zu suchen.

Project: Marijana Cvetković → Formats: publication, discussion → Date: 20 May 2016 → Venue: ACTOPOLIS apartment, Bulevar Despota Stefana 36, Belgrade → Participants: Jelena Vesić and Miloš Miletić (public discussion guests); Marijana Cvetković (discussion moderator); Katarina Popović (designer) → Acknowledgements: Dalija Aćin Thelander, Dragana Alfirević, Zoe Gudović, Vida Knežević, Milan Marković Matiss, Marko Miletić, Irena Ristić, Mirjana Boba Stojadinović, Jelena Vesić, Ana Vujanović, and other colleagues from Druga Scena

DRUGA SCENA

...a savremeni neoliberalni kapitalistički sistem
...kulturi, subverzivni potencijal koji se
...ogleda u njenom iskustvu rada u jednom
drugačijem modelu kulturne produkcije
od onog poželjnog, kontrolisanog i
dominantnog. Iako u tim okolnostima
ona nije proizvela neku trajnu promenu,
proizvela je znanje i iskustvo koje se još
uvek mogu iskoristiti.

NASTAVIĆE SE....

Marijana Cvetković
Beograd, maj 2016.

Expiration Date

The inherent instability of institutional memory in the case of Serbia's cultural institutions

Der instabile Charakter des institutionellen Gedächtnisses serbischer Kulturinstitutionen

The starting point of this documentary-analytical artwork is the inherent instability of institutional memory in Serbia's cultural institutions vis-à-vis the state-organised removal of artworks from the invaded areas of Croatia in 1991 and their discreet return after the war. The production of the term "memory" can be traced in two ways: the non-existence of nearly all state culture means that actors in the society are required to adopt identities via impermanent social structures, while personal, generationally structured memory—compounded by the effects of economic and digital rot—erodes the pre-digital, liberal cultural institutions in Serbia. The counterpoint to these processes framing the impermanence of culture as conquest is an investment in the structuring of the new Serbian national and cultural narrative through the projections of the dominant socio-economic stakeholders—state, private, and international—charting the subtle shifts in focus and objectives.

Ausgangspunkt dieses dokumentarisch-analytischen Kunstwerks ist die dem institutionellen Gedächtnis serbischer Kulturinstitutionen innewohnende Instabilität, wie sie sich in der staatlich organisierten Beseitigung von Kunst aus den im Jahr 1991 besetzten Gebieten Kroatiens und ihrer diskreten Rückführung nach dem Krieg manifestiert. Die Produktion des Begriffs „Gedächtnis" lässt sich auf zweierlei Weise nachzeichnen: Da es so gut wie keine Staatskultur gibt, müssen gesellschaftliche Akteure ihre Identität mithilfe unbeständiger Sozialstrukturen ausformen, während das persönliche, nach Generationen strukturierte Gedächtnis die prädigitalen, liberalen Kulturinstitutionen Serbiens aushöhlt; die Auswirkungen von wirtschaftlichem Niedergang und „Datenfäule" kommen erschwerend hinzu. Den Gegenpol zu diesen Entwicklungen, bei denen die Unbeständigkeit von Kultur als Sieg hingestellt wird, bildet eine Investition in die Ausgestaltung des neuen nationalen und kulturellen serbischen Narrativs. Denn durch die Projektionen der herrschenden sozioökonomischen Akteure – auf staatlicher, privater und internationaler Ebene – lassen sich die subtilen Veränderungen im Hinblick auf Schwerpunkte und Zielsetzungen erfassen.

99 Project: Nikola Radić Lucati → Format: installation → Dates: 18–29 May 2016 → Venue: ACTOPOLIS apartment, Bulevar Despota Stefana 36, Belgrade

Gaudeamus igitur: The Self-Organised Artist in a State of Domestic Agoraphobia

Self-organisation of the individual—an artist in the process of establishing her own artistic practice: state of affairs

Selbstorganisation des Individuums – eine Künstlerin entwickelt ihre eigene künstlerische Praxis: zum Stand der Dinge

The project *Gaudeamus igitur: The Self-Organised Artist in a State of Domestic Agoraphobia* is an artist's book titled *Gaudeamus igitur* and brought out in a limited edition, accompanied by a lecture performance. The artist's book consists of photos depicting tiles and floors, by and large from all the institutions the artist has passed through in the process of becoming a self-organised individual artist originating her own artistic practice. The text in the book is accompanied by a popular student song that is mainly performed at university/school graduation ceremonies—*Gaudeamus igitur*. In this way, the project questions the role of (educational) institutions in the age of self-organisation in art.

Das Projekt Gaudeamus igitur: The Self-Organised Artist in a State of Domestic Agoraphobia *besteht aus einem Kunstband in limitierter Auflage, der von einer Performance in Form einer Lesung begleitet wird. Der Kunstband enthält Fotos von Kacheln und Fußböden aus fast allen Institutionen, die die Künstlerin im Laufe ihrer Entwicklung zum selbst organisierten Individuum mit eigenen künstlerischen Praktiken durchlaufen hat. Der Text des Buches wird von dem bekannten Studentenlied* Gaudeamus igitur *begleitet, das hauptsächlich in Universitäten und Schulen bei Examensfeiern gesungen wird. Auf diese Weise hinterfragt das Projekt die Rolle von (Bildungs-) Einrichtungen im Zeitalter der künstlerischen Selbstorganisation.*

Project: Mariela Cvetić → Formats: artist's book, lecture performance, public discussion → Dates: 18–29 May 2016 & 27 May 2016 → Venue: ACTOPOLIS apartment, Bulevar Despota Stefana 36, Belgrade → Participants: Irena Ristić (dramaturgy) → Collaborating organisation: Faculty of Architecture

Vivant omnes virgines

Gaudeamus igitur

Researching

Researching is following one's curiosity. It is a process of inquiry into a particular field of interest, revisiting acquired knowledge and experiences beyond one's own, aiming at creating a bridge between known concepts and practices and those that still lie ahead of us, all the while establishing meaning and sense.

> *Mit dem Erforschen befriedigt man seine Neugier. Es ist ein Prozess, bei dem man ein bestimmtes Interessensgebiet erkundet, erworbene Kenntnisse auffrischt und neue Erfahrungen macht. Dadurch soll eine Brücke entstehen, die uns von bereits bekannten Konzepten und Praktiken zu solchen bringt, die noch vor uns liegen, während gleichzeitig Bedeutung und Sinn gestiftet werden.*

Boba Mirjana Stojadinović

Sharing

"Sharing is caring" is a popular phrase commonly used when you have something and your friend wants a part of it. So we share not only food, cigarettes, tram tickets, and taxi rides but also, more importantly, ideas and emotions. Sharing is a practical concept inextricably connected with the roots of solidarity and the practice of commons. But what happens when sharing, of goods or services, stops meaning caring? In what is called the "sharing economy", peer economy or collaborative consumption, owners rent something they are not using—a car or a house—to a stranger. Airbnb is a poster child of the sharing economy sector, where travellers can rent out a room, an entire house, or even a castle. Originally the product of the open-source community, nowadays the term "sharing economy" can be misleading, as most of the peer-to-peer exchange services are primarily profit-driven.

„Sharing is caring" ist eine häufig benutzte Redewendung, wenn man etwas hat, von dem ein Freund etwas abhaben möchte. Wir teilen nicht nur Essen, Zigaretten, Fahrscheine und Taxifahrten, sondern auch Wichtigeres wie Ideen und Gefühle. Teilen ist ein praktisches Konzept, das untrennbar mit Solidarität und gemeinschaftlich genutzten Gütern (commons) verbunden ist. Was passiert aber, wenn beim Teilen von Gütern und Dienstleistungen der soziale Gedanke verloren geht? Bei dem, was heute unter den Bezeichnungen sharing economy, *Peer-Ökonomie oder gemeinschaftliche Nutzung bekannt ist, geht es vor allem darum, dass jemand sein Auto, sein Haus, seine Wohnung oder etwas Ähnliches, das er gerade selbst nicht braucht, an einen Fremden verleiht oder vermietet. Ein Aushängeschild für den* sharing economy-*Sektor ist Airbnb, ein Onlineportal, das Zimmer, ganze Häuser oder sogar Schlösser an Reisende vermittelt. Das Konzept des* sharing *stammte ursprünglich aus der Open-Source-Gemeinschaft, aber heute kann der Begriff* sharing economy *irreführend sein, da die meisten dieser Tauschdienste in erster Linie profitorientiert sind.*

Ana Dana Beroš

Talking

Talking—uttering, producing discourse—is a meaning-making system. It is also an act of silencing by displacing one narrative with another; it can produce certain subjects and make others obsolete. Thus talking is a site of conflict and a terrain to be won.

Sprechen – eine Äußerung, ein Diskurs – ist ein bedeutungsgebendes System. Indem es ein Narrativ durch ein anderes ersetzt, bringt es aber auch etwas zum Schweigen. Sprechen kann bestimmte Themen auf den Tisch bringen und andere obsolet machen. Damit ist ein Gespräch ein Ort des Konflikts und ein Terrain, das es zu erobern gilt.

Elpida Karaba

How to Organise
an Organisation

**Self-organisational capacity-building
programme for young people active
in the field of urban development
and improvement**

*Selbst organisiertes Programm
zur Kompetenzerweiterung junger
Menschen auf dem Gebiet der
Stadtentwicklung und städtebaulicher Verbesserungsmaßnahmen*

Within the ACTOPOLIS Belgrade
Project, the Urban Incubator Association in cooperation with the Goethe-
Institut has developed a capacity-
building programme based on
generational and non-formal learning
methods in order to help young
people improve their self-organisational, directorial, management, and
communication skills. The target
group is young people already active
in the field of urban development
and improvement, working actively
with peers who are running or about
to establish new organisations or
non-formal groups.

Project: Urban Incubator: How to Organise an Organisation → Formats: workshops, exhibition,
presentation → Dates: April–May 2016 → Venues: Kraljevića Marka 8, Savamala, Belgrade;
ACTOPOLIS apartment, Despota Stefana 36, Belgrade → Participants—"How to Organise an Organisation"
(workshop): Urban Incubator (Ana Đorđević-Petrović, Ljubica Slavković, Miloš Starčević, Andrija
Vranić) and members of City Guerilla (Mirjana Utvić, Katarina Živković, Ivana Andrejić, Milan Stanimirović,
Ivan Avdić, Marija Brđović, Irena Ostojić, Katarina Kragović, Nina Vujasin, Olivera Petrović); Marijana
Cvetković, Marko Pejović, Urban Incubator, in collaboration with City Guerilla (workshop leaders);
—"Retrospective Loops" (exhibition): Branislav Mihajlović, Gallery KM8, Urban Incubator (curator);
Sara Radonja, Ivan Šuletić (artists);—"Our Belgrade Waterfront" (Camenzind Belgrade video): Ana
Đorđević-Petrović, Camenzind Belgrade, Urban Incubator, in collaboration with Katarina Ćirilović-
Popović, Luka Tilinger, Ljubica Slavković (project authors); Ivica Vujadinović (contributor), Luka
Tilinger (illustrations), Milan Popović (compositing), Damjan Ćirilović and Maja Klisinski (sound),
Caspar Wijnberg at Gaspard Music (narrator);—"Bike Kitchen Belgrade" (workshop): Miloš Starčević
(workshop leader); Zorica Milisavljević, Goethe-Institut Belgrade (project coordinator)

Im Rahmen des Belgrader ACTOPOLIS-Projekts hat die Urban Incubator Association in Zusammenarbeit mit dem Goethe-Institut ein Programm zur Kompetenzerweiterung entwickelt, das auf generationsübergreifenden und informellen Lernmethoden basiert. Es möchte jungen Menschen helfen, ihre Fähigkeiten zur Selbstorganisation, ihre Leitungs- und Führungskompetenzen sowie ihre Kommunikationsfähigkeit zu verbessern. Die Zielgruppe sind junge Menschen, die bereits auf dem Gebiet der Stadtentwicklung und städtebaulicher Verbesserungsmaßnahmen tätig sind; sie sollen aktiv mit Gleichaltrigen zusammenarbeiten, die neue Organisationen oder informelle Gruppen leiten oder gerade neu gründen.

Project: Vahida Ramujkić & Noa Treister → Formats: discussions in the public space → Dates: 19 May 2016 & 21 July 2016 → Venues: plato in front of the Faculty of Philosophy, Čika-Ljubina 18–20, Belgrade; plato in front of the local municipalities of Stevan Sinđelić and Vojvoda Putnik, Ustanička 194, Belgrade → Participants—Discussion 1: Branko Dimitrijević, Ognjen Dukić, Zoran Gajić, Branka Ćurčić, Đokica Jovanović, Saša Kostić, Vladimir Miladinović, Matija Medenica, Miloš Miletić, Nebojša Milikić, Vladimir Novaković, Dragomir Olujić Oluja, Milovan Pisarri, Danilo Prnjat, Mirjana Radovanović, Predrag Raljević; Vahida Ramujkić and Noa Treister (moderators);—Discussion 2: Radmila Gujaničić, Marko Jakovljev, Đokica Jovanović and Saša Petrović, Ana Džokić, Ognjen Đukić, Vladimir Novaković; Vahida Ramujkić and Noa Treister (moderators)

Indivisible Unalienable Property in the Context of Knowledge Production

The normalisation of private property in all spheres of social relations and human existence keeps us from imagining any other concept of property.

Die Normalisierung von Privateigentum in allen Bereichen des gesellschaftlichen und menschlichen Lebens verhindert den Entwurf alternativer Eigentumskonzepte.

Socially owned property is a guarantee of self-governance and self-management as well as of the protection of common societal relations, as opposed to self-organisation driven by joint individual/private interests. The normalisation of private property in all spheres of social relations and human existence keeps us from imagining any other concept of property. Two round tables on the topic of socially owned property in relation to knowledge, physical or financial capital, ways of self-organisation, and social capital have been organised in the public space.

Im Gegensatz zur Selbstorganisation, die von gemeinsamen Partikular- bzw. Privatinteressen geleitet ist, garantiert gesellschaftliches Eigentum Selbstverwaltung und Selbstmanagement sowie den Schutz allgemeiner sozialer Zusammenhänge. Die Normalisierung von Privateigentum in allen Bereichen des gesellschaftlichen und menschlichen Lebens verhindert den Entwurf alternativer Eigentumskonzepte. Zwei Diskussionsrunden im öffentlichen Raum widmeten sich dem Thema gesellschaftlichen Eigentums im Zusammenhang mit Wissen, Sach- und Finanzkapital, Formen der Selbstorganisation und Sozialkapital.

Initiatives

One-day assembly of colleagues involved in art and culture to discuss work conditions and the functioning of the local visual arts scene

Eintägiges Treffen von Kunst- und Kulturschaffenden zum Austausch über Arbeitsbedingungen und die Funktionsweise der lokalen Kunstszene

One of the important characteristics of the Belgrade art scene is association. In order to provide an insight into a broader picture of the current state of culture and a general diagnosis of the situation, I included in my research a number of close colleagues and associates in a one-day assembly with the intention of presenting and noting their experiences and observations regarding working conditions and the functioning of the local visual arts scene (artists, consumers, institutions, laws, money, etc.). This was documented in photo and video materials that were the product of our joint efforts.

Eines der wesentlichen Merkmale der Belgrader Kunstszene sind Zusammenschlüsse. Um einen umfassenden Einblick in die aktuelle kulturelle Lage und eine allgemeine Diagnose der Situation liefern zu können, lud ich im Rahmen meiner Recherchen eine Reihe von Künstler/innen zu einer eintägigen Veranstaltung ein, um ihre Erfahrungen und Eindrücke in Bezug auf ihre Arbeitsbedingungen und die Funktionsweisen der lokalen Kunstszene (Künstler/innen, Publikum, Einrichtungen, Gesetze, Finanzierung usw.) mitzuteilen. Die Ergebnisse dieses Treffens wurden in Form von Foto- und Videoaufnahmen dokumentiert.

Project: Anica Vučetić → Format: discussion → Date: 29 May 2016 → Venue: private house in Belgrade suburb of Grocka → Participants: Dragica Vuković, Svetlana Volic, Jasna Petrović, Miško Petrović, Ana Srbinović, Gordana Baškot, Olivera Parlić, Mirjana Denkov, Nina Todorović, Dragoslav Krnajski, Predrag Blagojević, Radoš Antonijević, Predrag Terzić, Milica Simonović, Mirjana Boba Stojadinović (discussion); Anica Vučetić (moderator); Slobodan Stefanović (project assistant); Svetlana Volic, Nina Todorović, Mirjana Boba Stojadinović (photo documentation); Mirjana Boba Stojadinović (audio documentation)

KAMEN-DIN-AMIKE

Kamendynamics
A Schematic Depiction of
Class Struggle in Kamendin

How to contextualise and visualise some problems pertaining to the social housing project in Zemun Polje?

Ein soziales Wohnungsbauprojekt in Zemun Polje – Probleme der Sichtbarmachung und des breiteren Kontextes

The activist research explores the possibility of creating a mural about class relations and class struggle in the neighbourhood of Kamendin in the suburb of Zemun Polje, where large numbers of poor people, particularly Roma families, live in social-housing apartments.

The research and documentary approach is focused both on relations towards problems of class society on the capitalist periphery and on communal or institutional capacities for the realisation of a critical political work in the public space. The idea is discussed with the inhabitants of Kamendin, local authorities, and the institutions in charge of social housing.

Das aktivistische Forschungsprojekt lotet Möglichkeiten aus, ein Wandgemälde zum Thema Klassenverhältnisse und Klassenkampf im Viertel Kamendin des Vorortes Zemun Polje zu gestalten. Hier leben viele arme Menschen, insbesondere Roma-Familien, in Sozialwohnungen.

Der dokumentarische Forschungsansatz fokussiert sich nicht nur darauf, wie Probleme der Klassengesellschaft an der kapitalistischen Peripherie angegangen werden, sondern richtet den Blick auch auf die kommunalen und institutionellen Möglichkeiten, um ein kritisches politisches Werk im öffentlichen Raum zu realisieren. Die Idee wird mit den Bewohner/innen von Kamendin, den Behörden vor Ort und den Institutionen des sozialen Wohnungsbaus diskutiert.

Project: Nebojša Milikić & Tadej Kurepa → Format: activist research, discussion → Dates: February–June 2016, 29 May 2016 (discussion) → Venue: ACTOPOLIS apartment, Bulevar Despota Stefana 36, Belgrade → Participants: Vahida Ramujkić (drawings); Zorana Pavlović, Slobodan Mitrović, Đorđe Popović, Milovan Pavlović (interviewees)

Low-Fi Video Remembered

Exploring possible ways of adequately enabling the archive of the Low-Fi Video movement online, carefully developed to evoke the particular continuity of "radical amateurism" in SFR Yugoslavia

Wege und Möglichkeiten, das Archiv der Low-Fi-Video-Bewegung adäquat online zu stellen und an die besondere Kontinuität der „radikalen Laienbewegung" der Sozialistischen Föderativen Republik Jugoslawien zu erinnern

The term Low-Fi Video (1997–2003) refers to the organised and coordinated production, distribution, and presentation of film and video, whose models of production and representation, in continuity with Yugoslav cine-amateurism and in collaboration with the international micro-cinema movement, enabled the inclusion of self-organised, amateur, vernacular production together with artistic creation in the process of forging a new language of alternative culture in Serbia. In order to increase the development of the Low-Fi Video archive and evoke the emancipatory models of cinema revived by the movement in keeping with the tradition of cine-amateurism, the Media Archaeology team is organising a live two-day event gathering together members of the movement from its original period and new artists and activists who can offer their contemporary response to the ideas of the movement.

Der Begriff Low-Fi-Video (1997–2003) bezieht sich auf die organisierte und koordinierte Produktion, den Verleih und die Vorführung von Filmen und Videos. In Fortsetzung des Amateurfilmschaffens im ehemaligen Jugoslawien und in Zusammenarbeit mit der internationalen Mikrokino- bewegung wurde es dank der Pro- duktions- und Darstellungsmodelle von Low-Fi-Video möglich, selbst organisierte, landesspezifische Amateurproduktionen mit künstleri- scher Schöpfungskraft zusammen- zubringen und so eine neue, alterna- tive Kultursprache in Serbien zu prägen. Um die Entwicklung des Low-Fi-Videoarchivs voranzubringen und an die emanzipatorischen Modelle des Kinos zu erinnern, die gemäß der Amateurfilmtradition von der Bewegung wiederbelebt wurden, organisiert das Team Medienarchäo- logie eine zweitägige Veranstaltung. Sie vereint Mitglieder der Bewegung aus der Anfangszeit und neue Künstler/innen und Aktivist/innen, die sich aus heutiger Sicht zu den Ideen der Bewegung äußern.

Project: Ivica Đorđević & Aleksandra Sekulić → Format: exhibition, archive, screening → Dates: 29 May 2016 & 3 June 2016 → Venues: Matrijaršija, Đorđa Čutukovića 13 & Center of Urban Culture IMAGO, Dečanska 14 → Participants: Miroslav Lakobrija (Low-Fi Video exhibition editor), Adam Ranđelović (musical programme editor), Mileta Mijatović (Fijuk organiser and curator of the exhibition by Aleksandar Opačić at Matrijaršija), Nikola Cakić (technical coordinator), Igor Stanojević (volunteer) → Collaborating organisation: Fijuk, fair for small and independent publishers → Acknowledgements: The Cyclist Conspiracy, The Red Step

ZBR / STRIP / ANIMACIJA
TURUMEN.WORDPRESS.COM
MARKO TURUMEN [FI]
DA / 1. OKTOBAR / 19H00 / KULTURM CENTAR REX [JEVREJSKA 16, BG]
UD DOBA 2014 DIMENZIJA LUDILO 29. 09. - 05. 10. 2014
AR ZA KULTURNU DEKONTAMINACIJU / MATRIJARŠIJA / ZMUC / KULTURNI CENTAR REX
RAD / DRUGSTORE / ULIČNA GALERIJA / CIGLANA / ELEKTRIKA PANČEVO / APOLO
naša kuća WWW.NOVODOBAFESTIVAL.NET INSTITUT FRANÇAIS
HEAVY TRASH
SPRING 2016 EU ROCKABILLY REVENGE

st/diverzitet/polifonost...
ivost granica
ivnist u funkciji korektiva
namičnost
cionalnost kriterijuma
pojedinca

bliski termini:
-nezavisna
-druga scena
-vaninstitucionalna
-samoinicijativa
-zajednica
-samoupravlja-
nje

RAZMOTRENI
MODELI:
a) zadruga
b) kooperative
c) komunistička
    zajednica
d) skupština
   stanara

u distribuciji zadataka
amostvaranje

ra
   sigurnost
ka autonomija
nja
svrha
vranje
zivnost
st

Ideološka matrica
zajednička ili ne?

nema
zajedničke
ideologije,
postoji samo?
a) praksa ideo
   koketir
b) zahte
c) pre

CIJA
VAI
UZ
E
avisnosti

očitavanje
ideologije
kroz
praksu

nužnost
jasne
eksplicitn
formuliso
pozicije

The Rehearsal Superstructure and Modelling of the Self-Organised Scene in Belgrade

An as-if inquiry that leads to polymedia work about modelling a self-organised cultural scene in Belgrade

Modelle einer selbst organisierten Kulturszene in Belgrad – eine Als-ob-Untersuchung mit künstlerischen Werken in verschiedenen Medien

In the context of the "great divides" in which Belgrade's cultural scene reproduces existing social relations, what is evident is the vast fragmentation and focus on different, more or less convincing attempts by individual entities to sustain themselves and consolidate regardless, and perhaps even because, of the weakening of others. Thus the question of what the self-organised cultural scene is, is expressed in the conditional form: What could it be? Why should it exist? What would it aim for? What principles would it be founded on? Can we even begin to imagine it? What would it look like if we tried?

Ten artists and cultural workers responded to this line of questioning aimed at articulating a new construct. Their answers were used as a starting point for the polymedia work in which the focus is on questioning the needs of the participants involved, as well as possible models for the self-organised cultural scene in Belgrade.

Die Kulturszene in Belgrad reproduziert die „großen Spaltungen", von denen die aktuelle gesellschaftliche Lage geprägt ist. Daher ist auch sie selbst weitgehend zersplittert. Darüber hinaus ist sie von unterschiedlichen, mehr oder weniger überzeugenden Versuchen einzelner Akteur/innen geprägt, ihre Stellung zu bewahren und zu festigen, auch wenn – oder gerade weil – sie dadurch andere schwächen. Daher wäre die Frage nach der selbst organisierten Kunstszene eigentlich besser im Konjunktiv zu formulieren: Was würde eine selbst organisierte Kunstszene bedeuten? Was wären ihre Existenzgründe, was ihre Ziele? Auf welchen Prinzipien würde sie beruhen? Können wir uns eine solche Kunstszene überhaupt vorstellen? Wie sähe eine solche Szene aus, wenn wir sie wirklich zu etablieren versuchten?

Zehn Künstler/innen und Kulturschaffende reagierten auf die Fragestellung, die auf die Gestaltung eines neuen Konstrukts zielte. Ihre Antworten waren der Ausgangspunkt für Arbeiten in vielzähligen Medien, die vor allem die Bedürfnisse der Beteiligten sowie mögliche Modelle der selbst organisierten Kulturszene Belgrads hinterfragen.

Project: Irena Ristić → Format: research, sound installation, report with public discussion → Dates: 18–29 May 2016 & 23 May 2016 → Venue: ACTOPOLIS apartment, Bulevar Despota Stefana 36, Belgrade → Participants: Dragan Protić, Igor Koruga, Mariela Cvetić, Vahida Ramujkić, Nikola Radić Lucati, Tanja Marković, Boba Stojadinović, Nebojša Milikić, Noa Treister, Vlada Novaković (dialogues); Milica Ivić (public discussion guest); Dragan Novković (sound designer); Anđelka Nikolić (associate) → Acknowledgements: Sandra Stojanović, for ZOOM

A Study of an Individual Case Drawing Exhibition with a Publication

There is a need to cast light on the unsustainable conditions of cultural models in order to redefine them and find a way to bring them back as an organic part of the social environment.

Es gilt, die unhaltbaren Bedingungen von kulturellen Modellen zu beleuchten, um sie neu zu definieren und sie nach Möglichkeit wieder organisch in das soziale Gefüge zu integrieren.

In the temporary, floating space of the ACTOPOLIS project, which is devoted to the topic of self-organisation in culture, we have chosen to put on a small, symbolic exhibition of intimate drawings. Among numerous possible ways of dealing with the topic of self-organisation in local conditions, we, as perennial participants in this Frankensteinian, transitional non-system of culture, wanted to point out the importance of an individual, personal experience and thus detect the flaws in the system's poor structural design.

Remont has been in existence since 1999 as an independent, self-organised structure. The most important thing that the staff at Remont had to work out through their practice was how to operate in an unstable, changeable, undefined environment and, at the same time, to act as a support for many others.

Project: Marija Radoš and Miroslav Karić (Remont—Independent Artist Association) →
Format: research, exhibition → Dates: 26–29 May 2016 → Venue: ACTOPOLIS apartment, Bulevar Despota Stefana 36, Belgrade → Participants: EmaEmaEma, Mario Kolarić, Andrej Bunuševac, Goran Stojčetović → Acknowledgements: Marko Stojanović, Željko Maksimović

Im temporären, fließenden Raum des ACTOPOLIS-Projekts, der sich dem Thema Selbstorganisation in der Kultur widmet, haben wir uns zu einer kleinen, symbolischen Ausstellung von intimen Zeichnungen entschlossen. Es gibt vielfältige Möglichkeiten, das Thema Selbstorganisation unter lokalen Bedingungen anzugehen; als ständige Mitwirkende an diesem Frankenstein'schen vorübergehenden Nicht-System der Kultur wollten wir auf die Bedeutung individueller, persönlicher Erfahrungen hinweisen und so Schwachpunkte in der Statik des Systems aufdecken.

Die unabhängige, selbst organisierte Künstlervereinigung Remont (zu Deutsch: Wartung) wurde 1999 gegründet. Ihre wichtigste Aufgabe war es, durch die praktischen Erfahrungen ihrer Mitglieder das Arbeiten unter instabilen, unbestimmten und veränderlichen Bedingungen zu meistern und gleichzeitig vielen anderen weiterhin Unterstützung zu bieten.

SPECIAL EDITION, MAY 2016

ISSN 2406-1174

ZIDNE NOVINE

THE WALL NEWSPAPERS, english translation of Issue 11, May 2016

www.zidne.udruzenjekurs.org

A CARNIVAL AMIDST RUINS

Author: Iskra Krstić
Artwork: KURS

The hierarchy of power in international affairs and economy is reflected in the domain of culture. The unconvincing means used to legitimise creative industries in the *core* countries are even more questionable in the pauperised post-socialist *periphery*, producing more dramatic effects all the while. By adopting harsh austerity measures and imposing a hostile attitude towards local cultural institutions formed during real socialism, the official cultural politics provide the local and international organizations for cultural management with extensive privileges in cultural production, thus leaving the cultural workers to their free will.

CREATIVE INDUSTRIES – A SOLUTION OR A PART OF THE PROBLEM?

The beneficial effects of creative industries on the local economy, urban revitalisation, youth unemployment, and attracting foreign investments are promoted in statements made by cultural managers, public strategies, and academic curricula alike. They consider creative industries to be the booster of *urban regeneration*, which induces the development of *cultural tourism* and the *implementation of the creative cities concept*. [1]

By describing creative industries as an activity based on active and autonomous contribution of free individuals to their economic and social surroundings, the creative industries' advocates blur the structures of political and economic power which restrain and instrumentalise the activities of cultural workers. Their optimistic interpretations, limited to the economic significance of creative industries and *cultural entrepreneurship*, de-contextualise the rising importance of the tertiary sector of the economy from the preceding crisis of agriculture and industry which preceded it; and the positive aspects of creating new business opportunities from the downsides of the aggressive expansion of the free market to all social functions and goods – more concretely, the commercialisation of *art, culture, fun, communications, free time and urban space*.

Most of the contemporary explanations of the phenomenon of creative industries vary elements of the definition formulated by the so-called *Creative Industry Task Force* in the late nineties, at a time when Great Britain expressed its resolution to back up the economic growth in this newly acknowledged domain. From early on, this concept was criticised and exposed as a result of a "mature Thatcherism", since it narrowly focused on extracting and enlarging economic profit from the activities which had rarely been identified as commercial and entrepreneurial previously. [2] A negative meaning of *cultural industry*, [3] from which the concept of creative industry evolved, has also been brought into question during the nineties, when *cultural imperialism* was replaced by a more subtle concept of *globalisation*.

COMMODITY-CULTURE AND COMMODITY-CITY

Globalisation stands for a high level of global economic integration and the emergence of hybrid cultural forms forged under the influence of the cultures of the developed countries. Parallel to these integrations, which cause the transformation of relations between different administrative entities, a *financialisation* of economy takes place, motivating cities to compete for a portion of the financial resources provided by the global financial markets. The *creative city* concept, namely, signifies a city which relies on attracting direct investment and rich consumers, instead of relying on the material production (the primary and the tertiary sector of the economy) in its geographical surroundings. By identifying the abovementioned local culture as an *economic resource*, such cities compete for funding for carnivals (such as the European capital of culture), allow the *spectacularisation* of their historical heritage, and initiate the processes of *gentrification*.

The process of gentrification renders the poor and derelict neighbourhoods more attractive for rich investors, while the previous inhabitants get thrown out either by crude force, rising rent, or cost-of-living increases. The so-called *creative class* (mostly young workers in culture and IT industry) is encouraged to inhabit the area in the primary phase of gentrification, thus contributing to the rise in its symbolic capital and increasing the visibility of such a neighbourhood on the seemingly endless map of potential space for investment. The *creative class* provides marketing for the neighbourhood in exchange for the temporary right of occupancy. In the following phase, this class is wiped out by the *financial class*, the moment the latter recognises the possibility to profit by flipping or indebting the *regenerated space* in question. Such gentrified neighbourhood soon becomes too expensive, or even physically inaccessible for "plain" inhabitants, who, nevertheless, still have to invest in it since the city retains the obligation to provide for the infrastructure and communal services.

The destruction of humanistic and universal narratives, and the proclamation of the failure of the welfare state and real socialism, together with the already described restructuring of the levels of management, legitimised the narrow perspective which so cynically focuses on the increase of money flow in particular city areas.

CULTURAL MANAGEMENT BETWEEN LABOUR AND CAPITAL

Global integrations, followed by the difficulties in harmonizing the institutions and actors in different levels, inaugurated the significance of cultural managers, who appear as the link between labour and capital also in Belgrade. During the last few years, different organisations for cultural management have concentrated their activities in Savamala, initiating the first phase of gentrification. Independent cultural spaces (Magacin, KC Grad…) were followed in step by foreign cultural centres' and foundations' projects, after which the used-to-be industrial warehouses and stores were flooded by coffee shops and night clubs, transforming Savamala into a nightlife centre and tourist attraction.

In their projects the creative industries often address the "issues of the day" and practices of public importance, such as civic participation and urban activism. They successfully present themselves in public as democratic and participatory, although the testimonies of their participants (Mixer, Urban incubator) speak in favour of a conclusion that they are, in fact, hierarchically organised structures with a bureaucratic division of tasks. The actual *absence of small actors* has been frequently pointed out – what exists are, in fact, groups of cultural workers organized artificially, *from above*. [4] Horizontal organising and activism usually only serve a marketing strategy for attracting liberal and affluent young public, whose need for socialisation through revolt has been a source of profit for the cultural industry at least since the sixties. The *coalition of creative entrepreneurs* of Savamala, in fact, expresses their surprise with the Belgrade waterfront project – or at least its endangering scale – failing to notice their own contribution to the *spectacularisation* of this neighbourhood. They invite the investors' from the UAE to a dialogue with "the people who have erected Savamala from the ashes and made it a true urban pearl of the Balkans", presenting the defence of their own benefit as a struggle for public interest.

SPECTACULAR UPROOTEDNESS

A certain amount of animosity towards the projects of these organisations is provoked by their hypermodern, superficial aesthetics which suggests a brake up with all forms of local culture. Something in their attitude radiates despise towards the more traditional types of art and modernist, socialist aesthetics alike, causing an impression that the spectator is dealing with a fake, an uprooted form which exclusively serves and belongs to neoliberal globalisation. That something isn't the minimalism and *contemporaneity* of their form *per se* – these could in fact also be used in a progressive manner – but the separation of their aesthetics from the logic of function and production, *blassé attitude*, [5] a smug and careless carnival amidst ruins. Organisations such as Mixer, Urban incubator, KC Grad, HUB 12, Nova Iskra (to mention a few) advocate market liberalisation and individual entrepreneurship, following the example of more affluent surroundings – failing to notice that the success of such models in the given, local context, is highly questionable, and omitting the fact that they largely rely on local and foreign public funds, and use lent state owned spaces.

Inspired by the rise of urban standard in the "more humanely" gentrified communities in Berlin, Prague or Budapest, the advocates for creative industries in Belgrade

skip a few important facts. These Mid-European cities received large, politically motivated, donations in the beginning of the nineties, at the time of economical prosperity in Europe. Prague and Budapest, also, belonged to a group of cities whose economy has been rapidly *tertiarising* since the seventies, and which attracted a number of affluent businesspeople from abroad, due to their favourable geographic position. Besides the fact that Belgrade, whose relative importance plummeted since the beginning of the nineties, could not possibly expect similar development, the ethical justification for promoting harsh spatio-social stratification, such as the one that followed gentrification in Prague and Budapest, is questionable to say the least.

IS THERE AN ALTERNATIVE?

The local and regional organisations for cultural management contribute to the commercialisation of culture, free time and urban space in cooperation with a (neo)liberally oriented state and city administration, thus, with the help of foreign foundations, sucking the cultural production and city space into neoliberal modes of governing, and preparing them for direct privatisation. Foreign foundations, all the while, reap profit from a palpable social anomy and distrust towards the society and the institutions, and a combination of local revanchist attitude towards the institutions of the socialist *public sphere* (houses of culture, etc.) and a bureaucratic blindness of the supranational organisations for the local specificities and more nuanced needs. The hierarchy of actors and the institutional frame prevent limited activism to overstep its strict boundaries towards a critique of a system within which international relations from the domain of politics and economy reflect on culture, enabling a patronising relationship towards the poorer parts of the post-socialist region.

In a time to which Bauman refers to as *fluid modernity* – an epoch in which the fast changes of rules outrun the person's ability to adapt – creative ingenuity might be a general necessity, but it bears fruit to just a few. An authentic creative strategy which would challenge the ongoing capitalist crisis must abandon the TINA (there is no alternative) dogma and the modes of grouping and production which conform to it, including the creative industries, and reclaim a right to

[1] Program Creative Europe http://www.kreativnaevropa.rs
[2] Simon Roodhouse, "The Creative Industries: Definitions, Quantification and Practice", in: Christiane Eisenberg, Rita Gerlach and Christian Handke (ur.), *Cultural Industries: The British Experience in International Perspective*, Humboldt University, Berlin, 2006.
[3] Theodor Adorno, Max Horkheimer, "The Culture Industry: Enlightenment as Mass Deception" (1944) in: *The Dialectics of Enlightement*, Stanford University Press, Stanford, 2002.
[4] http://www.transeurope-express.eu/sve-ce-to-umetnost-pozlatiti/
[5] http://www.gradbeograd.eu/clanak_vest.php?id=177
[6] Georg Simmel, "The Metropolis and Mental Life" (1903.) in: Gary Bridge and Sophie Watson (ur.) *The Blackwell City Reader*, Wiley-Blackwell, Oxford MA, 2002.
* Text on the poster: Paraphrase of the text from the Assembly of artists in Paris Commune. More at: http://www.redwedgemagazine.com/online-issue/manifesto-federation-artist-commune

This number is produced under the project ACtopolis BEoGRAD organised by Goethe-Institut and Urbane Künste Ruhr, production Goethe-Institut Belgrad.

ZIDNE NOVINE,
(The Wall Newspapers);
Publisher: KURS - Đorđa Lobačeva 7, Beograd, kurs.org@gmail.com, www.udruzenjekurs.org;
Editors: Miloš Miletić, Mirjana Radovanović;
Translation: Iskra Krstić;
Graphic design/artwork: KURS (Miloš Miletić, Mirjana Radovanović);
Print: SGR Standard2, Beograd; 300 copies

CIP – Каталогизација у публикацији
Народна библиотека Србије, Београд

316.7:766

ZIDNE novine / Udruženje KURS. - God. 1, br. 1 (nov. 2013)-   . - Beograd : Udruženje KURS, 2013-
. - 1 presavijen list : ilustr. u boji ; 66 x 47 cm

Povremeno izlaze prevodi određenih brojeva na eng. jezik.
ISSN 2406-1174 = Zidne novine (Udruženje KURS)
COBISS.SR-ID 210632972

Wall Newspaper
A Carnival amidst Ruins

Wall Newspaper uses texts and illustrations to rethink various social issues and critically refer to the processes of neo-liberal capitalism.

Wall Newspaper _reflektiert mithilfe von Text und Illustrationen gesellschaftliche Themen und verweist kritisch auf die Abläufe im neoliberalen Kapitalismus._

Wall Newspaper is a visual and informative media form that considers different social issues. The main goal of _Wall Newspapers_ is to increase the visibility of contents that critically assess the processes of neo-liberal capitalism, by producing sharply defined texts and illustrations.

For the Belgrade edition of ACTOPOLIS, KURS produced an issue of _Wall Newspaper_ in cooperation with Iskra Krstić. This issue asks how cultural production, in particular creative industries, backed up by international foundations, serves the aims of cultural privatisation. The topic is broad: many of these processes are universal and could be related to other cities in which ACTOPOLIS takes place.

Wall Newspaper ist ein visuelles Informationsmedium, das sich mit verschiedenen gesellschaftlichen Themen auseinandersetzt. Seine Texte und Illustrationen beziehen klar Position, ordnen die Abläufe im neoliberalen Kapitalismus kritisch ein und machen diese Themen stärker sichtbar.

Im Rahmen der Belgrader ACTOPOLIS-Ausgabe hat das Projekt KURS in Zusammenarbeit mit Iskra Krstić eine Ausgabe der Wall Newspaper _erstellt. Sie widmet sich der Frage, wie die aktuelle Kulturproduktion und vor allem die Kreativindustrie mithilfe internationaler Stiftungen dem Ziel der Kulturprivatisierung dient. Das Thema ist auf breiter Ebene aktuell: Viele dieser Vorgänge sind universell und lassen sich auch in anderen ACTOPOLIS-Städten beobachten._

Project: KURS (Miloš Miletić and Mirjana Radovanović) → Format: publication and public discussion → Dates: May 2016 → Venues: ACTOPOLIS apartment, Bulevar Despota Stefana 36, Belgrade; October Social Centre, Strahinjića Bana 33, Belgrade; CZKD—Centre for Cultural Decontamination, Birčaninova 21, Belgrade → Participants: KURS (Miloš Miletić and Mirjana Radovanović) (editing); KURS (Miloš Miletić and Mirjana Radovanović) (illustrations); Iskra Krstić (text); Iskra Krstić, Danilo Prnjat, Selman Trtovac (public discussion guests)

U10 Art Collective

Seven artists present their artwork and themselves as organisers, curators, and members of the art collective through a group show.

Sieben Künstler/innen zeigen ihr Werk und treten im Rahmen einer Gruppenausstellung als Organisator/innen, Kurator/innen und Mitglieder des U10 Kunstkollektivs auf.

In the framework of the ACTOPOLIS project, the U10 Art Collective realised seven individual art works on the theme of self-organisation. Completed works are presented at the exhibition, with a discussion and presentation of the artistic group's experiences to date in the field of self-organisation.

Im Rahmen von ACTOPOLIS realisiert das U10 Kunstkollektiv sieben Einzelarbeiten zum Thema Selbstorganisation. Die Ausstellung zeigt die fertigen Werke, außerdem finden eine Diskussion und Präsentation der bisherigen Erfahrungen der Künstlergruppe auf dem Gebiet der Selbstorganisation statt.

Project: U10 Art Collective → Format: exhibition → Dates: 18–29 May 2016 → Venue: ACTOPOLIS apartment, Bulevar Despota Stefana 36, Belgrade → Participants: U10 Art Collective (Lidija Delić, Nina Ivanović, Sava Knežević, Isidora Krstić, Iva Kuzmanović, Nemanja Nikolić, Marija Šević)

Education

Education is the production and reproduction of culture and society through the legitimisation of certain knowledges and narratives and the invalidation of others. It is a commodity within the global economy, indispensable to productive power relations, and a method to organise the division of labour.

Education can also be para-academic, an apparatus to question canon-making forces and claim its own views on history, art, gender, and class. It is a tool that can be used not only to investigate the everyday functioning and effects of power relations or forms of knowledge but also to call certain narratives into question while at the same time devising new ones.

Bildung ist die Produktion und Reproduktion von Kultur und Gesellschaft, indem bestimmte Kenntnisse und Narrative legitimiert und andere gleichzeitig entwertet werden. Innerhalb der globalen Wirtschaft ist sie eine für produktive Machtbeziehungen unabdingbare Ware und eine Methode zur Organisation von Arbeitsteilung.

Als Instrument zur Hinterfragung der den Lehrkanon bestimmenden Kräfte und zur Geltendmachung eigener Sichtweisen zu Geschichte, Kunst, Gender und Gesellschaftsschicht kann Bildung auch para-akademisch sein. Mit diesem Werkzeug können nicht nur Funktionsweisen und Auswirkungen von Machtbeziehungen oder Wissensformen untersucht werden, sondern auch bestimmte Narrative infrage gestellt und gleichzeitig neue erdacht werden.

Elpida Karaba

Heritage

Be it natural, historical, national, or cultural, heritage refers to a specific value or meaning given by a group, a state, or society as a whole to natural resources, flora and fauna, a place, an event, a building, an artefact, or a memory. Heritage can be built heritage, such as houses, cemeteries, factories, and monuments, or intangible, i.e. living cultural heritage that can include performing arts, rituals, social practices, individual stories, oral traditions and expressions, language, digital heritage, traditional craftsmanship, and other knowledge and practices. Since the 1972 World Heritage Convention—which emerged from two separate movements, one focusing on the preservation of cultural sites and the other dealing with the conservation of nature—the main aim of the heritage movement has been to preserve, protect, and pass on our world heritage through the generations.

Jegliches Erbe – sei es natürlich, historisch, national oder kulturell – bezieht sich auf einen bestimmten Wert oder eine Bedeutung, die natürlichen Ressourcen, Flora und Fauna, einem Ort, einem Ereignis, einem Bauwerk, einem Artefakt oder einer Erinnerung von einer Gruppe, einem Staat oder der Gesellschaft insgesamt beigemessen werden. Bei dem Erbe kann es sich um Bauten wie Häuser, Friedhöfe, Fabriken und Denkmäler handeln oder um immaterielles Erbe, das heißt lebendiges Kulturerbe wie darstellende Künste, Rituale, gesellschaftliche Gepflogenheiten, einzelne Erzählungen, mündliche Überlieferungen und Ausdrucksformen, Sprache, digitalisierte Kulturgüter, traditionelle Handwerkskunst sowie andere Kenntnisse und Praktiken. Die UNESCO-Welterbekonvention von 1972 entstand aus zwei unterschiedlichen Bewegungen, von denen sich die eine auf den Erhalt von Kulturstätten konzentrierte und die andere mit Naturschutz befasste. Wichtigstes Ziel des Abkommens ist es, das Kultur- und Naturwelterbe zu erhalten, zu schützen und über Generationen weiterzugeben.

Danijela Dugandžić

Infrastructure

Infrastructural decisions create the basis for how we live together: infrastructures not only enable actions; they regulate the potential for action. Infrastructures privilege certain uses and complicate others. Infrastructures organise access to and participation in many areas of society. Because of their scale and the different (political and economic) interests involved, infrastructural decisions often escape political control. Moreover, infrastructures can obstruct the conditions of their functioning. Or, to put it differently: because there are houses, people live in them; because there are streets, there are cars driving past; because there are banks, there are bank robberies.

Infrastrukturelle Entscheidungen sind das Fundament unseres Zusammenlebens: Infrastrukturen ermöglichen nicht nur Handlungen, sondern steuern auch die Handlungsmöglichkeiten. Sie erleichtern bestimmte Handlungen und erschweren andere. Infrastrukturen regeln Zugang und Teilhabe in vielen Bereichen der Gesellschaft. Aufgrund ihrer Größenordnung und unterschiedlicher (politischer und wirtschaftlicher) Interessen entziehen sich infrastrukturelle Entscheidungen häufig der politischen Kontrolle. Darüber hinaus können Infrastrukturen die Umstände für ihr Funktionieren erschweren. Oder anders gesagt: Weil es Häuser gibt, wohnen Menschen in ihnen, weil es Straßen gibt, fahren Autos vorbei, weil es Banken gibt, gibt es Banküberfälle.

geheimagentur

BUCHAREST

Bucharest-South:
Build Your Own City

Twenty sixteen was a year of elections—presidential, parliamentary, and local elections, referendums, reruns of elections: throughout the world it seemed like the last democratic instrument for people to express their will on governance issues and government representatives was reduced to its purely symbolical role. Harsh anti-democratic and nationalist agendas, algorithms and voting bots, fake news and neo-fascism have appropriated the popular vote to institute and legitimise regimes based on fear, segregation, the acceleration of poverty, and all the other characteristics of the apocalyptic societies in which we seem to be struggling to survive. In some cases, as in Austria, there were reasons for hope—a little more than half the voters chose not to give in to an openly far-right president. In other cases, as in Bucharest, local elections brought in the first woman mayor—alas, a pseudo-leftist, conservative, business-as-usual figure. There were common threads linking the campaigns in all the different countries, the exit polls, and the after-commentaries: from the vilification of the immigrant and the return to the empty, yet exacerbated notion of the nation to the bitter blaming of old or poor people for the results and the perplexing gaps that were evident between urban and rural voters, between metropolises and provinces.

Before all of this happened, rather than putting all our money on bottom-up, grass-roots, self-organised processes and institutions (even if we have learned to trust them more), we decided to propose a project for ACTOPOLIS | The Art of Action that would rely on the democratic process via which certain elected representatives make decisions about the city's fate. We live in a place that is still highly centralised—so why not use and repurpose the institutions that we have for the greater good rather than dismiss them? We took inspiration from an American TV series which tried to show that only through (sometimes unpopular) political will can segregation be fought, and we challenged ourselves to find out how much segregation is kept in place by our economy, infrastructure, and media.

Bucharest-South: Build Your Own City was first of all an exercise in imagination, but it was also a lesson in realism and trust, which we—the project team—have learned and been amazed by. We wanted to circumvent the eternal lament about bureaucracy, corruption, and the impossibility of being a good citizen, a lament that makes mileage out of the question, How do you see your city, Bucharest? So we decided to change the question to, How would you see your city were you in a position to make decisions about it? Our project was participative in that it relied on people to embody the role we proposed to them but it did not sell any promise (of entertainment, experience, wonder, or any of the usual icing that participative projects come with). It was situated at the crossroads of sociological survey, architectural manifestation, and artistic intervention; it was short-lived, though it had many outcomes; it was present but not imposing, inviting but not intrusive, a bit too fancy for the general chaos in which it took place, but nonetheless manifesting a serious (even if imagined) institution that people were invited to inhabit for their ten minutes of glory and responsibility.

At the beginning we set out to discuss the area we work in: tranzit.ro/bucuresti has had its space for the past four years close to the northern border of Bucharest-South, and Zeppelin is developing a long-term project in Halele Carol, a factory space in the same area. We had of course visited Văcărești Park (popularly known as the Bucharest Delta), the Berceni market and shopping mall, and the Bellu cemetery, where several famous people are buried, as well as some (quite a few and fairly recent) artistic and cultural spaces spread around this southern area. Some of us had even made it to Ferentari, the segregated neighbourhood with a bad reputation. You can read more about some of these places in the stories architect and writer Mihai Duțescu tells in the texts commissioned for our project. Or you can understand the geographical positioning and varied profiles of initiatives in various other places from the map conceived by Cosmina Goagea, Maria Alexandrescu, and Claudiu Forgaci—once you visit these places, you realize how outstanding and pioneering they are, appearing as they do in the middle of dormitory neighbourhoods, post-industrial deserts, and infrastructural voids. The Bucharest-South stories and map, together with Vlad Petri's documentary film *10 Minutes' Mayors*, represent three complementary accounts offering a glimpse of this part of the city, which is considered to be the bad, poor, not-fancy, distant, uninteresting, hard-to-reach, dangerous, wild, derelict, provincial slice of Bucharest, even though it represents half the city. With these three tools one (i.e. an inhabitant of the Bucharest-North) can hopefully cut through the maze of prejudices and understand this area as more than the network of streets one has to drive through on the way out of the city to the Danube or the sea.

We have, however, hoped and dared to believe that ACTOPOLIS was neither just a pretext for us to learn more nor a large-scale international deployment of forces designed to bring knowledge to the usual places where knowledge is consumed (i.e. to the northern part of the city). We dared to believe that even a very brief relocation of attention to Bucharest-South would shift the agenda, that mapping and pointing and narrating are very good at evoking a subject but are not enough if they are not accompanied by real encounters with those who actually live in the place and make it their everyday constituency. *Be a Mayor for Ten Minutes*, the main action of *ACTOPOLIS: Bucharest-South*, was a platform for us to find out how this city might look if it were to be governed by its regular citizens. Most of the people who took up the seat and insignia of temporary mayor described a city with more equitable distribution of resources, more social justice and education, less bureaucracy, one that is greener and friendlier and perhaps even less rigid in terms of its social norms (the legalisation of marijuana was proposed by one of our mayors). Contrary to the expectations fed by a media focused too much on cultivating forms of class and race hate, an impressive number of participants (many of whom were children) underlined the need for measures that help the homeless and the poor. It could have been that the responsibility of the role and the presence of the video camera attracted some political correctness but we doubt this was the real reason, as the few lunatics we had as participants or passers-by did not shy away from expressing their ideas. Bucharest-South's ten-minute mayors also spoke about their dissatisfactions and the things they saw as urgent, from the lack of jobs and the dysfunctionality of traffic and public transport to the need for better hospitals, more green spaces, and playgrounds. They portrayed the ideal mayor as someone who is open to dialogue with local citizens and civic organizations. They recognised the "good places" (proposing to value them by promoting local information and cultural programmes) and offered solutions for how to change the "bad places" (education, social care, and culture being some of the most frequent instruments that were mentioned as a means to implement such change). Some of the mayors wrote follow-up emails, showing they had also continued to think about these issues after they had left their "office". Others came for the screening of Vlad Petri's film, in which they were portrayed, and once again agreed with their own ideas six months later. One of the mayors stood next to us in the metro at the end of one day "in office" and looked at the diploma we offered him— did he feel recognised? Was that the only diploma he had received in a long time? Was he wondering if real mayors have such diplomas in their offices?

The office that "our" mayors occupied was an open pavilion, designed by architect Constantin Goagea and artist Daniela Pălimariu to be transparent and functional, with a touch of gold, a wall clock, and a map of Bucharest-South, with comfortable furniture and a councillor's area. Daniela Pălimariu and sociologist Iuliana Dumitru conceived the hospitality programme and all the papers the mayors had to fill out or sign. Passers-by took between thirty seconds and thirty minutes to listen to our team explaining the project and telling us their problems—some were convinced to take over the mayor's or councillor's seat, others just left. Despite the visual pollution in each of the places where the pavilion was installed, it succeeded in becoming a point of attraction, but in terms of the widespread and committed participation of people in the actual game, it was also more than just a street curiosity.

It was important that this carefully constructed structure did not get junked at the end of the project, and it didn't. It was given to the Arhipera Association, which works with participative architecture projects in rural areas that are subject to extreme poverty. Our mayor's office was transformed into a public-space facility in Belciugatele village, not far from Bucharest, where other decisions will be taken, collectively.

A pavilion (with an afterlife), three days of intense citizen participation, a list of realistic ideas that we hope will eventually make it to the table of the official mayors, a non-academic but still very relevant sociological survey, a documentary film, and a research project together with a map that is actually usable both for locals of Bucharest-South and for tourists, as well as five short stories that are not only picturesque depictions of this place but also good literature: this was *Bucharest-South: Build Your Own City*. We continue to work in this city, to cross the lines that divide it, to shop at the markets in the vicinity of which our pavilion stood, and to visit the good places from our map and from our mayors' mental maps.

RALUCA VOINEA, ȘTEFAN GHENCIULESCU

Bukarest-Süd:
Baue deine eigene Stadt

2016 war ein Jahr der Wahlen. Präsidentschafts-, Parlaments-, Kommunalwahlen, Referenden, Wahlwiederholungen – weltweit schien das letzte demokratische Instrument, mit dem Menschen ihre Meinung zu Regierungsfragen und Regierungsvertretern äußern können, auf eine rein symbolische Rolle reduziert worden zu sein. Radikal anti-demokratische und nationalistische Agenden, Algorithmen und Wahlbots, Fake News und Neofaschismus haben sich die Stimmen der Menschen zu eigen gemacht und zur Wahl und Legitimierung von Regimen geführt, die auf Angst, Segregation, der Beschleunigung von Armut und all den anderen Charakteristika apokalyptischer Gesellschaften beruhen, in denen wir ums Überleben zu kämpfen scheinen. In manchen Fällen gab es Anlass zur Hoffnung, so etwa in Österreich, wo sich etwas mehr als die Hälfte der Wähler gegen einen offen rechtsaußen stehenden Präsidenten entschied. In anderen Fällen, wie zum Beispiel in Bukarest, wurde bei den Kommunalwahlen zwar das erste Mal eine Frau zur Bürgermeisterin gewählt – leider allerdings eine pseudo-linke Konservative, unter der alles so weiter gehen wird wie bisher. In verschiedenen Ländern wiesen die Kampagnen, Abstimmungen über einen Austritt und nachfolgenden Kommentare gewisse Ähnlichkeiten auf: von der Diffamierung von Migranten und der Rückkehr zu einem hohlen, gleichzeitig aber zugespitzten Begriff der Nation bis zur bitteren Beschuldigung alter oder armer Menschen, für das Wahlergebnis verantwortlich zu sein, und erstaunlichen Unterschieden zwischen den Wähler/innen in städtischen und ländlichen Regionen, in den Metropolen und der Provinz.

Anstatt unser gesamtes Geld in selbst organisierte Bottom-up- oder Graswurzel-Prozesse und Institutionen zu stecken (auch wenn wir ihnen inzwischen mehr Vertrauen entgegenbringen), entschieden wir uns noch vor all diesen Geschehnissen, ein Projekt für ACTOPOLIS – Die Kunst zu Handeln vorzuschlagen, das den demokratischen Prozess widerspiegelt, auf dessen Grundlage bestimmte gewählte Vertreter über das Schicksal der Stadt entscheiden. Wir leben in einer immer noch stark zentralisierten Stadt. Warum also sollten wir die vorhandenen Institutionen nicht zum Wohle der Allgemeinheit nutzen bzw. für diesen Zweck umfunktionieren, anstatt sie abzulehnen? Angeregt durch eine amerikanische Fernsehserie, die zeigte, dass sich Segregation allein durch (manchmal unpopulären) politischen Willen bekämpfen lässt, wollten wir herausfinden, in welchem Maße Segregation durch Ökonomie, Infrastruktur und Medien aufrechterhalten wird.

Bukarest-Süd: Baue deine eigene Stadt war in erster Linie ein imaginatives Experiment, für uns als Projektteam aber auch eine Lehrstunde in Realismus und Zuversicht, die wir staunend annahmen. Wir wollten das ewige Lamento über Bürokratie, Korruption und die Unmöglichkeit guter Bürgerschaft hinter uns lassen oder uns vielmehr die ständigen Klagen auf die Frage „Wie sehen Sie Ihre Stadt, Bukarest?" zunutze machen. Daher beschlossen wir, die Frage umzuformulieren: „Wie würden Sie Ihre Stadt sehen, wenn Sie Entscheidungen fällen könnten?" Unser Projekt hatte insofern partizipativen Charakter, als die Beteiligten die von uns vorgeschlagene Rolle spielten; zugleich machten wir jedoch keinerlei Versprechungen etwa in Bezug auf Unterhaltung, Erfahrung, Staunen und die anderen üblichen Bonbons partizipatorischer Projekte. Das Projekt stellte eine Schnitt-

stelle zwischen soziologischer Studie, architektonischer Präsenz und künstlerischen Eingriffen dar; es war kurzlebig und zeitigte dennoch viele Ergebnisse; es war präsent, aber nicht überwältigend, einladend, aber nicht aufdringlich; es war etwas zu ausgefallen für das allgemeine Chaos ringsum, ließ jedoch eine ernsthafte (wenngleich nur imaginierte) Institution entstehen, die die Menschen zu zehn Minuten Ruhm und Verantwortung einlud.

Zunächst diskutierten wir über die Gegend, in der wir arbeiten: tranzit.ro/bucureşti befindet sich seit vier Jahren in Räumen an der nördlichen Grenze zu Bukarest-Süd und Zeppelin entwickelt ein Langzeitprojekt in Halele Carol, einem Fabrikgelände in derselben Gegend. Natürlich hatten wir den Văcăreşti Park (im Volksmund auch Delta von Bukarest genannt) besucht, ebenso den Markt und das Einkaufszentrum von Berceni und den Bellu-Friedhof mit den Gräbern berühmter Persönlichkeiten sowie eine ganze Reihe relativ neuer Räume für Kunst und Kultur, die sich hier im Süden der Stadt befinden. Einige von uns waren sogar in Ferentari gewesen, einem segregierten Viertel mit schlechtem Ruf. Näheres über diese Orte können Sie in den für unser Projekt entstandenen Erzählungen des Architekten und Schriftstellers Mihai Duţescu erfahren. Alternativ können Sie sich auf der von Cosmina Goagea, Maria Alexandrescu und Claudiu Forgaci entwickelten Karte über die geografische Lage und die unterschiedlichen Profile von Initiativen an anderen Orten informieren. Bei einem Besuch werden Sie begreifen, wie herausragend und wegweisend diese Projekte aufgrund ihrer Lage in Schlafstädten, postindustriellen Wüsten und Räumen ohne irgendeine Infrastruktur sind. Zusammen mit Vlad Petris Dokumentarfilm 10 Minutes' Mayors bieten die Erzählungen und die

Karte von Bukarest-Süd drei komplementäre Darstellungen, die einen Einblick in diesen Teil der Stadt ermöglichen. Obwohl er die Hälfte der Stadt ausmacht, gilt er als schlechter, armer, nicht angesagter, abgelegener, uninteressanter, schwer zu erreichender, gefährlicher, wilder, heruntergekommener, provinzieller Teil von Bukarest. Mit diesen drei Instrumenten sollten die Menschen (bzw. die Bewohner/innen von Bukarest-Nord) imstande sein, sich einen Weg durch das Labyrinth der Vorurteile zu bahnen und mehr in diesen Vierteln zu sehen als nur ein Straßengeflecht, das man auf dem Weg an die Donau oder ans Meer durchqueren muss.

Dabei hofften wir, dass ACTOPOLIS uns nicht lediglich als Vorwand dienen würde, um mehr über diesen Teil der Stadt zu erfahren. Ebenso wenig sollte es ein groß angelegter, internationaler Einsatz von Kräften sein, um Wissen an die üblichen Orte des Wissenskonsums (nämlich den Norden der Stadt) zu transportieren. Wir wagten zu glauben, dass sogar eine sehr kurze Verlagerung der Aufmerksamkeit auf Bukarest-Süd die Agenda verändern würde, dass Kartierung, Verweis und Narration gute Mittel zur Vermittlung eines Themas wären, jedoch nicht ausreichen, wenn sie nicht durch reale Begegnungen mit den Bewohner/innen und Wähler/innen dieser Viertel ergänzt werden. Be a Mayor for Ten Minutes, das zentrale Projekt für ACTOPOLIS: Bukarest-Süd, diente uns als Plattform, um mögliche Erscheinungsformen einer Stadt auszuloten, die von ihren ganz normalen Einwohner/innen regiert würde. Die meisten Menschen, die den Sitz und die Insignien einer/eines temporären Bürgermeisterin/Bürgermeisters übernahmen, beschrieben eine Stadt mit gerechterer Ressourcenverteilung, mehr sozialer Gerechtigkeit und Bildung, weniger Bürokratie, eine grünere, freundlichere und im

Hinblick auf gesellschaftliche Normen vielleicht sogar weniger strenge Stadt (einer der Bürgermeister schlug die Legalisierung von Marihuana vor). Entgegen der durch das übermäßige mediale Schüren von Klassen- und Rassenhass entstandenen Erwartungen unterstrich eine beeindruckende Zahl von Teilnehmer/innen, darunter viele Kinder, die Notwendigkeit von Maßnahmen für Obdachlose und Arme. Möglicherweise haben das mit der Rolle einhergehende Verantwortungsgefühl und die Präsenz einer Videokamera für eine gewisse politische Korrektheit gesorgt; zugleich bezweifeln wir dies, da die wenigen verwirrten Geister, die als Teilnehmer/innen oder Passant/innen auftauchten, kein Geheimnis aus ihren Ansichten machten. Die Zehn-Minuten-Bürgermeister/innen von Bukarest-Süd sprachen auch über ihren Unmut und dringende Anliegen, vom Mangel an Arbeitsplätzen und nicht funktionierendem Verkehr bzw. unzureichenden öffentlichen Verkehrsmitteln bis zum Bedarf an besseren Krankenhäusern, mehr Grünflächen und Spielplätzen. Den/die ideale/n Bürgermeister/in schilderten sie als jemanden, der offen für den Dialog mit Bürger/innen und Bürgervereinigungen vor Ort ist. Sie identifizierten „gute Orte" (und schlugen vor, sie durch lokale Infostände und Kulturprogramme zu fördern) und machten Verbesserungsvorschläge für die „schlechten Orte" (Bildung, soziale Betreuung und Kultur waren die meistgenannten Instrumente, um diese Veränderungen umzusetzen). Einige Bürgermeister schrieben im Anschluss an ihr „Amt" E-Mails, die zeigten, dass sie über diese Themen auch nach Ablauf ihrer „Amtszeit" noch nachdachten. Andere kamen zur Aufführung von Vlad Petris Film und bekräftigten ihre sechs Monate zuvor geäußerten Ideen. Einer der Bürgermeister/innen stand nach

einem Tag „im Amt" neben uns in der U-Bahn und besah sich das ihm verliehene Diplom – fühlte er sich anerkannt? War es das einzige Diplom, das er seit langer Zeit erhalten hatte? Fragte er sich, ob echte Bürgermeister/innen solche Diplome in ihren Büros haben?

Das Büro „unserer" Bürgermeister/innen war ein von dem Architekten Constantin Goagea und der Künstlerin Daniela Pălimariu entworfener offener Pavillon. Er war transparent und funktional, mit etwas Gold, einer Wanduhr, einer Karte von Bukarest-Süd, bequemem Mobiliar und einem Bereich für den Stadtrat ausgestattet. Daniela Pălimariu und die Soziologin Iuliana Dumitru entwickelten das Programm und die Formulare, die die Bürgermeister/innen ausfüllen und unterzeichnen mussten. Passant/innen verweilten zwischen 30 Sekunden und 30 Minuten, um sich das Projekt von unserem Team erklären zu lassen und uns ihre Probleme zu schildern; einige konnten überzeugt werden, den Sitz der/des Bürgermeisterin/Bürgermeisters oder Stadträtin/Stadtrats zu übernehmen, andere gingen einfach weiter. Obwohl das städtische Umfeld an den verschiedenen Standorten des Pavillons denkbar unattraktiv war, wurde er doch zu einem Anziehungspunkt. Bedenkt man die umfassende und engagierte Teilnahme der Menschen an dem eigentlichen Spiel, so war der Pavillon mehr als ein reines Kuriosum.

Uns war es wichtig, dass dieses sorgfältig konstruierte Gebilde nach Projektende nicht einfach entsorgt werden würde, und das wurde es auch nicht. Der Pavillon wurde der Arhipera Association übergeben, die partizipative Architekturprojekte in ländlichen und extrem ärmlichen Gegenden durchführt. Unser Bürgermeisterbüro wurde im unweit von Bukarest gelegenen Dorf Beciugatele in einen öffentlichen Raum umgewandelt, in dem nun

*andere – kollektive – Entscheidungen
getroffen werden.*

*Ein Pavillon (mit einem Nachleben),
drei Tage intensive Bürgerbeteiligung,
eine Liste realistischer Ideen, die,
so hoffen wir, schließlich auf dem Tisch
der offiziellen Bürgermeisterin landen
wird, eine nicht-wissenschaftliche, aber
dennoch sehr aussagekräftige sozio-
logische Studie, ein Dokumentarfilm
und ein Forschungsprojekt, das in einer
für die Bewohner/innen von Bukarest-
Süd ebenso wie für Tourist/innen
nutzbaren Karte resultierte, sowie fünf
Kurzgeschichten, die nicht nur pittores-
ke Darstellungen dieser Viertel liefern,
sondern darüber hinaus auch noch gute
Literatur sind. Das war Bukarest-Süd:
Baue deine eigene Stadt. Wir setzen
unsere Arbeit in dieser Stadt fort, um die
Trennlinien zu überschreiten, um auf
den Märkten der Viertel einzukaufen,
in denen unser Pavillon stand, und um
die guten Orte unserer Karte und die
der geistigen Stadtpläne unserer
Bürgermeister/innen zu besuchen.*

RALUCA VOINEA, ŞTEFAN GHENCIULESCU

Be a Mayor for Ten Minutes (Mayor's) Pavilion

A temporary pavilion set up in three public places becomes the mayor's office for the imaginary city of Bucharest-South for a few days.

Ein jeweils wenige Tage an drei öffentlichen Orten aufgebauter Pavillon dient als Bürgermeisteramt der imaginären Stadt Bukarest-Süd.

Entering the space, the participants are invited to act, advance proposals, and consult advisers. They assume the power of decision-making. The pavilion is a light, temporary structure that is easy to transport to different locations. It is as transparent and friendly as possible, while also playing with the usual clichés associated with administration (in Romania): the big chair and desk, the map behind the desk, the all-important door to the higher authority, etc.

Besucher/innen, die den Raum betreten, werden aufgefordert, Bürgermeisteraufgaben zu übernehmen und etwa Vorschläge zu machen oder sich mit Expert/innen zu beraten. Sie übernehmen die Entscheidungsgewalt. Der Pavillon lässt sich aufgrund seiner leichten Struktur problemlos an verschiedene Orte transportieren. Mit seiner Transparenz schafft er eine freundliche Umgebung. Gleichzeitig spielt er mit den Stereotypen, die mit Verwaltungseinrichtungen (in Rumänien) verbunden sind: dem großen Stuhl und Tisch, der Landkarte hinter dem Tisch, der Tür, die pompös auf Autorität verweist usw.

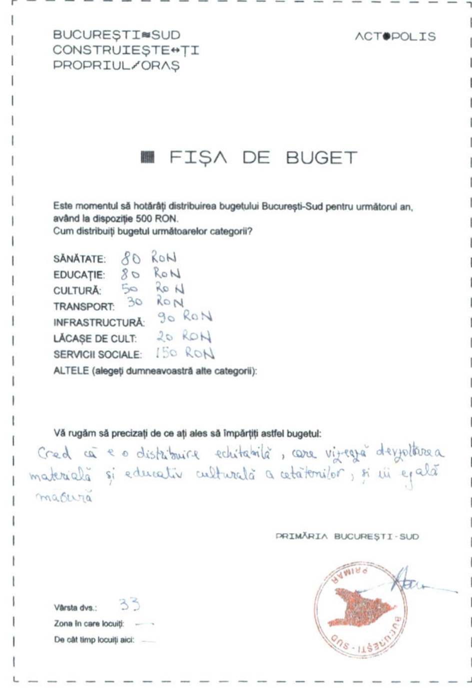

BUCUREȘTI≈SUD
CONSTRUIEȘTE↔ȚI
PROPRIUL/ORAȘ

ACT●POLIS

▥ FIȘĂ DE BUGET

Este momentul să hotărâți distribuirea bugetului București-Sud pentru următorul an, având la dispoziție 500 RON.
Cum distribuiți bugetul următoarelor categorii?

SĂNĂTATE: 80 RON
EDUCAȚIE: 80 RON
CULTURĂ: 50 RON
TRANSPORT: 30 RON
INFRASTRUCTURĂ: 90 RON
LĂCAȘE DE CULT: 20 RON
SERVICII SOCIALE: 150 RON
ALTELE (alegeți dumneavoastră alte categorii):

Vă rugăm să precizați de ce ați ales să împărțiți astfel bugetul:
Cred că e o distribuire echitabilă, care vizează dezvoltarea materială și educativ culturală a cetățenilor, și ii egală maßură

PRIMĂRIA BUCUREȘTI-SUD

Vârsta dvs.: 33
Zona în care locuiți: —
De cât timp locuiți aici: —

Project: Ștefan Ghenciulescu, Raluca Voinea, Cosmina Goagea, Constantin Goagea, Daniela Pălimariu, Mihai Duțescu, Iuliana Dumitru → Format: intervention in public space → Dates: 23, 26, 28 May 2016 Monday, 23 May, 12–7 p.m.: outside the former Flamura Cinema, across the street from Flamura Park and Toporasi tram stop (trams 7 and 25); Thursday, 26 May, 12–7 p.m.: entrance to Sebastian Park, on Sebastian Avenue, across the street from Kaufland–Vulcan stop (bus route 173); Saturday, 28 May, 12–7 p.m.: Piata Sudului, outside the Big Berceni store, near the Piata Sudului metro exit from the square → Venues: outside the former Flamura Cinema, across the street from Flamura Park; entrance to Sebastian Park, on Sebastian Avenue; Piata Sudului, outside the Big Berceni store → Participants: Matei Popescu, Sorina Dumitru (pavilion construction); Dragoș Dragnea (design); Floriana Genes, Bogdan Stănescu, Sorin Popescu (installation operators)

The Other Map
of (South) Bucharest

Cultural and social entrepreneurship,
DIY and maker space, circular
economy

*Kulturelles und soziales Unterneh-
mertum, Do-it-yourself- und
Makerkultur, Kreislaufwirtschaft*

For an outsider, the places we are talking about are rather difficult or even impossible to find. In recent years different kinds of places have arisen in the neighbourhood situated south of the city centre—from spaces for cultural events or the maker movement, production workshops for social design, contemporary art centres, and a radio broadcasting station to a large natural urban delta in need of protection. The current phenomenon represented by all these initiatives and places should eventually turn the "bad" part of the city into an appealing one, a place to be, a cool destination. We are researching and mapping these energy points. *The Other Map of (South) Bucharest* shows the spots that are generating urban change and becoming an artwork in themselves.

136　Project: Cosmina Goagea → Format: print and online publication, research → Dates: 23–28 May 2016 →
Participants: Maria Alexandrescu (artworks); Marius Weber (graphic design)

Für Außenstehende sind die Plätze, um die es hier geht, kaum oder überhaupt nicht zu finden. In den vergangenen Jahren sind im Stadtteil südlich des Stadtzentrums verschiedene neue Orte entstanden – Räume für Kulturveranstaltungen, Makerspaces, Produktionsworkshops für Social Design, Zentren für zeitgenössische Kunst, ein Radiosender sowie ein großes naturbelassenes Areal, das geschützt werden soll. Die Dynamik, die von all diesen Initiativen und Orten ausgeht, soll aus dem „schlechten" Teil der Stadt letztendlich einen attraktiven, angesagten, coolen Stadtteil machen. Wir erforschen diese Orte und erstellen eine Karte ihrer Energiepunkte. *The Other Map of (South) Bucharest weist die Orte aus, von denen städtischer Wandel ausgeht und die selbst zu Kunstwerken werden.*

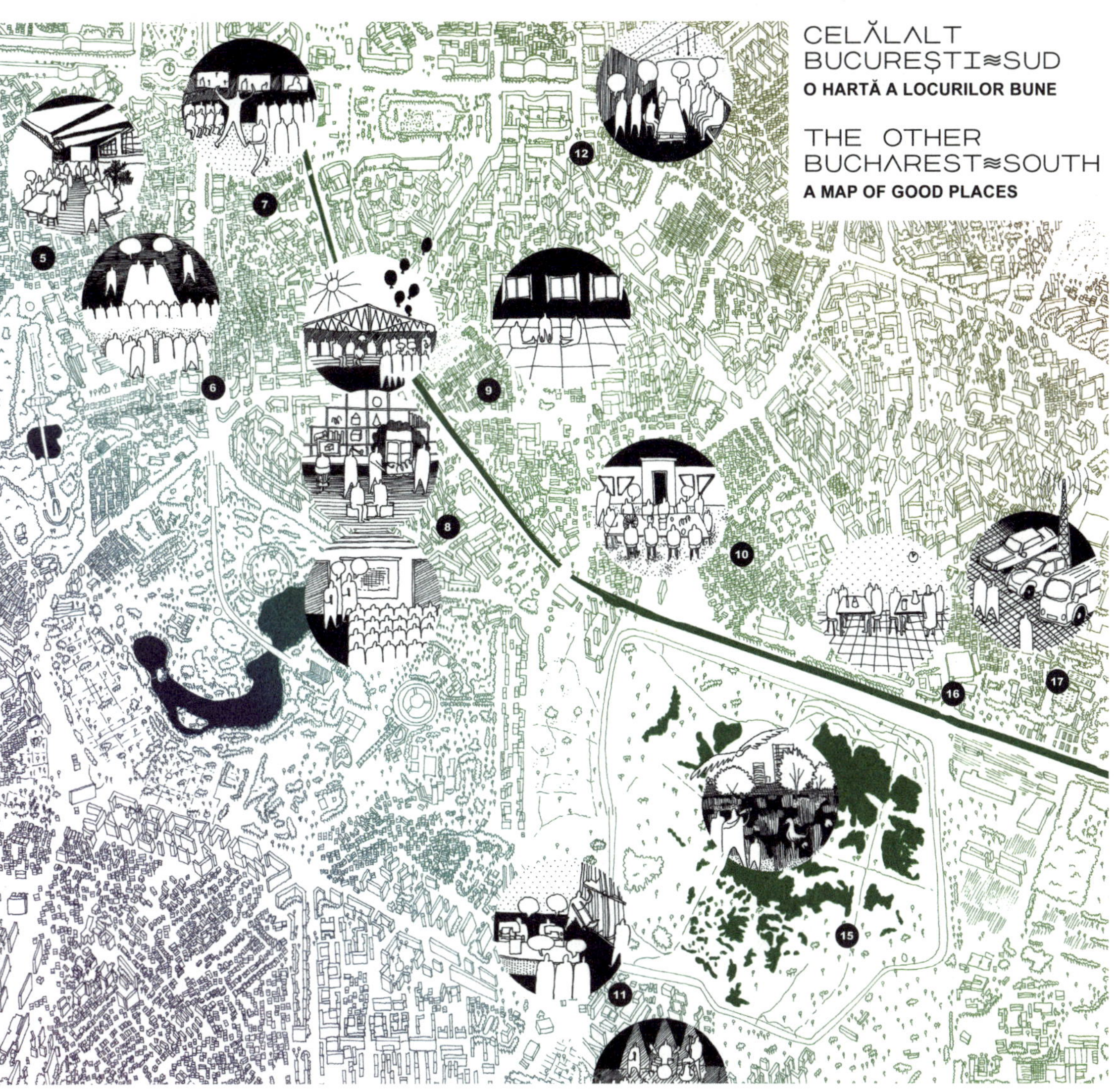

Southern Stories
Five Texts and Photo-reportages

A journey through the less European Bucharest

Eine Reise durch das weniger europäische Bukarest

My personal contribution to the Bucharest-South project consists of a set of narratives about several key points on the map of Bucharest. Each of these stories documents one neighbourhood of southern Bucharest and, more particularly, one specific aspect of that neighbourhood. The stories are about places but always involve people—they are actually about people using, inhabiting, and transforming these spaces. I live in this part of the city. I both like it and hate it, and as an architect and writer I believe I can understand and (sometimes) anticipate its transformations.

Mein persönlicher Beitrag zum Projekt Bukarest-Süd besteht aus Geschichten über zentrale Punkte auf der Karte von Bukarest. In jedem Text geht es um ein Viertel im Süden Bukarests, genauer gesagt um einen konkreten Aspekt dieses Viertels. Doch auch wenn das Hauptaugenmerk auf Orten liegt, geht es immer um Menschen, die diese Orte nutzen, hier wohnen und sie transformieren. Auch ich lebe in diesem Teil der Stadt, mit dem mich eine Hassliebe verbindet. Als Architekt und Schriftsteller kann ich, glaube ich, seine Transformationen verstehen und zuweilen vorwegnehmen.

Format: texts and images → Dates: March–November 2016 → Venue: Bucharest-South →
Participants: Mihai Duțescu (texts—literary reportage); Andrei Mărgulescu (images—photo-reportages)

10 Minutes' Mayors
The Documentary

Inhabitants of the southern (the less privileged and lesser-known) part of Bucharest were invited to imagine that the area has become an independent city and that they were elected its mayors. They received a (mobile) office and some official insignia. The game turned into a serious business when the mayors had to swear an oath, come up with a vision, and, more importantly, take tough decisions.

Die Bewohner/innen des südlichen, weniger privilegierten und unbekannteren Teils von Bukarest wurden aufgefordert, sich vorzustellen, ihr Stadtteil wäre unabhängig und sie wären zum Bürgermeister bzw. zur Bürgermeisterin gewählt worden. Sie erhielten ein (mobiles) Büro und die offiziellen Amtsinsignien. Aus dem Spiel wurde Ernst, als die Teilnehmer/innen einen Schwur leisten, eine Vision entwickeln und vor allem harte Entscheidungen treffen mussten.

Project: Vlad Petri → Collaborators: Raluca Voinea, Ștefan Ghenciulescu → Format: film screening → Date: 22 November 2016 → Venue: JAZZ PONG → Translation: Andra Matzal

Cătălina Ioniță Park

Re-use of the ACTOPOLIS pavilion as park furniture in Belciugatele, as part of the Arhipera Summer School 5.0

Die Arhipera Summer School 5.0 erweckt den ACTOPOLIS-Pavillon im Park von Belciugatele zu neuem Leben

Project: Lorin Niculae → Format: community intervention, installation → Dates: 25–30 July 2016 → Venue: Belciugatele village, Călărași County → Participants: Diana Laura Rizea, Teodora Lică, Alexandra Maxim, Alexandru Brătescu, Alexandru Popa, Sebastian Veldhuisen, with support from Diana Costache, Ionuț Paraschiv, Andrei Ardeleanu, and Ștefania Simu

Labour

The entire world is made up of labour—if we refer to the
global aggregate of human efforts used in the production
of goods and services. Life in our societies is all about work
diffusing into and penetrating every human activity. However, labour should be distinguished from work and defined
as a repeated process that never finishes, aimed at meeting
the need for consumption. Work, on the other hand, can
be determined by categories of means and end, as a process
that leaves behind a durable object. Today we are constantly
pushed to define ourselves by the work we do, to perform
immaculately in meeting needs. Assuming the roles
of "job-holders", we internalise instrumental reasoning in
which it becomes normal to think of everything as a potential means to be used to some further end. Not only do
we substitute "use value" for "worth" in economic discourse
but intrinsic worth—relative to human demand or need—
is being abandoned. By accepting such a condition, we are
agreeing to become engines in the cyclical production
of "labour" and perpetual (self-) exploitation through jobs
that are often insecure and precarious. In the end, are we
worker or "animal laborans"?

*Die ganze Welt besteht aus Arbeit – wenn wir damit die
Gesamtheit der globalen menschlichen Anstrengungen für
die Erzeugung von Waren und Erbringung von Dienstleistungen meinen. In unseren Gesellschaften ist Arbeit Sinn und
Zweck des Lebens; sie reicht in jede menschliche Aktivität
hinein und durchdringt sie. Lohnarbeit sollte jedoch von
schöpferischer Arbeit unterschieden und als wiederholter, nie
endender Prozess definiert werden, der auf die Erfüllung von
Konsumbedürfnissen ausgerichtet ist. Schöpferische Arbeit
ist dagegen kein Mittel zum Zweck, sondern ein Prozess, bei
dem ein dauerhaftes Objekt entsteht. Wir werden heutzutage
ständig gedrängt, uns über unsere Arbeit zu definieren
und einwandfrei zu funktionieren, um den gesellschaftlichen*

Anforderungen zu entsprechen. Indem wir die Rolle von „Arbeitnehmer/innen" annehmen, internalisieren wir ein zweckdienliches Denkmodell, in dem es als normal gilt, alles und jedes als potenzielles Mittel zu begreifen, das einem bestimmten Zweck dient. Im ökonomischen Diskurs setzen wir nicht nur den Begriff „Wert" mit „Gebrauchswert" gleich, sondern geben auch den auf menschliche Bedürfnisse bezogenen inneren Wert auf. Indem wir uns derartigen Bedingungen unterwerfen, akzeptieren wir, zu Maschinen im Produktionskreislauf von „Lohnarbeit" und ständiger (Selbst-)Ausbeutung durch oft unsichere und prekäre Jobs zu werden. Was sind wir dann? Arbeitende oder Arbeitstiere?

Ana Dana Beroš

Migration

In the animal world, migration is a behavioural adaptation, a long-distance movement that helps individuals and groups survive in new-found lands, irrespective of natural boundaries. Dominant discourses on human migration, however, portray migrants as key figures in abolishing concepts of the nation-state and geopolitical borders by demanding freedom of movement as an essential human right. Transnational migration to the industrialised countries of the West, as a form of postcolonial backlash, is still not widely recognised as a regulatory tool of the labour market. There are various kinds of migrant—nomadic, circulatory, refugee, settler— who are all part, willingly or not, of the light infantry of global capitalism. The ambiguous condition of the migrant is reflected in his or her representation either as a symbolic figure of "fearism", responsible for the (un)conscious production of fear in others, or as a human being invariably in need of care. Questioning the contradictory perspectives on migrants should bring a new historical consciousness, as this apparently marginal figure deserves to be viewed as a central political agent of change in our time.

In der Tierwelt ist Migration eine Verhaltensanpassung, eine Bewegung über längere Entfernungen und natürliche Grenzen hinweg, die einzelnen Tieren und Tiergruppen das Überleben in neu entdeckten Gebieten sichert. In den vorherrschenden Diskursen über menschliche Migration werden Auswandernde und Flüchtlinge jedoch als Schlüsselfiguren dargestellt, die das Konzept der Nationalstaaten und geopolitischen Grenzen abschaffen, indem sie Bewegungsfreiheit als ein essenzielles Menschenrecht einfordern. Die in Form einer postkolonialen Gegenbewegung stattfindende transnationale Migration in die westlichen Industrieländer wird noch nicht als Regulierungsinstrument des Arbeitsmarktes anerkannt. Es gibt verschiedene Arten von Migration – nomadische und zirkuläre, Flüchtlinge, Aussiedler/innen –, die alle freiwillig oder unfreiwillig Teil der leichten Infanterie des globalen Kapitalismus sind. Ihre zwiespältige Situation spiegelt sich darin wider, dass sie entweder als Symbolfiguren für das „Angstmachende" dargestellt werden, die für die (un)bewusste Angsterzeugung bei anderen verantwortlich sind, oder aber als Menschen, die grundsätzlich auf Fürsorge und Unterstützung angewiesen sind. Das Hinterfragen der widersprüchlichen Sichtweisen auf Migrant/innen sollte zu einem neuen historischen Bewusstsein führen, da diese offensichtlichen Randfiguren es verdienen, als zentrale Triebkraft für politische Veränderungen in unserer Zeit betrachtet zu werden.

Ana Dana Beroš

Nationalism

Nationalism can be expressed as a belief or political ideology that involves individuals identifying with their nation, often characterising themselves by excluding or opposing others.

Some people maintain that the idea of the nation originally came about as a response to colonialism. Today it is at the foundation of the state constitutions of most countries in the world, particularly democratic ones. Nations essentially constitute "imagined communities".

Nationalismus kann als Glaube oder politische Ideologie zum Ausdruck kommen, wobei sich Einzelpersonen mit ihrer Nation identifizieren und durch die Abgrenzung von anderen definieren.

Einige behaupten, dass der Gedanke der Nation ursprünglich eine Reaktion auf den Kolonialismus war. Heute dient der Begriff als Grundlage für die Verfassungen der meisten Staaten der Welt, insbesondere der demokratischen. Im Grunde sind Nationen „imaginierte Gemeinschaften".

Boba Mirjana Stojadinović

OBERHAUSEN

A Day in the New City

We usually open the *City Centre* (which is what we called our festival centre) at around 12 p.m.—the *City Centre* is in a vacant former restaurant in Oberhausen's main station, the nucleus around which the old city was built. Midday is still quite early in the new city and everything is quiet. But if you walk past the abandoned platform, you might hear Denise Ritter's sound installation *Gutehoffnungsgeister* starting to play. Some of the artists, some visitors, and some random passers-by come into the city centre to chat, to explore, or to eat something—there is always plenty of food and drink in the new city. Some of it is free, and for some of it people can pay what they want. Nobody seems to be in a hurry. At around 2 p.m. Mark and Felix from We Are Visual collect their tools for *Everything as of Tomorrow.* Somebody picks up the keys for Dirk Schlichting's *Parzelle 1*, intending to spend the afternoon in the garden in the high street of the old city. Close by, Susanne Kudielka and Kaspar Wimberley's *Archaeological City Museum* opens its doors to visitors. Lots of things happen that we don't know about. The weather is usually nice, it's even hot sometimes. Perhaps that's why nobody is in a hurry. Visitors from the other ACTOPOLIS cities come by. We drink and eat together. We go on guided tours through the new city. We go rollerskating. We go for a picnic. We go looking for Lars Moritz's monster, a huge —but most likely peaceful—mysterious creature. We destroy the old city together with school children. We enjoy the view together. We meet friends and strangers. We listen to music. We sing old songs and learn new dances. We look for the new in the old. And for the old in the new. We listen to stories from elsewhere. We write love letters.

Everything seems peaceful. Perhaps it is all too calm? The new city stays up late, goes to bed late. Much later than the old city. It is a city of leisure, of talking to each other, of walking, of the night.

Infrastructures for a New City

For ACTOPOLIS, we invited artists and artist groups to come up with an infrastructure for a new city. An infrastructure that a new city should have. Infrastructures not only enable actions to take place but also regulate the potential for action. Infrastructures privilege certain uses and complicate others. Infrastructures regulate access to and participation in many areas of society. By creating new infrastructures, converting existing ones, or revitalising those that are derelict, would we also be able to envision and facilitate new urban practices?

Constructing the New City

1) Infrastructures for the new city were proposed and built by the five artists, groups, or collectives we had invited.
2) The city centre was our contribution to the infrastructure of the new city: a place to hang out, to party, to discuss things, to get information, and to gather for city tours, etc.
3) Presentations and interventions came from artists from all the other ACTOPOLIS cities as part of the micro-residency programme.
4) People from Oberhausen were asked to become ambassadors for the new city, to contribute something to the new city, and, where needed, we set aside a small budget to make sure these ideas could be manifested—a picnic, an observation desk, a new dance, or an "amorous writer in residence", a

contribution from local performance artist Marie-Luise O'Byrne-Brandl, who offered to help write love letters for passers-by in front of the train station.

A New City 1

"In the musical *Sweat Shop*, which we put on in Oberhausen in 2015, we told the tragic love story of a city left behind by its lover, industry. When we told that love story, we realised that one of the problems cities have is that they themselves cannot leave. They can't go away. They are stuck with what's already there and that often means with what's no longer working. What's to be done with all those infrastructures of a once booming steel and coal industry? What's to be done about a city centre where half the shops are empty? And how should we deal with an image or self-image defined by what's lost? With the infrastructural impositions of the past? So we started asking ourselves what a city would look like that was built according to the desires and demands of its citizens today. What if we could build a new city? That became the motto of our proposal: We are building a new city, *Wir bauen eine neue Stadt*. There is a German post-punk song with that title (by Palais Schaumburg) which probably gave us the idea—but for us the promise behind it was to escape to some extent, at least from the demands imposed on our practice of again and again having to deal or engage with something that is already fucked up."

Utopia

One reason why the concept of building a "new city" appealed to us was that we thought it would allow us to ask fundamental questions such as "How do we want to live together?"—and in doing so, at least potentially, extend the focus and scope beyond what we have increasingly come to see as the limitations of site-specific arts practices (including our own): being called in to a place, as "community nurses" or amateur city planners, to fix something that is assumed to be broken, and running the danger of again and again reiterating or putting a focus on these assumptions about a place.

A New City 2

"A new city: Oberhausen was only built when coal and steel industries settled in the area in the eighteenth century. In the 1990s, Oberhausen was re-imagined as a shopping and leisure paradise, when a shopping mall was conceived as its 'new' city centre, a decision that is blamed by many for the emptiness and decay of Oberhausen's old city centre. With the demise of the industry that shaped the city for many years, Oberhausen seems to have lost its purpose. What does it mean for a city when the very thing it is founded on has disappeared?"

Old and New

Of course, nobody wanted to ignore the old city. Not the artists we had invited —some of whom developed concepts that were in-depth explorations of the old city, while others presented ideas that would have worked in any city, but that nevertheless engaged, in their execution, with the context of the old city in different ways. And not us: when asked about our ambitions for the project (did we want to activate people?), we answered that, no, our ambition was to produce visibility for activities that were already happening, to provide a framework in which actors who were already engaging with the city in various ways could realise ideas.

A New City 3

"Ladies and gentlemen, 'there is no alternative'—T.I.N.A. With this slogan, Margaret Thatcher formulated a principle that is still constitutive for an understanding of politics in which the only option for action is to simply keep going. 'It is easier to imagine the end of the world than the end of capitalism.' We've heard that a lot recently. Capitalism is crisis. And crisis is a justification for the politics of austerity and exclusion. Everywhere in Europe. Ladies and gentlemen, here in Europe, in Germany, in Oberhausen, it has become easy to forget that the future is radically open, that tomorrow doesn't have to be like today and that everything can always end differently. Because reality first and foremost is one thing: it is improbable. … Today, we propose a different slogan: no longer T.I.N.A., there is no alternative, but T.I.N.O., this is not Oberhausen. The end of history was yesterday. We are building a new city. On the territory of the old city, for ten days, because we don't believe cities have to be forever, because we don't want to swap one eternity for another. But nevertheless, it is time to say goodbye to the old city. Please follow me …"

A New City 4

"It is difficult to imagine a new city without taking a big pen to the map of the old city. We have decided to take a finer pen, and we did not draw any new streets into the city map, but a Möbius strip—a figure that doesn't allow you to distinguish between up and down, inside and outside. Take this paper strip—now draw 'old' on one side and 'new' on the other. If you join the ends like that, you get a circle. But by twisting this part a bit before joining the ends, a Möbius strip is created. If we follow this side long enough, the side that has old written on it, we arrive at the new, and at the old again. If we walk through the streets of the old city for long enough, we arrive in the new city, and vice versa."

GEHEIMAGENTUR

Ein Tag in der neuen Stadt

Normalerweise öffnet das Stadtzentrum (so nennen wir unser Festivalzentrum) gegen 12 Uhr. Es befindet sich in einem leer stehenden ehemaligen Restaurant im Oberhausener Hauptbahnhof mitten in der Altstadt. Es ist später Vormittag in der neuen Stadt und alles ist ruhig. Aber wenn man an den verlassenen Gleisen vorbeigeht, kann man eventuell hören, wie Denise Ritters Klanginstallation Gutehoffnungsgeister zu spielen beginnt. Einige Künstler/innen und Besucher/innen und ein paar Leute, die sich eher zufällig hierher „verirrt" haben, kommen ins Stadtzentrum, um zu plaudern, sich umzusehen oder etwas zu essen – in der neuen Stadt gibt es immer reichlich zu essen und zu trinken. Manches ist kostenlos, bei anderem kann man selbst entscheiden, wie viel man dafür zahlen möchte. Niemand scheint es eilig zu haben. Gegen 14 Uhr suchen Mark und Felix von We Are Visual ihre Utensilien für Alles ab morgen zusammen. Jemand, der den Nachmittag im Musterkleingarten mitten in der Fußgängerzone verbringen möchte, holt die Schlüssel für Dirk Schlichtings Parzelle 1 ab. In der Nähe öffnet das Archäologische Stadtmuseum von Susanne Kudielka und Kaspar Wimberley seine Türen für die Besucher/innen. Viele Dinge passieren, von denen wir gar nichts wissen. Das Wetter ist meist schön, manchmal

*ist es sogar richtig heiß. Vielleicht hat
es deswegen niemand eilig. Besucher/
innen aus anderen ACTOPOLIS-Städten
kommen vorbei. Wir trinken und essen
zusammen. Wir machen Führungen durch
die neue Stadt. Wir laufen Rollschuh.
Wir machen ein Picknick. Wir begeben
uns auf die Suche nach Lars Moritz'
Monster, einer riesigen, höchstwahrscheinlich jedoch friedfertigen Kreatur.
Wir zerstören zusammen mit Schul-
kindern die alte Stadt. Wir genießen
gemeinsam die Aussicht. Wir begegnen
Freunden und Fremden. Wir hören
Musik. Wir singen alte Lieder und lernen
neue Tänze. Wir suchen das Neue im
Alten. Und das Alte im Neuen. Wir hören
uns Geschichten aus anderen Städten
an. Wir schreiben Liebesbriefe. Alles
scheint friedlich. Ist es vielleicht sogar
zu ruhig? Die neue Stadt bleibt lange
auf und geht spät schlafen, viel später
als die alte Stadt. Sie ist eine Stadt
der Muße, des Miteinanderredens, des
Spazierens, der Nacht.*

Infrastrukturen für
eine neue Stadt

*Für ACTOPOLIS baten wir Künstler/
innen und Künstlergruppen, eine
Infrastruktur für eine neue Stadt vorzuschlagen. Eine Infrastruktur, wie eine
neue Stadt sie haben sollte. Infrastrukturen ermöglichen nicht nur Handlungen,
sondern steuern auch die Handlungsmöglichkeiten. Infrastrukturen erleichtern
bestimmte Handlungen und erschweren
andere. Infrastrukturen regeln Zugang
und Teilhabe in vielen Bereichen der
Gesellschaft. Wären wir durch die Schaffung neuer, die Umnutzung bestehender
oder die Revitalisierung aufgegebener
Infrastrukturen auch in der Lage, neue
urbane Praktiken zu entwickeln und zu
begünstigen?*

Die Konstruktion der
neuen Stadt

*1) Infrastrukturen für die neue Stadt
wurden von den fünf von uns eingela-
denen Künstler/innen, Gruppen
und Kollektiven vorgeschlagen und
errichtet.*

*2) Das Stadtzentrum war unser Beitrag
zur Infrastruktur der neuen Stadt:
ein Ort zum Abhängen und Diskutieren,
für Partys und Informationen, ein
Treffpunkt für Stadtführungen usw.*

*3) Am Mikro-Residenzprogramm nah-
men Künstler/innen aus allen ACTO-
POLIS-Städten teil und brachten
Präsentationen und Interventionen ein.*

*4) Oberhausener Bürger/innen wurden
gebeten, Botschafter/innen für die
neue Stadt zu werden und etwas zur
neuen Stadt beizutragen. Wo nötig,
stellten wir ein kleines Budget für
die Umsetzung dieser Ideen zur Verfügung: ein Picknick, eine Aussichts-
plattform, einen neuen Tanz oder die
„amouröse Stadtschreiberin", einen
Beitrag der Oberhausener Performancekünstlerin Marie-Luise O'Byrne-Brandl,
die Passant/innen vor dem Bahnhof
Hilfe beim Schreiben von Liebesbriefen
anbot.*

Eine neue Stadt 1

*„Im Musical Sweat Shop, das wir 2015
in Oberhausen inszenierten, erzählten
wir die tragische Liebesgeschichte einer
Stadt, die von ihrer großen Liebe, der
Industrie, verlassen wurde. Bei der Entwicklung dieser Geschichte wurde uns
ein wesentliches Problem von Städten
klar: Sie können ihren Ort nicht verlassen. Sie können nicht weggehen. Sie
stecken in dem fest, was schon da ist,
und oft funktioniert das nicht mehr. Was
soll man also tun mit all der Infrastruktur einer einst boomenden Stahl- und
Kohleindustrie? Was macht man mit*

einem Stadtzentrum, in dem die Hälfte
der Geschäfte leer steht? Und wie geht
man mit einem Image oder Selbstbild
um, das von Verlust geprägt ist? Mit den
infrastrukturellen Altlasten der Vergangenheit? Wir fragten uns also, wie eine
Stadt aussähe, die nach den Wünschen
und Bedürfnissen ihrer Bürger/innen
heute erbaut würde. Was, wenn wir eine
neue Stadt bauen könnten? Daraus
entstand das Motto unseres Vorschlags:
Wir bauen eine neue Stadt. Wahrschein-
lich inspirierte uns ein deutscher Post-
Punk-Song gleichen Titels (von Palais
Schaumburg) dazu – dahinter stand
für uns jedoch das Versprechen, den
Zwängen unserer künstlerischen Praxis
bis zu einem gewissen Grad entrinnen
zu können und uns nicht immer wieder
mit Dingen befassen zu müssen, die
längst den Bach runtergegangen sind."

Utopia

Einer der Vorzüge des Konzepts einer
„neuen Stadt" lag darin, dass es uns
unserer Meinung nach fundamentale
Fragestellungen erlaubte, wie zum
Beispiel: „Wie wollen wir zusammenleben?". Es würde also zumindest
potenziell den Fokus und den Rahmen
über das hinaus erweitern, was wir
zunehmend als Begrenzung ortsspezifischer künstlerischer Praktiken
(auch unserer eigenen) empfinden:
als „Gemeindeschwestern" oder Ama-
teurstadtplaner/innen an einen Ort
gerufen zu werden, um etwas in Ordnung zu bringen, was man für kaputt
hält, und dabei Gefahr zu laufen, sich
ständig zu wiederholen oder diese
Annahmen über einen Ort in den Vordergrund zu stellen.

Eine neue Stadt 2

„Oberhausen entstand erst im 18. Jahrhundert, als sich die Kohle- und Stahl-
industrie im Ruhrgebiet ansiedelte. Im
letzten Jahrzehnt des 20. Jahrhunderts
sollte Oberhausen zum Shopping-
und Freizeitparadies werden, als ein Einkaufszentrum zur ‚neuen' Stadtmitte
gemacht wurde – eine Entscheidung,
die viele als Grund für die Leere und
den Verfall der Oberhausener Altstadt
ansehen. Mit dem Verlust der Industrien,
die die Stadt über viele Jahre prägten,
scheint Oberhausen seine Bestimmung
verloren zu haben. Was bedeutet es
für eine Stadt, wenn man ihr den Grund-
pfeiler nimmt?"

Alt und neu

Selbstverständlich wollte niemand die
alte Stadt ignorieren. Weder die eingela-
denen Künstler/innen – deren Konzepte
sich zum Teil intensiv mit der alten Stadt
befassten, während andere Ideen zwar
in jeder Stadt funktioniert hätten, sich
in ihrer Ausführung aber trotzdem auf
unterschiedliche Weise mit der alten
Stadt auseinandersetzten – noch wir
selbst: Die Frage, ob wir die Menschen
aktivieren wollten, verneinten wir und
entgegneten, unser Ziel liege darin,
bereits stattfindende Aktivitäten sichtbar zu machen, einen Rahmen zu
bieten, in dem Akteur/innen, die sich
bereits auf verschiedene Weise mit der
Stadt befassten, ihre Ideen verwirkli-
chen könnten.

Eine neue Stadt 3

„Meine Damen und Herren, es gibt keine
Alternative – ‚There Is No Alternative',
abgekürzt T.I.N.A. Mit diesem Slogan
formulierte Margaret Thatcher ein Prinzip,
das auch heute noch für ein Politikver-
ständnis steht, welches ein Weiter-so

als einzige Handlungsmöglichkeit sieht. ‚Es ist einfacher, sich das Ende der Welt vorzustellen als das Ende des Kapitalismus.‘ Diese Behauptung hört man in letzter Zeit oft. Kapitalismus bedeutet Krise. Und diese Krise dient als Rechtfertigung für Austeritäts- und Ausgrenzungspolitik. Überall in Europa. Meine Damen und Herren, hier in Europa, in Deutschland, in Oberhausen vergisst man leicht, dass die Zukunft radikal offen ist, dass morgen nicht wie heute sein muss und dass alles stets ganz anders enden kann. Denn die Realität ist vor allem eines: unwahrscheinlich. … Heute schlagen wir einen neuen Slogan vor: nicht mehr T.I.N.A., There Is No Alternative, sondern T.I.N.O., This Is No Oberhausen (Dies ist kein Oberhausen). Das Ende der Geschichte war gestern. Wir bauen eine neue Stadt. Auf dem Boden der alten, zehn Tage lang, weil wir nicht glauben, dass Städte ewig fortbestehen müssen, weil wir nicht eine Ewigkeit gegen eine andere tauschen wollen. Trotzdem wird es Zeit, der alten Stadt Lebewohl zu sagen. Bitte folgen Sie mir …“

Eine neue Stadt 4

„Es ist schwierig, sich eine neue Stadt vorzustellen, ohne sich mit einem dicken Stift an den Plan der alten Stadt zu machen. Wir haben beschlossen, einen feineren Stift zu verwenden. Wir haben in den Stadtplan keine neuen Straßen, sondern ein Möbiusband eingezeichnet – eine Figur, bei der sich oben und unten, innen und außen nicht unterscheiden lassen. Man nehme einen Papierstreifen und schreibe ‚alt‘ auf die Vorder- und ‚neu‘ auf die Rückseite. Klebt man die Enden aneinander, erhält man einen Ring. Aber wenn man das eine Ende vor dem Verbinden umdreht, erhält man ein Möbiusband. Folgt man ihm lange genug auf der Seite, auf der

‚alt‘ steht, gelangt man zu ‚neu‘ und dann wieder zu ‚alt‘. Spaziert man nur lange genug durch die Straßen der alten Stadt, gelangt man in die neue Stadt und umgekehrt.“

GEHEIMAGENTUR

Archaeological City Museum

An archaeological museum for the new city

Ein archäologisches Museum für die neue Stadt

As a visitor to Oberhausen, one inevitably ends up coming face to face with the city's industrial past. Europe's first chewing-gum museum bids farewell to the past and tells the story of today. Instead of digging deeper, it investigates the uppermost "stratum". However, the museum is not just an area for viewing chewing-gum exhibits. It also prompts ideas and discussions about the role of museums and about identity politics in the local context.

Als Besucher/in Oberhausens landet man unweigerlich in der industriellen Vergangenheit der Stadt. Das erste Kaugummimuseum Europas verabschiedet sich vom Alten und erzählt die Geschichte von heute. Anstatt in der Tiefe zu graben, untersucht es die oberste „Erdschicht". Das Museum dient nicht nur als Ausstellungsfläche für Kaugummiexponate, sondern gibt Anstoß zu Gedanken und Gesprächen über die Rolle des Museums und über Identitätspolitik im lokalen Kontext.

Project: Susanne Kudielka and Kaspar Wimberley → Format: installation →
Dates: 1–11 September 2016 → Venue: Marktstraße 107, Oberhausen

BALLISTOL
-52°C
HUFA

UNB.
T1
SS1
CCC1
UNB.

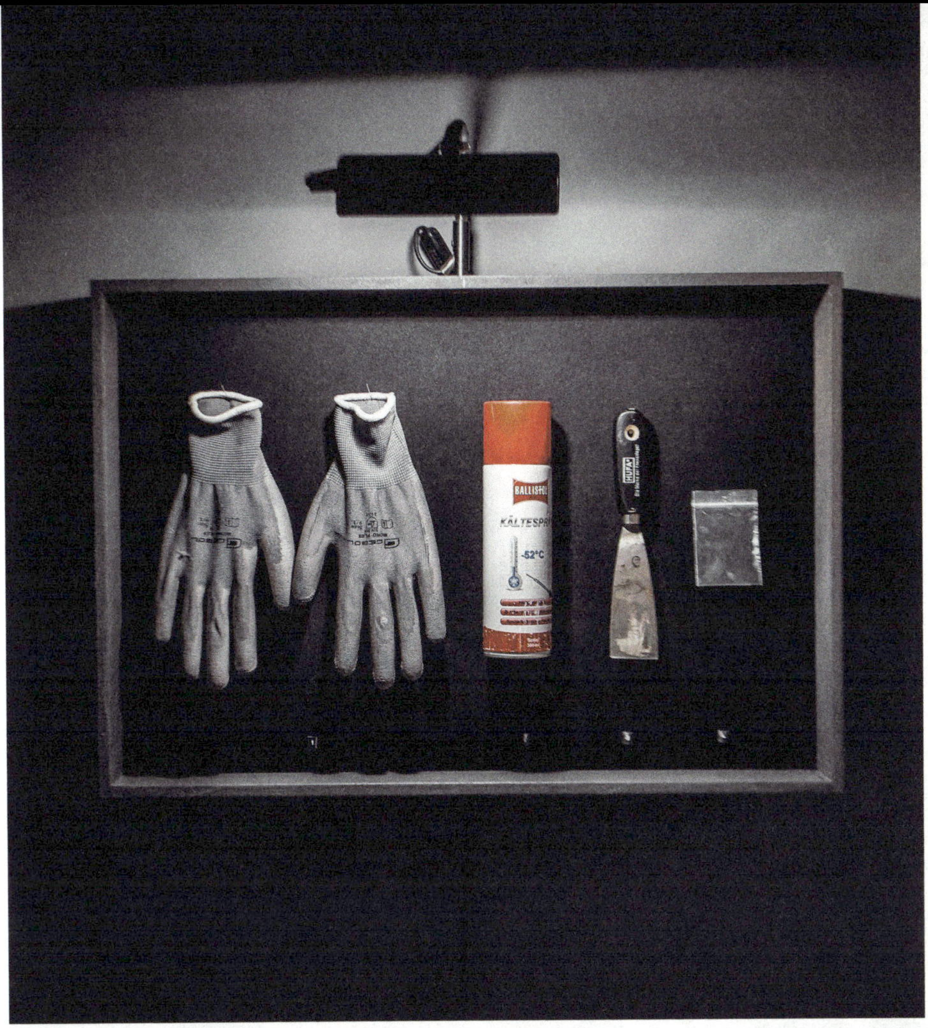

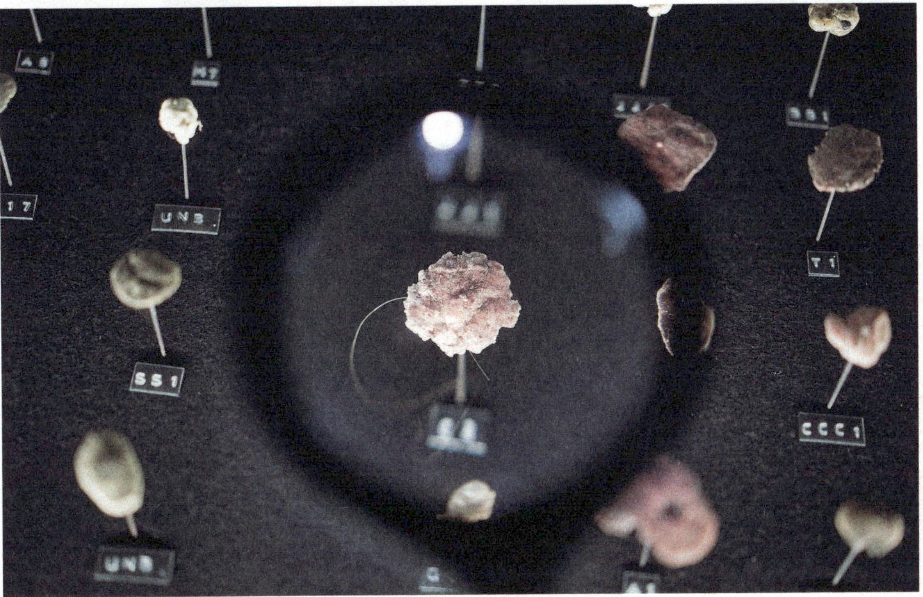

City Centre

The centre of the new city

Das Zentrum der neuen Stadt

geheimagentur is establishing a *City Centre* in Oberhausen's main train station, intended as a focal point and place of social interaction for all the new city's residents and visitors. All the information relevant to the new city can be found here, in addition to a programme of workshops, parties, performances, and presentations. You can play table tennis, try the drink of the day, or rent a bicycle to explore the new city.

Im Oberhausener Hauptbahnhof richtet die geheimagentur ein Stadtzentrum ein. Das Zentrum ist Anlaufstelle und Ort des Austauschs für alle Bewohner/innen und Besucher/innen der neuen Stadt. Hier gibt es alle relevanten Informationen zur neuen Stadt. Hier findet ein Programm aus Workshops, Partys, Performances und Präsentationen statt. Und hier kann man Tischtennis spielen, den Drink des Tages verkosten und Fahrräder zur Erkundung der neuen Stadt leihen.

 Project: geheimagentur → Format: installation → Dates: 1–11 September 2016 → Venue: Willy-Brandt-Platz 1, Oberhausen

Everything as of Tomorrow

Solutions for tomorrow's problems

Lösungen für die Probleme von morgen

We Are Visual research and imagine the problems of tomorrow and claim to know what to do before the problems manifest themselves. They are hosting a workshop in a futuristically designed trailer that also serves as a showroom and laboratory. Here, they design and produce the tools and everyday objects that can be used to provide expert solutions for tomorrow's problems.

We Are Visual recherchieren und imaginieren Probleme von morgen und behaupten zu wissen, was zu tun ist, schon bevor die Probleme sich manifestieren. In einem futuristisch gestalteten Anhänger eröffnen We Are Visual eine Werkstatt, die gleichzeitig als Showroom und Labor fungiert: Hier entwerfen und produzieren sie Werkzeuge oder Alltagsgegenstände, mit denen die Probleme von morgen fachkundig gelöst werden können.

Project: We Are Visual (Felix Jung and Marc Einsiedel) → Format: installation, intervention → Dates: 1–11 September 2016 → Venues: Will-Quadflieg-Platz; Altmarkt; station forecourt, Oberhausen

Gutehoffnungsgeister

**Multichannel sound installation
with audio recordings of the old city**

*Mehrkanalige Klanginstallation
mit Audioaufnahmen der alten Stadt*

Denise Ritter is realising a multi-channel, electro-acoustic sound installation on the abandoned platforms 4 and 5 of Oberhausen's main railway station. The installation is based on field recordings from the city's leisure and entertainment culture, thereby rendering audible the "ghosts" that have supplanted Oberhausen's cultural and historical identity.

Denise Ritter wird auf den verlassenen Gleisen 4 und 5 des Hauptbahnhofs Oberhausen eine mehrkanalige elektroakustische Klanginstallation realisieren, die auf Audioaufnahmen der Freizeit- und Vergnügungskultur in Oberhausen basiert – als Hör-barmachung der „Geister", die in Oberhausen an die Stelle von kultureller und historischer Identität getreten sind.

Project: Denise Ritter → Format: sound installation → Dates: 1–11 September 2016 →
Venue: Willy-Brandt-Platz 1, Museum Platforms 4 and 5, Oberhausen

OBERHAUSEN HBF
Oberhausen HBf
WC

Parzelle 1

A row of garden plots in the pedestrian zone

Schrebergartenzeile in der Fußgängerzone

A row of garden plots is planted in the middle of the city's former pedestrian zone. The initial phase features the creation of a "sample garden", whereby a prominent area of the urban space is repurposed, creating a juxtaposition of show and privacy, of old and new urban space. The sample garden can be rented by residents for a while and used to host a spontaneous barbecue or simply spend a summer afternoon relaxing in the garden.

In der Mitte der ehemaligen Fußgängerzone wird eine Schrebergartenzeile geplant. Als Auftakt entsteht ein „Musterkleingarten". Eine exponierte Stelle des Stadtraums wird umgenutzt. Es entsteht ein Gegenüber von Repräsentation und Privatheit, von altem und neuem Stadtraum. Der Musterkleingarten kann von den Anwohner/innen zeitweise gemietet und genutzt werden – für Grillfeste oder einfach für einen entspannten Sommernachmittag im Garten.

Project: Dirk Schlichting → Format: installation → Dates: 1–11 September 2016 → Venue: Marktstraße, at number 16, Oberhausen

The Monster

A monster for the new city

Ein Monster für die neue Stadt

There is a monster living in the new city. It resembles a giant lizard but nobody knows which species it belongs to. Sometimes at night it crawls up the Knappenhalde (slag heap) and you may even come across it in the pedestrian zone. People say the monster lives in the city's former mining shafts and tunnels. It embodies the uncanny, the sinister, ready to burst out at any moment. And that is exactly why it has become one of the new city's major tourist attractions. Book a monster safari or buy a popular monster souvenir in the new city centre.

In der neuen Stadt lebt ein Monster. Es erinnert an eine riesige Echse, doch niemand weiß, welcher Spezies es angehört. Manchmal kriecht es nachts die Knappenhalde hinauf und sogar in der Fußgängerzone kann man ihm begegnen. Das Monster, sagt man, lebe in den stillgelegten Schächten und Stollen der Stadt. In ihm verkörpert sich das Unheimliche, das jederzeit hervorbrechen kann. Und natürlich ist es gerade deshalb eine der großen Sehenswürdigkeiten der neuen Stadt. Im Stadtzentrum können Monstersafaris gebucht werden und auch das Geschäft mit Monstersouvenirs blüht.

164 Project: Lars Moritz → Format: intervention, performance → Dates: 1–11 September 2016 → Venue: Knappenhalde, Oberhausen

Why We Travel

Saša Šimpraga exhibits his work
Why We Travel at the main station:
a small metal plaque listing reasons
why people should travel, extracted
from an old guidebook.

Saša Šimpraga zeigt in Why We
Travel *(Warum wir reisen) eine kleine
metallene Plakette am Hauptbahnhof, die Gründe aus einem alten
Reiseführer zitiert, warum Menschen
auf Reisen gehen sollten.*

Project: Saša Šimpraga → Format: installation → Dates: 1–11
September 2016 → Venue: Willy-Brandt-Platz 1, Oberhausen

ACTOPOLIS Radio

A live radio show about ACTOPOLIS,
composed of interviews and field
recordings conducted in participating cities

*Aus Interviews und Field Recordings
aus beteiligten Städten entsteht live
eine Radiosendung über
ACTOPOLIS.*

Project: Haris Sahačić → Format: live radio show → Dates:
1–11 September 2016 → Venue: city centre, Oberhausen

Polio: The Official
ACTOPOLIS Dance

Together with interested inhabitants,
Jörg Luchtenberg creates his own
dance for the new city.

*Jörg Luchtenberg entwickelt zusam-
men mit interessierten Bewohner/
innen einen eigenen Tanz für die
neue Stadt.*

Project: Jörg Luchtenberg → Format: interactive
performance → Date: 3 September 2016 → Venue: city centre,
Oberhausen

The Rehearsal

Irena Ristic's *Sociodrama Workshop*
is an interactive presentation of her
research on the self-organisation
of the cultural scene in Oberhausen
and Belgrade.

Irena Ristics Sociodrama Workshop
*ist eine interaktive Präsentation ihrer
Forschung zur Selbstorganisation
der kulturellen Szene in Oberhausen
und Belgrad.*

Project: Irena Ristić → Format: workshop →
Date: 9 September 2016 → Venue: city centre, Oberhausen

Build Your Own City

In *Build Your Own City* Ștefan
Ghenciulescu reports on "citizen
mayors", gold fever, guerilla
restoration, post-apocalyptic wild-
life, and other urban adventures
in Romania.

*Ștefan Ghenciulescu berichtet
in* Build Your Own City *über Bürger-
Bürgermeister/innen, Goldrausch,
Guerilla-Restaurierung, postapoka-
lyptische Tierwelt und andere städtische Abenteuer in Rumänien.*

Project: Ștefan Ghenciulescu → Format: lecture →
Date: 9 September 2016 → Venue: city centre, Oberhausen

Work Like a Donkey, Live Like a Man!

Work Like a Donkey, Live Like a Man! is Önder Özengi's tale of the division of labour between humans and donkeys collecting rubbish on the streets of Mardin (Turkey).

Önder Özengi erzählt in Work Like a Donkey, Live Like a Man! *von der Arbeitsteilung zwischen Menschen und Eseln, die in den Straßen von Mardin (Türkei) den Müll aufsammeln.*

Project: Önder Özengi → Format: lecture →
Date: 9 September 2016 → Venue: city centre, Oberhausen

Amorous Writer in Residence

The new city not only has a post office, it also has an "amorous" writer in residence. During her performance Marie-Luise O'Byrne-Brandl helps people formulate their love letters and give them an imaginative flourish.

Die neue Stadt hat nicht einfach eine Postfiliale – sie hat eine amouröse Stadtschreiberin. In ihrer Performance hilft Marie-Luise O'Byrne-Brandl Menschen beim Formulieren und fantasievollen Ausschmücken ihrer Liebesbriefe.

Project: Marie-Luise O'Byrne-Brandl → Format: interactive performance → Date: 6 September 2016 → Venue: station forecourt, Oberhausen

Title Observation Deck

A private roof terrace is made open to the public. Visitors can savour a splendid view of the new city, while enjoying a cool drink.

Eine private Dachterrasse wird der Öffentlichkeit zugänglich gemacht. Hier kann man den Ausblick auf die neue Stadt genießen. Dazu werden kühle Drinks serviert.

Format: interactive performance → Dates: 1–11 September 2016 → Venue: 4th floor, Lothringer Straße 60, Oberhausen

With a Little Help

Panos Sklavenitis presents his poster series *With a Little Help* in the urban space. The series features the artist's friends, portrayed as exemplary citizens of a new city.

Panos Sklavenitis stellt im Stadtraum seine Posterserie With a Little Help *vor, auf der der Künstler seine Freunde als exemplarische Bürger/innen einer neuen Stadt präsentiert.*

Project: Panos Sklavenitis → Format: poster installation → Dates: 1–11 September 2016, presentation on 3 September 2016 → Venue: inner City Oberhausen

Segregation

From not being allowed to sit on the front seats of the bus
to having to raise their kids in unheated schools, people
are subjected to segregation in every urban structure, with
megalopolises acting as havens for all forms of ghettos,
while smaller versions of segregated societies are to be
found even in villages. Urban segregation can be manifested
in (sometimes paradoxical) phenomena such as people
retreating behind high fences in an obsession with security
and well-paid privacy, entire communities living without
access to basic amenities like running water, favelas having the best view from the hills of the city (Rio de Janeiro),
almost half a city enduring an underprivileged lifestyle
(Bucharest-South), people fighting for the right to the sun
(Norway). Generous public spaces, the equitable distribution of resources, and inclusive architecture are aspects
of policy-making that can prevent segregation and its
alienating effects.

*Vom Verbot, im Bus in den vorderen Reihen zu sitzen, bis
hin zur Beschulung ihrer Kinder in ungeheizten Räumen
sind Menschen in allen städtischen Gebilden der Segregation ausgesetzt. In Megalopolen sind alle Formen der
Ghettoisierung zu beobachten und selbst in Dörfern sind
kleinere getrennte Gesellschaften zu finden. Städtische
Segregation äußert sich in (manchmal paradoxen) Phäno-
menen: Menschen leben zurückgezogen hinter hohen
Zäunen und geben in ihrem Sicherheitswahn viel Geld für
den Schutz ihrer Privatsphäre aus, während ganze Stadtviertel nicht einmal Zugang zur Grundversorgung mit flie-
ßendem Wasser haben. In den Favelas von Rio de Janeiro
hat man nichts als einen wunderbaren Blick von den
Hügeln auf die Stadt, in Bukarest ist der gesamte Süden
und damit fast die halbe Stadt unterprivilegiert und in
Norwegen gibt es Menschen, die um ihr Recht auf Sonne
kämpfen. Zu den Aspekten einer Politikgestaltung, die*

Raluca Voinea

Self-organisation

Self-organisation is the daily production of a non-profit
climate of self-empowerment. Non-institutional individuals
who work in a self-empowered way are self-organised. They
do not receive any benefit from the system, but they still
work hard (to articulate the urge) to express themselves
through art and culture, directed towards the public from the
bottom up.

*Selbstorganisation ist die tägliche Erzeugung einer nicht auf
Profit ausgerichteten Atmosphäre der Selbstbefähigung.
Nichtinstitutionelle Individuen, die selbstbefähigt arbeiten,
sind selbstorganisiert. Sie erhalten keinerlei Leistungen vom
System, arbeiten aber trotzdem hart, weil sie das Bedürfnis
haben, sich durch Kunst und Kultur auszudrücken und sich
direkt an ein Publikum zu wenden.*

Boba Mirjana Stojadinović

Social Struggle

Social struggle is a layered agonism of a network of classes, ethnicities, religions, and communities that are connected with each other in rhizomatic relations of social process. Social struggle compounds a socio-spatial ramification.

Sozialer Kampf entsteht aufgrund vielschichtiger Rivalitäten zwischen Gesellschaftsschichten, Ethnien, Religionen und Gemeinschaften, die durch rhizomatische Zusammenhänge gesellschaftlicher Strukturen miteinander verbunden sind. Sozialer Kampf hat sozialräumliche Auswirkungen.

Pelin Tan

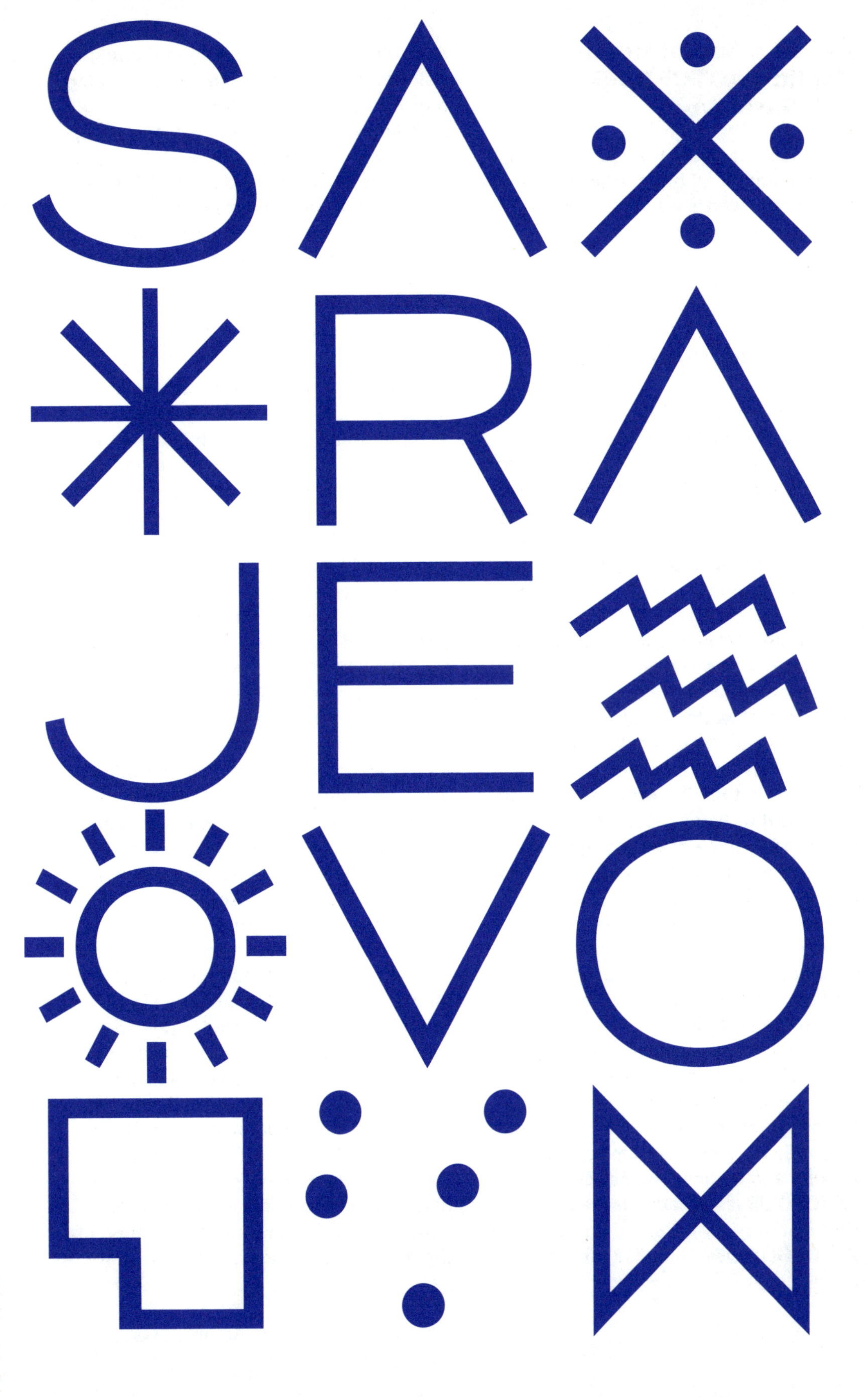

Art as a Social Healing Tactic—ACTOPOLIS Lab Sarajevo

"We shall not cease from exploration, and the end of all our exploring will be to arrive where we started and know the place for the first time."

T. S. Eliot

Posing the Question

Whose privilege is it to reflect on the city and decide what is in the public interest, what public space we wish for, and what public space we need today? A clue to answering this question may be found in Jane Jacobs's assertion that "cities have the capability of providing something for everybody, only because, and only when, they are created by everybody."[1] It is apparent that in contemporary societies, where most of the urban policies are designed for and by a class of white, wealthy, and healthy men, this becomes very hard to achieve. The idea that all those who live, love, and work in the city, who visit the city, who use it or have a feel for it are to be asked to think about the question seems very far-fetched and can be realised only when proper spaces, time, and resources are available, and when there is the political will to support it. When there is not, we adopt other tactics and try other methods in an attempt to find the answer.

Politically compelled to understand and reclaim public space, we started with long discussions whose aim was to pose questions that disturb us, while also reflecting on possible counter-actions and tactics. The period in which ACTOPOLIS is operating is a significant one, not only for Sarajevo and the other ACTOPOLIS cities but also for the world as a whole: it represents an uprising in defence of a public space. We are seeing a growing number of initiatives dealing with and reflecting on the city and recognise that the city has once again become the focus of our interests and struggles. ACTOPOLIS Sarajevo is just a continuation of the initiatives for the city that have emerged in recent years to enrich urban common spaces.

The Hospital

The first step was to find a space where questions could be publicly asked and potentially answered in a common forum. One such space is Hastahana Park. After a period of deliberation and discussion, the decision was taken to make it the focal point from which the city would be looked at and possibilities for improvement explored.

The history of this place is telling and served as a fundamental metaphor for ACTOPOLIS Sarajevo. It starts with the construction of the hospital in 1866, one of the first two hospitals built in Sarajevo.[2] It was built by Topal Osman Pasha as an Ottoman military hospital and constructed on land owned by several families consisting of gardens and houses.[3] It was built on a site with excellent natural air circulation, it had its own water and sewage system as well as the first modern pharmacy in Bosnia Herzegovina, and was a place where modern European medical treatments were applied at an early stage of their development.[4] Under Austro-Hungarian rule it also served as a military hospital, which then grew in size after World War I and during World War II as part of the Kingdom of Yugoslavia. In the socialist era, the hospital was modernised and developed further but had serious problems with a lack of space and the deteriorating condition of the hospital buildings. A new hospital was built nearby in 1979, rendering Hastahana obsolete as a medical facility.[5] During the 1992–5 war the building was heavily shelled and the resulting damage was never repaired. The rundown building was left to decay until it was finally removed after it became unsafe and a danger to passers-by.

Today, this centrally located urban site is a place of constant challenge—a huge parking lot, a park and a playground for youth, dogs, and kids, and a place for different sports activities and leisure, all in equal part. It is a city landmark, hosting the only BMX and skate park in Bosnia Herzegovina, and a place were different generations meet. It is also home to Helmut Lutz's sculptural work *Zvjezdani put*, which, after travelling through Santiago de Compostela, Rome, Athens, Jerusalem, and Istanbul, came to rest in Sarajevo bringing a powerful message about labour and creativity as well as the promise of love between people.[6]

Taking as our starting point the fact that Sarajevo today desperately needs spaces of comfort, of communion, of sociality, spaces that go "beyond markets" in a productive collaboration of thinkers, creators, users, and everybody else, we placed our laboratory right there in Hastahana, hoping to create a kind of symbolic "new hospital" for healing the city's problems.

The Laboratory

Healing often requires comprehensive research, proper diagnostics, knowledge, experimentation, trial and error, collaborative thinking, group and individual treatments, a great deal of practice, and empathy and communication with the patient; it needs the right questions to be asked and, last but not least, it requires proper technology. We all know Dr House, right?

Our ACTOPOLIS Lab Sarajevo was also a production laboratory where artists, urbanists, and activists joined together to answer questions relating to the present state and future possibilities of urban life and to test strategies for action. Through an Open Call, the team behind ACTOPOLIS Lab Sarajevo, working together with the jury, selected three projects: *Sarajevo Album*, *Green Pavilion*, and *Sarajevo Cloud*. The projects focus on the commons, citizen participation, networking with various groups and individuals, open dialogue, testing and acting, critical thinking, and collaborations. They set out not only to test methods for thinking about the city but also to explore various tools for problematising and transgressing borders and constructing transversal links between art, urban planning, and activism. Within the framework of the laboratory they operate together to find answers, diagnose problems, and come up with optimal therapies; they also have the potential to serve as a platform for dialogue, reflection, and the exchange of opinions and ideas about the meaning and transformation of space, history, and the present and future of the city.

Our laboratory was thus developed to enable everyone to become an investigator and to discover or rediscover something about his or her city. Of course, dealing with real-time/real-world/real-city/real-people situations and the complexity of cross-relations is always hard but someone wisely reminded us that everybody needs a laboratory and remarkable things come from experimentation. We knew that there would be difficulties at the beginning, multiple attempts and failures, but we never stopped looking forward.

Finding the Remedy

The process of healing can only start with the consent and determination of the patient and continues with the determination of healers to find the proper cure. If we understand our cities as a body politic, as David Harvey proposed, we learn that it can be attacked, wounded, remoulded, or rebuilt.[7] Different viruses and diseases can attack this body, but can it be cured, and how? In his introduction to the publication *Šta da napišem na zidu,* Dr Anton Halilović talks about experimentation and building tactics designed to create possibilities for coming together and breaking apart to create a collective vision of an emancipated future as a vision of transformation for ourselves with the help of our cities and together with them. He then adds "a disturbing unknown" when he says, "We cannot know if this future will be the future of the ultrapolis from dystopian films, brutal and exhausted of all humanity, or of a city that will cure mankind. We can handle this, the unknown, only with a determination to think and act. This means that we need to look at the conditions and forces, recognise the challenges, threats, and trends, and carefully read the signs, but it may also mean taking pugnacious individual and collective responsibility in the process of constructing the city as image, symbol, and form, which is the form of life itself."[8]

We must take time and proceed slowly, for contemporary viruses are, as we are learning, quite resistant and appear in mutated forms. We witness how the toughest of them all, the virus of capitalism, presents itself in sparkly commercials that exploit the values of love, family, friendship, and sharing, taking the stories of life and work achievements and presenting them to us in the form of a perfect body or a perfect world, all in order to sell a product and generate capital. This resistant virus, developed through time, occupies and contaminates our virtual and physical worlds and quickly spreads across our commons. As Marina Gržinić puts it, "capitalism not only produces different worlds and modes of living, but also cultural and artistic paradigms through which it is possible to say that wars between different worlds (also presented as the 'worldless' world) take place on the aesthetic level, through specific concepts that hegemonize the sphere of art and culture, imposing a certain political (anti)agency, a status quo that needs to be precisely defined."[9]

Today the space of Hastahana is not occupied by initiatives working with visions of the city, like that of *Sarajevo Cloud*, or initiatives aiming to create new public spaces to provoke debate about venues for cultural and art productions like *Green Pavilion*, nor by those who examine the past and present to create the future like *Sarajevo Album*, but rather by those who sell the magic[10] at a certain price. The price is the disqualification of those for whom this space is more than a seasonal affair—their exclusion from the process of deciding how it is governed and disposed. Here we are talking about nothing less than the foundations of a democracy. To quote a citizen of Sarajevo, "A struggle for the park, better schools and day care, streets without holes, water without scale, air free of poisons, as well as the struggle for freedom and for equality can only start as a resolute incursion into all the processes by which decisions about us are made without us: democracy as the ability to self-govern."[11]

It is in Hastahana that we saw this on a small scale and in a most immediate sense. Trapped again in the nostalgia for places we miss, we all learn again and again that this time round our public space is not destroyed by the war but by the very system that should fight for the public interest. In many ways, as Dr Jelena Petrović put it, "we can now be sure, it is the war by other means."[12] In this war, everything needs to be demanded again and again, until we find tactics and shape answers that will enable us to moderate participation in and about public space and preserve the very nature of the public space, which, as suggested, makes visible all the traumatic and sometimes painful things that have occurred and allows for constant constructive conflict in order to create new meanings.[13] We end and we continue, waiting for the bruises to disappear and hoping desperately for a different kind of magic.

DANIJELA DUGANDŽIĆ

1   Jane Jacobs, *The Death and Life of Great American Cities* (New York: Random House, 2002), p. 238.
2   See http://www.radiosarajevo.ba/vijesti/lokalne-teme /prve-bolnice-u-bih-sarajevske-hastahane -kojih-skoro-vise-i-nema-foto/196549.
3   Topal Osman Pasha, who was originally from Crete, was Ottoman Grand Vizier and served in Bosnia from 1861 to 1869. He built roads along the Neretva and Bosnia rivers, constructed the first brewery in Sarajevo in 1864, and was responsible for post offices, military buildings (the first buildings in the area of the former Maršal Tito barracks and now the university campus), sawmills, the famous Konak residence, and, in 1866, the first two hospitals in Bosnia Herzegovina (the Hastahana hospital for civilians located in the Bistrik neighbourhood, at Halilbašiča 16, and the Hastahana military hospital in Titova street), as well as the first printing company and many other projects that were a part of his urban modernisation plan. For more on this, see http://www.vakuf.ba/aktuelnosti/vakufske-bolnice-u -sarajevu-i-tuzli-kao-pretece--moguce-nove -vakufske-bolnice-u-bih/300.
4   This is described in more detail in the history section of the official website of the General Hospital Abdulah Nakaš in Sarajevo: http://www.obs.ba/index.php /historijat.
5   For more on the history of the hospital, see http://www.radiosarajevo.ba/metromahala/teme /historijat-opce-bolnice-primdr-abdulah-nakas -tradicija-duga-150-godina/212539.
6   Helmut Lutz's *Sternenweg*, a stage sculpture located in public space, was given to Sarajevo on 22 July 2005 during the Baščaršijske Noći (Nights of Bascarsija) festival. See http://novi.ba/clanak/12203 /znate-li-sta-predstavlja-jezivi-park-u-centru-sarajeva.
7   David Harvey, "The City as a Body Politic", in Jane Schneider and Ida Susser (eds.), *Wounded Cities: Destruction and Reconstruction in a Globalized World* (Oxford: Berg, 2003), pp. 25–43.
8   Dr Anton Halilović, "Obećanje grada i imaginacija praksi", introduction to Boriša Mraović (ed.), *Šta da napišem na zidu?*, Gradologija izdanje 03 (Sarajevo: CRVENA, 2015), pp. 8–13, here: p. 13 (my translation).
9   Marina Gržinić, "A War over the Location of the Void", in *Re-politicizing Art, Theory, Representation and New Media Technology* (Vienna: Schlebrügge, 2008), pp. 171–81, here: pp. 171–2.
10 For more on the Coca-Cola Sarajevo Holiday Market, see http://www.klix.ba/magazin/coca-cola-sarajevo -holiday-market-na-novoj-lokaciji-u-parku-hastahana -zimska-carolija-pocinje-7-decembra/161129060#12.
11 Interview with an inhabitant of the Pofalići neighborhood of Sarajevo, who grew up in Malta and the Koševsko neighbourhoods, "RAZGOVOR ZA RAZGOVOR: Gdje skrenuti?", *Zajednički grad* 1, (Sarajevo, October 2015) (my translation).
12 Dr Jelena Petrović, a member of the curatorial collective Red Min(e)d, private communication to the author, November 2016 (my translation).
13 As suggested by Nikola Bojić in a private conversation with the author in Sarajevo, 16 July 2016.

Kunst als Taktik der sozialen Heilung – ACTOPOLIS Lab Sarajevo

„Wir lassen niemals vom Entdecken, Und am Ende allen Entdeckens Langen wir, wo wir losliefen, an Und kennen den Ort zum ersten Mal."

T. S. Eliot

Die Fragestellung

Wessen Privileg ist es, über die Stadt nachzudenken und zu beschließen, was im öffentlichen Interesse ist, welchen öffentlichen Raum wir uns wünschen und welchen wir brauchen? Einen ersten Anhaltspunkt zur Beantwortung dieser Frage liefert die These von Jane Jacobs: „Städte haben nur dann die Fähigkeit, allen etwas zu bieten, wenn sie von allen gestaltet werden."[1] Das wird offenkundig ein schwieriges Unterfangen in heutigen Gesellschaften, in denen die meisten städtebaulichen Maßnahmen auf wohlhabende, weiße, gesunde Männer ausgerichtet sind und von ebensolchen entworfen werden. Die Vorstellung, dass alle, die in der Stadt leben, lieben und arbeiten, die sie besuchen, nutzen oder ein Gefühl für sie haben, gebeten werden sollen, über diese Frage nachzudenken, scheint äußerst abwegig und lässt sich nur dann umsetzen, wenn die entsprechenden Räume, die entsprechende Zeit und die entsprechenden Ressourcen zur Verfügung stehen und der politische Wille da ist. Ist das nicht der Fall, verfolgen wir eine andere Taktik und testen zur Klärung der Frage eine andere Methode.

Unter dem politischen Druck, den öffentlichen Raum zu begreifen und zurückzuerobern, begannen wir mit langen Diskussionen, um beunruhigende Fragen zu stellen und zugleich über mögliche Gegenaktionen und -taktiken nachzudenken. Der Zeitraum von ACTOPOLIS ist bedeutsam, sowohl für Sarajevo und die anderen ACTOPOLIS-Städte als auch für die Welt insgesamt: ACTOPOLIS gibt den Protesten zur Verteidigung des öffentlichen Raums ein Gesicht. Eine wachsende Zahl von Initiativen beschäftigt sich mit der Stadt, reflektiert über sie und erkennt, dass sie einmal mehr zum Fokus unserer Interessen und Auseinandersetzungen geworden ist. ACTOPOLIS Sarajevo ist lediglich eine Fortsetzung der Initiativen für die Stadt, die sich in den letzten Jahren zur Bereicherung gemeinsamer städtischer Räume herauskristallisiert haben.

Das Krankenhaus

Der erste Schritt bestand darin, einen Ort zu finden, an dem man öffentlich Fragen stellen und sie in einem gemeinsamen Forum potenziell klären konnte. Ein solcher Ort ist der Hastahana-Park. Nach ersten Beratungen und Diskussionen beschloss man, ihn zum Mittelpunkt der Perspektiven auf die Stadt und der Sondierung möglicher Verbesserungen zu machen.

Die Geschichte dieses Ortes ist bezeichnend und diente als grundlegende Metapher für ACTOPOLIS Sarajevo. Sie beginnt 1866 mit dem Bau eines der ersten beiden Krankenhäuser in Sarajevo, dem Hastahana.[2] Errichtet als osmanisches Militärkrankenhaus unter Topal Osman Pascha befand es sich auf dem Land mehrerer Familien, das Gärten und Häuser umfasste.[3] Das Gelände bot hervorragende natürliche Luftzirkulation, verfügte über ein eigenes Wasser- und Abwassersystem sowie die erste moderne Apotheke in Bosnien-Herzegowina; hier wurde nach der modernen europäischen Medizin behandelt, die sich noch im Frühstadium ihrer Entwicklung befand.[4] Zur Zeit der österreichisch-ungarischen Monarchie diente Hastahana auch als Militärkrankenhaus und wurde nach dem Ersten und im Zweiten Weltkrieg als Teil des Königreichs Jugoslawien noch vergrößert. In der Ära des Sozialismus wurde das Krankenhaus modernisiert und fortentwickelt, litt allerdings unter großer Platznot und zunehmend verfallenden Gebäuden. 1979 entstand ein neues Hospital in der Nähe, das Hastahana als medizinische Einrichtung obsolet machte.[5] Während des Bosnienkrieges wurde das Gebäude stark beschossen und der entstandene Schaden nie behoben. Das marode Gebäude verfiel zusehends, bis es unsicher und zur Gefahr für Passant/innen wurde, was letztlich zu seinem Abriss führte.

Heute ist dieses zentral gelegene städtische Grundstück ein Ort der permanenten Herausforderung – ein riesiger

*Parkplatz, Park und Spielplatz für
Kinder, Jugendliche und Hunde und ein
Ort für diverse Sport- und Freizeit-
aktivitäten – all dies zu gleichen Teilen.
Es ist ein Wahrzeichen der Stadt, der
einzige BMX- und Skatepark in Bosnien-
Herzegowina und Treffpunkt verschiedener Generationen. Hier befindet sich
auch Helmut Lutz' Skulptur Zvjezdani
put (Sternenweg), die nach Stationen in
Santiago de Compostela, Rom, Athen,
Jerusalem und Istanbul nun in Sarajevo
angelangt ist und eine starke Botschaft
über Arbeit, Kreativität und das Liebesver-
sprechen zwischen Menschen vermittelt.[6]*

*Ausgangspunkt war für uns die
Tatsache, dass Sarajevo heute dringend
Räume der Geborgenheit, der Gemeinschaft, der Geselligkeit braucht; Räume,
die in produktiver Zusammenarbeit von
Denker/innen, Erfinder/innen, Nutzer/
innen und allen anderen über „Märkte"
hinausgehen. Daher errichteten wir
unser Labor genau hier in Hastahana
in der Hoffnung, eine Art symbolisches
„neues Krankenhaus" zu schaffen,
um die Probleme der Stadt zu heilen.*

Das Labor

*Eine Heilung verlangt häufig umfassende
Forschung, eine genaue Diagnose,
Wissen, Experimente, praktisches Aus-
probieren, gemeinsame Überlegungen,
Gruppen- und Einzelbehandlungen, sehr
viel Praxiserfahrung, Empathie und
Kommunikation mit dem Patienten oder
der Patientin; sie erfordert die richtigen
Fragen und nicht zuletzt die geeignete
Technik. Wir alle kennen Dr. House,
nicht wahr?*

*Unser ACTOPOLIS Lab Sarajevo
war auch ein Produktionslabor, in dem
sich Künstler/innen, Städteplaner/innen
und Aktivist/innen zusammentaten,
um Fragen zum aktuellen Zustand und
zu künftigen Möglichkeiten städtischen
Lebens zu beantworten und Handlungsstrategien zu erproben. Aus den im
Rahmen einer öffentlichen Ausschrei-
bung eingereichten Vorschlägen wählte
das Team des ACTOPOLIS Lab Sarajevo
gemeinsam mit der Jury drei Projekte
aus: Sarajevo Album, Green Pavilion
und Sarajevo Cloud. Der Schwerpunkt der
Projekte liegt auf den Gemeingütern,
auf Bürgerpartizipation, auf der Vernetzung mit verschiedenen Gruppen und
Einzelpersonen, auf offenem Dialog,
auf Testen und Handeln, auf kritischem
Denken und Kooperationen. Dabei
sollen nicht nur Methoden für das Nach-
denken über die Stadt getestet, sondern
auch verschiedene Hilfsmittel erprobt
werden, um die Grenzen zwischen Kunst,
Stadtplanung und Aktivismus zu pro-
blematisieren, zu überschreiten und Quer-
verbindungen zu schaffen. Im Rahmen
des Labors arbeiten die Beteiligten
gemeinsam an Antworten, der Problem-
diagnose und der Entwicklung optimaler
Therapien; die Projekte haben darüber
hinaus das Potenzial, als Plattform für
Dialog, Reflexion, den Austausch von
Meinungen und Vorstellungen über
Sinn und Wandel von Raum, Vergangenheit, Gegenwart und Zukunft der Stadt
zu dienen.*

*Daher wurde unser Labor so
gestaltet, dass jeder zum Forscher oder
zur Forscherin werden und etwas über
seine oder ihre Stadt (neu) entdecken
konnte. Natürlich ist es immer schwierig,
mit Problemen realer Städte und realer
Menschen in Echtzeit in der realen Welt
und mit der Komplexität von Querbe-
zügen umzugehen, doch klugerweise
erinnerte uns jemand daran, dass jeder
ein Labor benötigt und Experimente
Beeindruckendes hervorbringen. Wir
wussten, dass es zu Beginn Schwierig-
keiten, mehrere Anläufe und Fehlschläge
geben würde, doch das hielt uns nicht
davon ab, stets nach vorne zu schauen.*

177

Das Heilmittel finden

Der Genesungsprozess kann nur unter Zustimmung und mit der festen Absicht des Patienten oder der Patientin beginnen und sich in der Entschlossenheit der Heilenden fortsetzen, das richtige Heilmittel zu finden. Wenn wir unsere Städte als Gemeinwesen im Sinne David Harveys verstehen, erkennen wir, dass sie angreifbar und verletzbar sind, erneuert oder wieder aufgebaut werden können.[7] Viren und Krankheiten können diesen Körper angreifen, doch lässt er sich heilen? Und wenn ja, wie? In seiner Einleitung zu dem Band Šta da napišem na zidu *spricht Anton Halilović über Versuche und Baustrategien, Möglichkeiten der Begegnung und der Trennung zu schaffen, um eine gemeinsame Vision einer emanzipierten Zukunft als Perspektive eines Wandels für uns selbst mithilfe unserer Städte und gemeinsam mit ihnen zu entwerfen. Dann fügt er noch etwas „beunruhigend Unbekanntes" hinzu: „Wir können nicht wissen, ob diese Zukunft die Zukunft der Ultrapolis dystopischer Filme sein wird, brutal und bar jeder Menschlichkeit, oder die Zukunft einer Stadt, die die Menschheit heilen wird. Diesem Unbekannten können wir nur begegnen, wenn wir entschlossen denken und handeln. Wir müssen uns also die Bedingungen und Kräfte ansehen, Herausforderungen, Bedrohungen und Trends erkennen und die Zeichen sorgfältig lesen; vielleicht müssen wir aber auch kämpferisch allein oder gemeinsam Verantwortung übernehmen beim Aufbau der Stadt als Bild, Symbol und Form, einer Stadt, die selbst die Lebensform ist."[8]*

Wir müssen uns Zeit nehmen und Schritt für Schritt vorgehen, denn die heutigen Viren sind, wie wir gerade lernen, überaus resistent und erscheinen auch in mutierter Form. Wir erleben, wie der widerstandfähigste Virus von allen, der Kapitalismus, sich in glitzernden Werbespots präsentiert, die sich Werte wie Liebe, Familie, Freundschaft und Teilen zu eigen machen und Geschichten von privatem und beruflichem Erfolg in Form eines perfekten Körpers oder einer perfekten Welt präsentieren, um ein Produkt zu verkaufen oder Kapital zu generieren. Dieser resistente Virus, wie er sich im Lauf der Zeit entwickelt hat, besetzt und kontaminiert unsere virtuellen und realen Welten und verbreitet sich rasant über alle unsere Gemeingüter. Marina Gržinić beschreibt es so: „Der Kapitalismus erzeugt nicht nur verschiedene Welten und Lebensweisen, sondern auch kulturelle und künstlerische Paradigmen; man kann also sagen, dass Kriege zwischen verschiedenen Welten (die auch als ‚weltlose' Welt dargestellt werden) auf einer ästhetischen Ebene mittels konkreter Konzepte stattfinden, die den Bereich Kunst und Kultur hegemonisieren und eine gewisse politische (Anti-)Handlungsmacht etablieren, einen Status quo, der genau definiert werden muss."[9]

Heute wird der Raum von Hastahana nicht von Initiativen besetzt, die wie etwa Sarajevo Cloud mit Visionen für die Stadt arbeiten oder wie der Green Pavilion die Schaffung neuer öffentlicher Räume anstreben, um Debatten über Orte für Kunst und Kultur anzuregen. Genauso wenig findet man hier Menschen wie bei Sarajevo Album, die Vergangenheit und Gegenwart untersuchen, um eine Zukunftsvision zu entwickeln; vielmehr begegnet man Menschen, die die Magie[10] zum Festpreis verkaufen. Der Preis disqualifiziert jene, für die dieser Raum mehr als eine saisonabhängige Angelegenheit ist – er schließt sie aus dem Entscheidungsprozess aus, wie dieser Raum verwaltet und eingeteilt wird. Wir sprechen hier über nicht weniger als die Grundfesten

178

einer Demokratie. Ein Bürger Sarajevos formulierte es so: „Das Ringen um den Park, um bessere Schulen und Kinderbetreuung, Straßen ohne Schlaglöcher, Wasser ohne Kalkablagerungen, Luft ohne Schadstoffe und auch der Kampf für Freiheit und Gleichheit können nur durch energische Eingriffe in all jene Prozesse beginnen, bei denen Entscheidungen ohne uns gefällt werden: Demokratie als Fähigkeit, sich selbst zu regieren."[11]

In Hastahana haben wir dies im Kleinen und ganz unmittelbar erlebt. Gefangen in der Sehnsucht nach früheren Orten, die wir vermissen, lernen wir ein ums andere Mal, dass unser öffentlicher Raum diesmal nicht vom Krieg zerstört wird, sondern von genau dem System, das sich eigentlich für das öffentliche Interesse einsetzen sollte. In vielerlei Hinsicht können wir heute, wie Jelena Petrović sagt, „sicher sein, dass es sich um Krieg mit anderen Mitteln handelt"[12]. In diesem Krieg muss alles immer wieder neu eingefordert werden, bis wir Strategien und Antworten finden, die es uns ermöglichen, Teilhabe im und um den öffentlichen Raum zu vermitteln und den Charakter dieses Raums zu wahren; denn wie dargelegt macht er all die traumatischen und mitunter schmerzhaften Dinge der Vergangenheit sichtbar und erlaubt einen ständigen konstruktiven Konflikt, um neue Bedeutungen zu schaffen.[13] Wir hören auf und machen weiter, warten auf das Abklingen der Schwellungen und hoffen verzweifelt auf eine andere Art von Magie.

Danijela Dugandžić

1   Jane Jacobs, The Death and Life of Great American Cities (New York: Random House, 2002), S. 238.

2   Vgl. http://www.radiosarajevo.ba/vijesti/lokalne-teme/prve-bolnice-u-bih-sarajevske-hastahane-kojih-skoro-vise-i-nema-foto/196549.

3   Der ursprünglich aus Kreta stammende Topal Osman Pascha war osmanischer Großwesir und diente zwischen 1861 und 1869 in Bosnien. Er baute Straßen an den Flüssen Neretva und Bosnia, errichtete 1864 die erste Brauerei Sarajevos und war zuständig für Postämter, Militärgebäude (die ersten Gebäude auf dem Gebiet der ehemaligen Marsal Tito Kaserne, dem heutigen Uni-Campus), Sägewerke, den berühmten Konak (Gouverneurssitz) und 1866 für die beiden ersten Krankenhäuser Bosnien-Herzegowinas (das Hastahana-Krankenhaus für die Zivilbevölkerung im Stadtteil Bistrik, Halilbašiča Nr. 16, und das Militärkrankenhaus Hastahana auf der Titovastraße). Auch die erste Druckerei und viele weitere Projekte waren Teil seines Plans zur Stadtmodernisierung. Weitere Informationen sind zu finden unter http://www.vakuf.ba/aktuelnosti/vakufske-bolnice-u-sarajevu-i-tuzli-kao-pretece--moguce-nove-vakufske-bolnice-u-bih/300.

4   Nähere Informationen sind unter dem Menüpunkt Geschichte auf der offiziellen Website des Krankenhauses Abdulah Nakaš in Sarajevo verfügbar: http://www.obs.ba/index.php/historijat.

5   Weitere Informationen über das Krankenhaus sind zu finden unter http://www.radiosarajevo.ba/metromahala/teme/historijat-opce-bolnice-primdr-abdulah-nakas-tradicija-duga-150-godina/212539.

6   Die Bühnenskulptur Sternenweg von Helmut Lutz, die im öffentlichen Raum ausgestellt ist, wurde der Stadt Sarajevo am 22. Juli 2005 während des Festivals Baščaršijske Noći (Nächte der Bascarsija) übergeben. Vgl. http://novi.ba/clanak/12203/znate-li-sta-predstavlja-jezivi-park-u-centru-sarajeva.

7   David Harvey, „The City as a Body Politic", in Jane Schneider und Ida Susser (Hrsg.), Wounded Cities: Destruction and Reconstruction in a Globalized World (Oxford: Berg, 2003), S. 25–43.

8   Anton Halilović, „Obećanje grada i imaginacija praksi", Einleitung zu Boriša Mraović (Hrsg.), Šta da napišem na zidu?, Gradologija izdanje 03 (Sarajevo: CRVENA, 2015), S. 8–13, hier S. 13 (Übersetzung der Autorin).

9   Marina Gržinić, „A War over the Location of the Void", in Re-politicizing Art, Theory, Representation and New Media Technology (Wien: Schlebrügge, 2008), S. 171–181, hier S. 171–172.

10 Weitere Informationen zum Coca-Cola Sarajevo Holiday Market finden sich unter http://www.klix.ba/magazin/coca-cola-sarajevo-holiday-market-na-novoj-lokaciji-u-parku-hastahana-zimska-carolija-pocinje-7-decembra/161129060#12.

11 Interview mit einem Bewohner des Viertels Pofalići in Sarajevo, der in den Stadtteilen Malta und Koševsko aufwuchs. „RAZGOVOR ZA RAZGOVOR: Gdje skrenuti?", Zajednički grad 1, (Sarajevo, Oktober 2015) (Übersetzung der Autorin).

12 Jelena Petrović, Mitglied des Kuratorenkollektivs Red Min(e)d. Privates Gespräch mit der Autorin, November 2016 (Übersetzung der Autorin).

13 So der Vorschlag von Nikola Bojić in einem privaten Gespräch mit der Autorin in Sarajevo, 16. Juli 2016.

Green Pavilion Sarajevo

The *Green Pavilion* is a public art project, creative laboratory, urban garden, and teaching tool for ecologically and socially sustainable practices.

Der Green Pavilion *ist ein öffentliches Kunstprojekt, ein Kreativlabor, ein städtischer Garten und ein Unterrichtsmittel für ökologisch und gesellschaftlich nachhaltige Praktiken.*

The *Green Pavilion* is a symbolic gallery growing in a public space, Hastahana Park, in the centre of Sarajevo. Covered with climbing plants, the pavilion offers the viewer an opportunity to remember its predecessor, to come up with an interpretation, and to conceive of it as a new space. The *Green Pavilion* project serves to commemorate Sarajevo's old Art Pavilion, which disappeared under mysterious circumstances in the late 1970s. It is intended to spark a debate about urban spaces and their role in art and culture. Our concern is to question local cultural policy and to encourage the citizens of Sarajevo to engage in conversations and activities, thus making this public space a forum for creative exchange and the production of art.

Der Green Pavilion *(Grüne Pavillon) ist eine symbolische Galerie, die auf einem öffentlichen Gelände, dem Hastahana-Park, im Zentrum von Sarajevo wächst. So entsteht ein mit Kletterpflanzen begrünter Pavillon, der dem Betrachter/der Betrachterin die Möglichkeit eröffnet, sich zu erinnern, ihn zu interpretieren und als neuen Raum zu denken. Das Projekt* Green Pavilion *dient der Erinnerung an einen ehemaligen Kunstpavillon in Sarajevo, der Ende der 1970er-Jahre unter ungeklärten Umständen verschwand; es soll eine Debatte über Stadträume und ihre Rolle für Kunst und Kultur anregen. Unser Anliegen ist es, die lokale Kulturpolitik infrage zu stellen und die Bürger/innen zu Gesprächen und Aktionen anzuregen, um so den öffentlichen Raum für kreativen Austausch und Kunstproduktion zu nutzen.*

Project: Lana Čmajčanin, Bojan Stojčić → Format: installation, intervention → Dates: 6 June – 30 September 2016 → Venue: Hastahana Park, Sarajevo

Sarajevo—ACTOPOLIS Lab Sarajevo

Sarajevo Album

Collective multimedia project about contemporary Sarajevo linking urban images and narratives

Kollektives Multimediaprojekt über das heutige Sarajevo, das Bilder und Erzählungen miteinander verbindet

Sarajevo Album is a collective, digital album of the city that brings together elements of pop culture, alternative and feminist ways of thinking about the city, and various practices and ideas. During the months of May, June, and July 2016, *Sarajevo Album* used the kiosk installation *CRVENA* to collect and analyse citizens' memories and narratives of the city. The project takes a critical look at urban spaces that are filled with good or bad memories and with personal images, ideas, and emotions. Together with the city's inhabitants, *Sarajevo Album* explores personal memories of places full of ruins and wild nature; it analyses abandoned urban spaces and how they have been transformed, individual and collective dreams, interiors, contemporary, temporary, and spontaneous architecture, darkness, noise and silence, and opinions, fictions, and fantasies about the city.

Sarajevo Album *ist ein kollektives, digitales Album der Stadt, in dem sich Elemente der Popkultur, alternative und feministische Denkweisen über die Stadt sowie verschiedene Praktiken und Ideen vereinen. Im Laufe der Monate Mai, Juni und Juli 2016 hat Sarajevo Album die Kioskinstallation CRVENA zum Sammeln und Analysieren von Erinnerungen und Erzählungen von Bürger/innen über die Stadt genutzt. Das Projekt hinterfragt Stadträume, die von guten oder schlechten Erinnerungen, von persönlichen Bildern, Ideen und Emotionen erfüllt sind. Sarajevo Album untersucht zusammen mit den Bewohner/innen die persönlichen Erinnerungen an Orte voller Ruinen und an wilde Natur; es analysiert verlassene städtische Räume und deren Transformationen, individuelle und kollektive Träume, Interieurs, zeitgenössische, temporäre und spontane Architektur, Dunkelheit, Lärm und Stille, Ansichten, Fiktionen und Fantasien über die Stadt.*

Project: Armina Pilav; Haris Sahačić, Katarina Bošnjak, Roberto Vertieri, Mirza Spuzić (co-authors) → Format: workshops, research, interventions → Dates: 6 June – 30 September 2016 → Venue: Sarajevo → Participants—"City as a Puzzle": Nardina Zubanović, Kolektiv Kreaktiva;—"City Games in Hastahana": Kolektiv Kreaktiva, Haris Fazlić, multimedialna domaćica, Semara Kikić

183

Sarajevo Cloud

What if we could observe individual experiences of common public space?

Was wäre, wenn wir individuelle Erfahrungen mit dem gemeinsamen öffentlichen Raum beobachten könnten?

Sarajevo Cloud is a multimedia installation that collects individual visions of Hastahana Park by using the physical space as a form of "augmented reality". The sculpture *Sarajevo Cloud*, mounted on the *Green Pavilion*, invites inhabitants and visitors to the city to share their visions with others via the smartphone app *Sarajevo Cloud*. The purpose of *Sarajevo Cloud* is not just to shape the space in Hastahana Park and to enable people to share their personal experiences and visions of the city with others but also to give all users of the app the opportunity to become designers of the public space and thus to override or blur the boundaries between shared physical and individual virtual space or even to dissolve them altogether.

184

Project: Asmir Mutevelić, Kenan Vatrenjak, Ibrica Jašarević, Vedad Islambegović →
Format: intervention, mobile app → Dates: 6 June – 30 September 2016 → Venue: Sarajevo

Sarajevo Cloud *ist eine Multimedia-installation, die individuelle Visionen des Hastahana-Parks sammelt, indem sie den physischen Raum als augmented reality nutzt. Die Skulptur* Sarajevo Cloud, *die am Green Pavilion angebracht ist, lädt die Bewohner/innen und Besucher/innen der Stadt dazu ein, ihre Visionen mit anderen zu teilen, indem sie die Smartphone-App* Sarajevo Cloud *nutzen. Die* Sarajevo Cloud *soll nicht nur erlauben, den Raum des Hastahana-Parks zu gestalten und persönliche Erfahrungen und Visionen der Stadt mit anderen zu teilen, sondern soll auch allen Nutzer/innen der App die Möglichkeit bieten, Designer/innen des öffentlichen Raums zu werden und so die Grenzen zwischen dem gemeinsam-physischen und dem individuell-virtuellen Raum außer Kraft zu setzen, zu verwischen oder ganz aufzuheben.*

Health Day in the Park:
Hatha Yoga with Semra Kikić

An opportunity to make your own
fruit and vegetable juices and
discuss healthy lifestyle choices

*Gespräche über eine gesunde
Lebensweise beim Herstellen von
Obst- und Gemüsesäften*

Project: Armina Pilav and Semra Kikić → Format: sport,
workshop → Date: 10 July 2016 → Venue: Hastahana Park,
Sarajevo

Sarajevo Seconds

Photo exhibition: photos of everyday life in Sarajevo as seen by the
younger generation, who love their
city but are also critical of it

*Fotoausstellung: Fotos des Alltags
in Sarajevo aus der Sicht einer
jungen Generation, die ihre Stadt
liebt, aber auch kritisiert*

Project: Adnan Bajramović and Zoe Ibrahimović
→ Format: exhibition → Date: 10 July 2016 →
Venue: Hastahana Park, Sarajevo

Skate Park

Volunteer action to fix up the skate
park in Hastahana

*Freiwilligenprojekt, um den
Skate Park in Hastahana wieder
in Ordnung zu bringen*

We invite you to help us fix up the
skate park and surrounding area.
The idea is to spend some time
together repairing the skate park,
giving it a fresh coat of paint, and
clearing up the surroundings.

*Wir laden euch ein, mit uns den
Skate Park und die Umgebung in
Ordnung zu bringen. Ziel der Aktion
ist es, den Skate Park zu reparieren,
die Anlage neu zu streichen, die
Umgebung sauber zu machen und
dabei Zeit miteinander zu verbringen.*

Project: Armina Pilav → Format: exhibition →
Date: 12–14 July 2016 → Venue: Hastahana Park, Sarajevo

Showcase the Skate Park:
Skating for Children

"What is a skate park, how is
it used?" Enes Vilić answers these
questions for children aged six
to twelve and explains the essentials
of skating to them.

*„Was ist ein Skate Park, wie wird
er benutzt?" Diese Fragen beantwortet Enes Vilić Kindern im Alter
von sechs bis zwölf Jahren und
erklärt ihnen die wichtigsten Sachen
zum Thema Skaten.*

Project: Enes Vilić → Format: skating →
Date: 15 July 2016 → Venue: Hastahana Park, Sarajevo

#SuS: Selfie u Sarajevo

#SuS: Selfie u Sarajevo is conceived
as a "quest game" in real space.
It is a way for participants to discover
new and forgotten places in the
city, such as cinemas. With #SuS
you'll have lots of fun, be constantly
on the move, and take plenty of
selfies. The goal is to explore the
city's past and present and to
develop new visions and ideas.

#SuS: Selfie u Sarajevo *ist als* quest
game *im realen Raum gedacht.*
Die Teilnehmer/innen sollen neue
und vergessene Orte wie zum
Beispiel Kinos in der Stadt entde-
cken. #SuS bietet viel Spaß, ständige
Bewegung und Gelegenheit zu
vielen Selfies. Ziel ist es, die Stadt
in ihrer Vergangenheit und Gegen-
wart zu betrachten und neue
Visionen und Ideen zu entwickeln.

Project: Fadil and Faruk → Format: urban game →
Date: 18 July 2016 → Venue: Hastahana Park, Sarajevo

South

A radical identity that has been somehow valorised today as a resistance to capital, South is a cultural construct that has been used to justify racial discrimination, geographical determinisms, and stereotypes and to reproduce uneven or repressive power relations.

> *Als radikale Identität, die heute gewissermaßen zum Widerstand gegen das Kapital hochstilisiert wird, ist der Süden ein kulturelles Konstrukt, das dazu dient, ethnische Diskriminierung, geografischen Determinismus und Stereotype zu rechtfertigen und unausgewogene oder repressive Machtbeziehungen zu reproduzieren.*

Elpida Karaba

Urban Geography

Sheep pasturing on industrial wasteland. Earthquakes changing urban grids. Rivers having their course redirected. The direction of winds disciplined. The return of food gardens in the city. Underground networks. Light pollution. Wild animals feeding on rubbish. Car fumes but no pesticides. The weight of people and their technosphere.

> *Schafe, die auf Industriebrachen weiden. Erdbeben, die Straßen- und Versorgungsnetze verändern. Umgeleitete Flüsse. Gebändigte Windrichtungen. Die Rückkehr von Nutzgärten in die Stadtzentren. U-Bahn-Netze. Lichtverschmutzung. Streunende Tiere, die sich von Abfällen ernähren. Autoabgase, aber keine Pestizide. Das Gewicht der Menschen und ihrer Technosphäre.*

Raluca Voinea

Urban Warfare

Cities in conflict are becoming spaces of exception, security zones, new economies, and areas of militarisation. A building or a master plan itself is already weaponised either through warfare or as an outcome of it. Urban warfare is a contemporary type of worship, where urban space, architecture, and infrastructural design are instrumentalised and serve the conflict.

Im Krieg werden Städte zu Ausnahmegebieten; es entstehen Sicherheitszonen, neue Wirtschaftsformen und militarisierte Bereiche. Selbst ein Bebauungs- oder Masterplan ist schon zu einer Waffe geworden – entweder als Bestandteil der Kriegführung oder als ihr Ergebnis. Urbane Kriegführung ist eine moderne Form von Religion, wobei städtischer Raum, Bauwerke und Infrastruktur instrumentalisiert werden und dem Kampf dienen.

Pelin Tan

Postscript of Invisible Belonging—From an "Artopia of Inclusion" to "Conflictual Participation"

As testing grounds for social change, cities continuously redefine what it means to belong to a place. If the sense of belonging to a city is easier to adopt than a national identity, we need to make use of this to foster the creation of a new belonging. The Zagreb group of cross-disciplinary practitioners working at the intersection of art, activism, design, technology, and urbanism investigated the possibilities inherent in contemporary concepts of urban citizenship with regard to the recent influx of migrants into the countries of the European West. If recognised as a process rather than a status, urban citizenship can nurture civic identities at local levels. It can change the meaning of the relationship of citizenship to space, to the urban heterogeneity and complexity that lie beyond categories of the national state.

The city of Zagreb—93.14 per cent of whose inhabitants are Croats, according to the last census in 2011—serves perfectly as a case study of a mono-ethnic city with a highly defined society on the European *limes*. Such ethnic homogeneity is especially interesting in light of today's social polarisation of indigenous and newcomer communities at the gateway to Fortress Europe. In the Zagreb ACTOPOLIS, part of the "art as urban praxis" platform situated on the Balkan route, re-emerging national-istic tendencies and the practice of everyday life in a nation-oriented society have been tested and challenged in a broad spectrum of artistic strategies and tactics. A heterogeneous body of localities was carefully chosen for the interventions, ranging from city-centre hotspots to peripheral communities, from invisible places and junk spaces to cyberspace, and from displaced sites in cities beyond the country's borders to the refuge of a gallery space. We courageously, and somewhat naively, undertook a collective mission to create a network of "inclusive urban territories"—of "spaces of otherness" —in what appeared to be a hegemonic environment.

It all started with a simple staircase.

Seminar for Walkers

Publicist and activist Saša Šimpraga, the founder of many (trans)local volunteer platforms aimed at improving city life, is the author of the *Seminar for Walkers*, the first city stroll programme. In his activist work, in contrast to spatial resistance "at the barricades", he uses a persistent, continuous series of almost invisible actions. Once a critical mass of citizens is reached, these actions are recognised by the city administration and take effect on an institutional level. A change, however small it may seem —for example, the (re)naming of city streets after women, heroines of the anti-fascist movement, or literary laureates—is crucial for citizen empowerment.

The *Seminar for Walkers* was conceived as an activist platform, summoned into being via an open call for members, but it also includes a wider public— that is, anyone capable of following Saša Šimpraga's rapid strides along less ordinary urban routes. The goal of the seminar is twofold, to introduce citizens to unfamiliar parts of the city, and to start public initiatives for the betterment of the city.

Within the *Seminar,* a site-specific intervention, *Connecting*, was realised as a showcase for tangible urban enhancements, encouraging citizens to imagine more desirable urban realities. In Zagreb's historic Upper Town a provisional staircase was erected, a scaffolding designed by the architect David Kabalin. The act of connecting created a direct pedestrian link between the park on the upper level and the promenade below the medieval fortifications. However simple it may have been, this ephemeral site-specific installation carried a symbolic meaning—in a time when fences and walls are being erected all over Europe, it defiantly showed that walls can be surmounted. The *Seminar for Walkers*, which gathered together up to a hundred "marching activists" per stroll, continued throughout the year and supported community organisations and initiatives to promote further concepts for fairer, more inclusive forms of cities.

Communities of Care

Another site-specific practice in the Zagreb ACTOPOLIS was a research-based workshop designed for the Folnegovićevo neighbourhood, one of the first post-war modernist settlements in Europe. Selma Banich, a performance artist who works in the medium of dance performance and action in public space, invited other artists and cultural workers —Marija Borovičkić, Mila Čuljak, Ivana Rončević, and Ana Vilenica—to work together in the *Communities of Care*. The workshop intended to invent, engineer, and share tools for everyday use to help overcome obstacles in local communities generated by the system. However, it encountered difficulties in finding agreement among the artists, who acted as "neighbourhood catalysts" themselves. The first question was this: In the process of creating human relations of care, what types of relationships are produced, for whom, and for what reason? We learned that relations set up in artistic cooperative systems do not necessarily need to be intrinsically collaborative, but they can open up to productive conflict as a means of authentically engaging a collective.

The physical presence of the workshop was embodied in a mobile camper set up next to a fenced-off playground at the edge of the neighbourhood, in the vicinity of the only mosque in Zagreb. Through a series of interviews with residents, dog walkers, and passers-by as well as prominent figures involved in the making of the settlement in the early 1960s, the researchers probed various aspects of life in the Folnegovićevo neighbourhood and its areas of conflict. It encompassed discussions on social housing, modernist urbanisation and contemporary (de/re)industrialisation processes, the nationalist imprint in public space, and the wider socio-political context that forms the everyday life of the community.

An interim public forum was staged on International Workers' Day, on a rainy Sunday morning, in front of the façade of the largest local supermarket, which has regular working hours on a holiday. Invited locals, who were able to witness the workshop process, could now see its progress and comment on its course, as it played out in front of the supermarket's red façade, windowless and plastered with posters. As many burning issues, both local and supra-local, were broached, the researchers, most of them coming from different localities, are now working in a synergy of pluralistic positions and searching for one specific local issue to be tackled in the community during the Zagreb ACTOPOLIS exhibition in 2017.

Road to Belonging

The *Road to Belonging* was a participatory light and landscape intervention, conceived as a "spatial experiment in belonging" by the artist Nikola Bojić.
 As a designer and researcher interested in spatial storytelling both on territorial and site-specific scales, he delved into an unfinished construction site in the hinterland of Novi Zagreb. It is the site of a never-built social housing project in the Podbrežje neighbourhood, located on the rim of the modernist extension of the city across the Sava river. All that was completed on-site was a useless one-kilometre-long road with a round-about, a surreal fragment of urban infrastructure immersed in an undefined landscape. With the simple gesture of planting a walnut tree in the centre of the defunct roundabout, the artist aspired to reconstruct the memory of eradicated groves of trees that a local man had taken care of for decades.

A participatory light event was performed on the roundabout to intro-duce the tree to the community living across from the construction site. Locals were invited to write caring messages to the walnut tree, via a light projector, so the tree would grow fearlessly as their symbol of resistance to authoritarian urbanisation. The messages were written in a simple application, programmed by the designer Damir Prizmić, which transformed regular text into Morse code, a combination of dots and dashes. The results were unique light messages projected from the roundabout into the silence of the night sky.

A tree is thus still standing at the defunct roundabout of Podbrežje, where the artist created a site out of a non-site, a place where the symbolic field of resis-tance and the physical location collapse into a single site. The *Road to Belonging* is impossible to fully comprehend without seeing it from the air, as the view from above showing the entire terrain of the construction site is an integral part of the work, one that is not easily acces-sible for the average spectator. The ques-tion still lingers, Is it possible to belong to the site of an unbuilt urban vision? Can belonging be designed and serve as an emotional tool for reclaiming the city?

Full Range Society

Full Range Society is a participatory audio work by Lightune.G, a duo com-prising multimedia artist Bojan Gagić and electro-acoustic engineer Miodrag Gladović. The artistic pair is best known for their innovative "lumino-acoustic" research into the transformation of light signals into sound. Although the artists' engagement with society took the form of "personal audio confessions" in the artist-run Greta gallery in central Zagreb, the *Full Range Society* project was devised both for cyberspace and physi-cal space, to be experienced in stages.

The first act, entitled *Soundentity*, took place in a fictional waiting room inside a gallery, where the audience par-ticipated in the anonymous filling out of fictional forms. A series of standardised questions—of the type found in most data forms designed to collect personal information—were asked about age, gender, marital status, level of education, and ethnicity. The data was then digi-tally converted into a personalised audio image, a *Soundentity* card. The exhibi-tion opening was an intrinsic part of the artwork with the *vernissage* crowd serving both as an ideal public and as performers. A collection of somewhat unique personal micro-compositions was created during the week the exhibi-tion was open. A real question emerges, about how diverse *Soundentity* cards can be in a homogenous society that accepts very few deviations from the norm.

The second act, devised for cyberspace to include a wider international public, is designed as an application, a computer game to manipulate societies in the making of the *Soundmap of Europe.* The focus of the web application is also on the transformation of data into sound, and each website visitor is invited to choose a particular country and historical period and manipulate the available demographic data. The artwork can be perceived as an exercise in social engineering that aims to question and influence attitudes and social behaviours on a large scale. Will the architect of the new social construct design an open society and produce the desired characteristics in a targeted European population? Will he or she create a different, a more humane "sound composition" of the world we live in or not?

Spaces between (Living) Places

A "displaced" socio-spatial exploration —a Zagreb satellite research project based in Stuttgart—artist Tonka Maleković's *Spaces between (Living) Places* examines the phenomenology of fluid identities in cultural and geographic "spaces between". The artist spent a year working as an economic migrant in Germany and used her experience, together with the experiences of protagonists she interviewed with similar biographies, to portray a common reflection on economic migration and the processes of reconstructing one's identity in relation to a sense of belonging in a new social milieu.

In collaboration with the cultural anthropologist Petra Kelemen, the artist examined methodological forms and formats of artistic and scientific research and their hybridisation. The artwork is based on encounters between the artist and migrant workers that took place during a series of urban walks. The dialogue between persons who share "placelessness" can be perceived as physical, cognitive, and emotional encounters that seek to find common ground. Matija Kralj, a video artist who followed Tonka Maleković and the anthropologist during their field research, documented a part of these narrations on film.

The *Spaces between (Living) Places* research also came to light within the framework of an exhibition at the Student Centre Gallery in Zagreb, as a media installation composed of three segments: a multichannel sound installation presenting fragments of interviews with numerous economic migrants, a video projection of the conversation with the artist and her reading of the *Bewerbung,* an official application form used for finding employment in Germany, and a selection of photographic fragments that bear witness to the artist's quest for her own (non-)identification with the figure of the migrant worker. In the context of the exhibition, the interviews with economic migrants engage the audience in a polylogue, whereby those that are absent from their community of origin somehow become fully present and their narrations create a potential for understanding the complexities of migrant processes in contemporary societies.

An Open End

The Zagreb ACTOPOLIS experience proved that operating with a spectrum of artistic interventions in concrete or abstract urban topographies, actual localities, or the wider public sphere only has meaning inside open forums, where the interventions need to be expressed, debated, and articulated. The

Zagreb public arena has been expanding and contracting, shape-shifting constantly, from large activist walking groups and community members in peripheral neighbourhoods to the usual gallery-goers in the city's cultural life. We have learned that such "publicness" needs to create simultaneous acts of reinvention, realignment, and reconnection in order to create vibrant networks of social and political positions that delve into and deal with the complexities of contemporary urban reality. When engaging organically with actual territories, our involvement also requires active participation in the spatial struggles of the places in question. We need to be sensitive to how these environments are entered, traversed, and left behind, once our process of research and engagement is over. Moreover, when a radical spatial experience is necessary, we need not only to engage but also to try to create new "practices of locality" for future society.

The Zagreb ACTOPOLIS experience clearly showed that intervening in socially complex realities involves a dynamic of productive conflicts—it is by no means simply an "artopia of inclusion". An undivided community, a unified collective, is a seductive figment, one that can only be achieved if differences are ignored. It was important to realise that collaboration sometimes emerges from the antagonistic interaction of agents rather than from their agreement within a collectively constructed utopia. Sitting together at the same table and conceiving collective frictionless actions is no longer considered to be community making. "Conflictual participation" should also be acknowledged as a relevant and productive concept of citizen engagement in the everyday life of the city. Moreover, it should be valued for its respectfulness of diversity and genuine openness to others and otherness, as the modus operandi of new subjectivities and sociabilities in the world.

ANA DANA BEROŠ

Postskript zu Invisible Belonging – Von einer „Kunstopia der Inklusion" zu einer „konfliktgeladenen Partizipation"

Als Versuchsgelände für gesellschaftlichen Wandel definieren Städte ständig neu, was es heißt, sich einem Ort zugehörig zu fühlen. Wenn es zutrifft, dass man sich in einer Stadt schneller heimisch fühlt als in einem Land, müssen wir diesen Umstand aufgreifen, um ein neues Zugehörigkeitsgefühl zu fördern. Vor dem Hintergrund des Migrantenstroms der letzten Zeit untersuchte die Zagreber Gruppe, die disziplinübergreifend an der Schnittstelle von Kunst, politischem Engagement, Gestaltung, Technologie und Stadtentwicklung arbeitete, die gegenwärtigen Vorstellungen einer „Stadtbürgerschaft" und die sich daraus ergebenden Möglichkeiten. Wird diese Stadtbürgerschaft eher als Prozess denn als Status begriffen, kann sie auf lokaler Ebene zur Herausbildung bürgerschaftlicher Identitäten beitragen. Sie kann die Beziehung von Bürgerschaft zum Raum, zu urbaner Heterogenität und Komplexität, die über die Kategorien des Nationalstaates hinausgehen, in ihrer Bedeutung verändern.

Der letzten Volkszählung von 2011 zufolge sind die Einwohner/innen Zagrebs zu 93,14 Prozent Kroat/innen. Damit ist die Stadt eine perfekte Fallstudie einer stark mono-ethnisch geprägten Gesellschaft an der Grenze Europas. Eine derartige ethnische Homogenität ist vor allem angesichts der heutigen sozialen Polarisierung von Einheimischen und Neuankömmlingen am Tor zur Festung Europa von besonderem Interesse. Die Zagreber Plattform von ACTOPOLIS und ihre „Kunst als urbane Praxis" befinden sich direkt auf der Balkanroute. Mit einer großen Bandbreite an künstlerischen Strategien und Taktiken wurden hier die wiederauflebenden nationalistischen Tendenzen und die Alltagspraktiken in einer nationalstaatlich ausgerichteten Gesellschaft unter die Lupe genommen und auf den Prüfstand gestellt. Die Orte der Interventionen wurden mit großer Sorgfalt ausgewählt – von Brennpunkten im Stadtzentrum zu Gemeinschaften am Stadtrand, von unsichtbaren Orten über „Junkspaces" zum Cyberspace, von der Galerie als Zufluchtsort bis hin zu einem über die Landesgrenze hinaus verlagerten Satellitenprojekt. Mutig und etwas naiv stellten wir uns der kollektiven Aufgabe, in einem scheinbar hegemonialen Umfeld ein Netz aus „inklusiven Stadtgebieten" – aus „Räumen des Andersseins" – zu schaffen.

Alles begann mit einer einfachen Treppe.

Seminar for Walkers

Urheber des Seminar for Walkers, des ersten Programms an Stadtspaziergängen, ist der Publizist und Aktivist Saša Šimpraga, der auch viele (über-)örtliche Plattformen für Freiwilligenarbeit gründete, die das Leben in der Stadt verbessern sollen. In seiner politischen Arbeit setzt er nicht auf räumlichen Widerstand „auf den Barrikaden", sondern verfolgt beharrlich die Strategie nahezu unsichtbarer Aktionen. Irgendwann wird die Stadtverwaltung aber auch auf diese Aktionen aufmerksam, sodass sie Wirkung entfalten. Für die Befähigung der Bürger/innen ist jede Veränderung wichtig, so klein sie auch sein mag – beispielsweise die (Um-)Benennung von Straßen nach Frauen, Heldinnen des antifaschistischen Widerstands oder preisgekrönten Literatinnen.

Das Seminar for Walkers wurde als Plattform für Aktionen konzipiert, für die in einem öffentlichen Aufruf um Mitglieder/innen geworben wurde. Gleichzeitig sollte aber auch ein breiteres Publikum angesprochen werden – das heißt alle, die in der Lage sind, Saša Šimpraga zu folgen, der mit großen und schnellen Schritten die weniger ausgetretenen Pfade der Stadt erkundet. Das Seminar verfolgte zwei Ziele: Zum einen sollten die Bürger/innen die unbekannten Ecken der Stadt kennenlernen, zum anderen sollten öffentliche Initiativen zur Aufwertung der Stadt angestoßen werden.

Als Beispiel für konkrete Verbesserungen im Stadtraum und als Ermutigung für die Bürger/innen, sich wünschenswertere städtische Bedingungen vorzustellen, erfolgte im Rahmen des Seminars eine ortsspezifische Intervention mit dem Titel Connecting: In Zagrebs historischer Oberstadt wurde eine provisorische Fußgängertreppe errichtet – ein vom Architekten David Kabalin entworfenes Gerüst. Damit entstand eine Verbindung zwischen dem auf der mittelalterlichen Festung gelegenen Park und der unterhalb der Anlage verlaufenden Promenade. Trotz ihrer Schlichtheit hatte diese kurzzeitige Installation einen hohen Symbolwert: In einer Zeit, in der überall in Europa Zäune und Mauern errichtet werden, zeigt sie geradezu provokativ, dass man Mauern überwinden kann. Das Seminar for Walkers, bei dem pro Spaziergang bis zu 100 „marschierende Aktivist/innen" zusammenkamen, fand das ganze Jahr hindurch statt und unterstützte kommunale Organisationen und Initiativen, um weitere Ideen für gerechtere, inklusivere Stadträume zu fördern.

Communities of Care

Ein anderes ortsspezifisches Projekt von ACTOPOLIS Zagreb war eine Forschungswerkstatt im Stadtviertel Folnegovićevo, eine der ersten modernen Neubausiedlungen Europas in der Nachkriegszeit. Selma Banich, eine Performancekünstlerin, die mit den Medien Tanz und Aktionen im öffentlichen Raum arbeitet, lud mit Marija Borovičkić, Mila Čuljak, Ivana Rončević und Ana Vilenica andere Kunst- und Kulturschaffende zur Zusammenarbeit an den Communities of Care ein. In der Werkstatt sollten Instrumente für den alltäglichen Gebrauch erfunden, entwickelt und gemeinsam dazu genutzt werden, systembedingte Widerstände in den lokalen Gemeinschaften zu überwinden. Die als „Nachbarschaftskatalysatoren" fungierenden Künstlerinnen hatten jedoch Mühe, sich auf eine Vorgehensweise zu einigen. Als erstes stellte sich die Frage, welche Art von Verhältnissen entstehen – für wen und aus welchen Gründen –, wenn sich fürsorgliche zwischenmenschliche Beziehungen entwickeln. Uns wurde klar, dass Beziehungen, die sich in Systemen künstlerischer Zusammenarbeit herausbilden, nicht zwangsläufig kooperativ sein müssen, sondern auch mit produktiven Konflikten einhergehen, mit denen sich die Arbeitsgruppe ganz authentisch auseinandersetzen muss.

Die Werkstatt war in einem Wohnmobil untergebracht, das neben einem eingezäunten Spielplatz am Rand des Viertels in der Nähe der einzigen Moschee Zagrebs aufgestellt wurde. Durch viele Gespräche mit Einwohner/innen,

mit Menschen, die ihre Hunde ausführen, und anderen Passant/innen sowie mit bekannten Persönlichkeiten, die in den frühen 1960er-Jahren an der Entstehung der Siedlung beteiligt waren, erforschten die Künstlerinnen verschiedene Aspekte des Lebens im Viertel und seiner Konfliktfelder. In den Gesprächen wurden viele Aspekte thematisiert: der soziale Wohnungsbau, die modernistische Urbanisierung und aktuelle (De- bzw. Re-)Industrialisierungsprozesse, die nationalistische Prägung des öffentlichen Raums und der breitere sozio-politische Kontext, der das Alltagsleben der Gemeinschaft ausmacht.

Am Tag der Arbeit, einem regnerischen Sonntag, fand ein temporäres öffentliches Forum vor einem der größten Supermärkte des Viertels statt, der auch an Feiertagen regelmäßig geöffnet hat. Die interessierten Stadtteilbewohner, die den Arbeitsprozess der Werkstatt mitverfolgt hatten, konnten jetzt die erzielten Fortschritte sehen, die vor der roten, fensterlosen und mit Plakaten beklebten Fassade des Supermarkts ausgestellt waren, und ihre Zielrichtung kommentieren. Da viele brennende lokale, aber auch überörtliche Fragen aufgeworfen wurden, arbeiten die forschenden Künstlerinnen, die überwiegend aus anderen Orten kommen, jetzt synergetisch an pluralistischen Positionen und suchen nach einem spezifischen lokalen Thema, das sie während der ACTOPOLIS-Ausstellung 2017 angehen wollen.

Road to Belonging

Bei Road to Belonging handelt es sich um eine partizipatorische Licht- und Landschaftsintervention, die der Künstler Nikola Bojić als ein „räumliches Experiment der Zugehörigkeit" konzipierte. Als Gestalter und Forschender, der sich für räumliche Erzählkunst auf territorialer, aber auch ortsspezifischer

Ebene interessiert, befasste er sich eingehend mit einem unvollendeten Bauvorhaben am Stadtrand von Novi Zagreb. Auf der Baustelle im Viertel Podbrežje, das auf der anderen Seite des Flusses Sava am Rand des Neubaugebiets liegt, sollten eigentlich Sozialwohnungen entstehen, die aber nie gebaut wurden. Fertiggestellt wurde nur eine nutzlose, einen Kilometer lange Straße, die in einen Kreisverkehr mündet – ein surreales Fragment einer städtischen Infrastruktur, das sich in einer unbestimmten Landschaft verliert. Der Künstler pflanzte auf der Mittelinsel des überflüssigen Kreisverkehrs einen Walnussbaum. Mit dieser simplen Geste wollte er an die Baumgruppen erinnern, um die sich ein Ortsansässiger jahrzehntelang gekümmert hatte, bevor sie für das Bauvorhaben gefällt wurden.

Um das Bäumchen den Bewohner/innen der gegenüber der Baustelle liegenden Siedlung vorzustellen, organisierte der Künstler ein partizipatorisches Lichtereignis. Er forderte die Anwohner/innen dazu auf, dem Walnussbaum mithilfe eines Lichtprojektors liebevolle Botschaften zu schreiben, damit der Baum angstfrei als Symbol des Widerstands gegen autoritäre Stadtentwicklungsmaßnahmen wachsen würde. Die Botschaften wurden mit einer einfachen App geschrieben, die der Designer Damir Prizmić programmiert hatte. Normaler Text wurde in Morsezeichen, in eine Kombination aus Punkten und Strichen, umgewandelt. Dabei entstanden einzigartige Lichtbotschaften, die von dem Kreisverkehr in die Stille des Nachthimmels projiziert wurden.

*So steht der Baum auch heute noch auf diesem unbefahrenen Kreisverkehr von Podbrežje, wo der Künstler einen Nicht-Ort in einen Ort verwandelt hat, an dem das symbolische Feld des Widerstands und der physische Stand-*ort eins werden. Die *Road to Belonging* ist aber erst aus der Vogelperspektive vollständig zu verstehen, weil sich nur dann die gesamte Baustelle als integralen Teil der Arbeit erfassen lässt. Dem bzw. der durchschnittlichen Betrachter/in bietet sich dieser Anblick natürlich so gut wie nie. Die Frage bleibt: Ist es möglich, zu einem Ort nicht gebauter urbaner Vision zu gehören? Kann Zugehörigkeit gestaltet werden und als emotionales Instrument zur Rückeroberung der Stadt dienen?

Full Range Society

Full Range Society ist ein partizipatorisches Audioprojekt des Künstlerduos Lightune.G, das aus dem Multimediakünstler Bojan Gagić und dem Elektroakustikingenieur Miodrag Gladović besteht. Das Künstlerpaar ist vor allem für seine innovative Licht-Akustik-Forschung bekannt, mit der es die Umwandlung von Licht- in Tonsignale untersucht. Auch wenn ihre Auseinandersetzung mit der Gesellschaft in Form von „persönlichen Audiogeständnissen" in der künstlergeführten Galerie Greta im Zentrum Zagrebs erfolgte, war das Projekt *Full Range Society* als Mehrakter sowohl für den Cyberspace als auch den realen Raum konzipiert.

Der erste Akt mit dem Titel Soundentity *fand in einem fiktiven Warteraum in einer Galerie statt. Das Publikum füllte anonym fiktive Formulare mit Fragen aus, die üblicherweise bei der Erhebung persönlicher Daten gestellt werden: Alter, Geschlecht, Familienstand, Bildung und Ausbildung sowie ethnische Zugehörigkeit. Die Daten wurden anschließend digital in ein individuelles Audiobild verwandelt – einen* Soundentity*-Ausweis. Wesentlicher Bestandteil des Kunstwerks war die Ausstellungseröffnung, bei der die Gäste*

der Vernissage das ideale Publikum
zum Ausfüllen der Fragebögen abgab.
Für die einwöchige Ausstellung wurde
so eine Sammlung einzigartiger persönlicher Mikrokompositionen geschaffen.
Sie warfen die Frage auf, wie unterschiedlich Soundentity-Ausweise in
einer homogenen Gesellschaft überhaupt sein können, wenn diese Gesellschaft nur sehr wenige Abweichungen
von der Norm akzeptiert.

Der zweite Akt war für den Cyberspace konzipiert, um ein breiteres
internationales Publikum anzusprechen.
Er ist als App, als Computerspiel
gestaltet, um Gesellschaften bei der
Erstellung der Soundmap of Europe
zu manipulieren. Auch bei der Webappli-
kation liegt der Schwerpunkt auf der
Umwandlung von Daten in Ton.
Hier ist jede/r Besucher/in der Website
eingeladen, ein bestimmtes Land und
eine historische Epoche auszuwählen
und die verfügbaren demografischen
Daten zu bearbeiten. Das Kunstwerk
kann als Experiment in Social Engineering verstanden werden, das Einstellungen und Sozialverhalten auf breiter
Basis hinterfragen und beeinflussen
will. Wird der oder die Architekt/in des
neuen sozialen Gefüges eine offene
Gesellschaft kreieren und die ge-
wünschten Merkmale der umrissenen
europäischen Zielgruppe erzeugen?
Wird er oder sie eine andere, menschli-
chere „Klangkomposition" der Welt, in
der wir leben, erzeugen oder nicht?

Spaces between (Living) Places

Als eine „verlagerte" sozialräumliche
Erkundung untersuchte die Künstlerin
Tonka Maleković mit ihrem Projekt
Spaces between (Living) Places in dem
in Stuttgart angesiedelten Satelliten-
projekt von ACTOPOLIS Zagreb die
Phänomenologie fließender Identitäten

in kulturellen und geografischen Zwi-
schenräumen. Die Künstlerin hatte
ein Jahr als Arbeitsmigrantin in Deutschland verbracht und nutzte ihre eigenen
Erfahrungen, aber auch die Erfahrungen
anderer von ihr befragter Personen
mit ähnlichen Biografien, um dann die
gemeinsamen Überlegungen zur Wirtschaftsmigration und die Prozesse
zur Rekonstruktion der eigenen Identität
vor dem Hintergrund eines Zugehörig-
keitsgefühls zu einem neuen sozialen
Milieu darzulegen.

In Zusammenarbeit mit der Kultur-
anthropologin Petra Kelemen untersuchte die Künstlerin methodische
Formen und Formate künstlerischer und
wissenschaftlicher Forschung sowie
deren Hybridisierung. Ihre Arbeit beruht
auf Begegnungen mit Arbeitsmigrant/
innen en bei einer Reihe von Stadtspaziergängen. Der Dialog zwischen
Menschen, die alle „ortlos" sind, kann
als physische, kognitive und emotiona-
le Begegnung und Suche nach einem
gemeinsamen Nenner verstanden
werden. Die Videokünstlerin Matija Kralj
begleitete Tonka Maleković und die
Anthropologin bei deren Feldforschung
und hielt einen Teil dieser Erzählungen
filmisch fest.

Die Forschungsarbeit Spaces
between (Living) Places war auch im
Rahmen einer Ausstellung in der Galerie
des Zagreber Studentenzentrums als
dreiteilige Medieninstallation zu sehen:
als Mehrkanal-Klanginstallation, die
Teile der Interviews mit zahlreichen
Arbeitsmigrant/innen präsentierte, als
Videoprojektion eines Gesprächs mit
der Künstlerin, bei dem sie ein offiziel-
les Bewerbungsformular für einen
deutschen Arbeitgeber vorliest, und als
Auswahl an Fotofragmenten, die Zeug-
nis ablegen vom Bestreben der Künstlerin, sich (nicht) mit der Figur einer
Arbeitsmigrantin zu identifizieren.
Im Rahmen der Ausstellung wird das

Publikum in die Gespräche mit den
Arbeitsmigrant/innen einbezogen. Dabei
entsteht ein Polylog, bei dem diejeni-
gen, die fern ihrer Herkunftsländer
leben, in gewisser Weise ganz gegenwärtig werden. Ihre Erzählungen lassen
die Komplexitäten von Migrationspro-
zessen in heutigen Gesellschaften
verständlich werden.

Offenes Ende

Die Erfahrung von ACTOPOLIS Zagreb
zeigte, dass die Arbeit mit einer Bandbreite an künstlerischen Interventionen
in konkreten oder abstrakten städtischen Topografien, an tatsächlichen
Orten oder in der breiteren Öffentlichkeit
nur innerhalb von offenen Foren sinn-
voll ist, weil die Interventionen dort
erklärt, debattiert und formuliert werden
müssen. Die öffentliche Bühne in Zagreb
vergrößerte und verkleinerte sich ständig, nahm immer wieder andere Formen
an und bezog viele verschiedene Menschen mit ein, von großen Gruppen politisch Engagierter, die zusammen Stadt-
spaziergänge unternahmen, über Bewoh-
ner/innen in den Außenvierteln bis hin
zu den üblichen Galeriebesucher/innen
des kulturellen Lebens der Stadt. Wir
haben gelernt, dass ein solches „Öffent-
lich-Sein" Neuerfindung, Neuausrich-
tung und Rückbindung zugleich bedeuten muss, um lebendige Netzwerke
sozialer und politischer Positionen zu
schaffen, die sich eingehend mit den
Komplexitäten der aktuellen städtischen
Wirklichkeit auseinandersetzen. Befasst
man sich auf natürliche Weise mit
tatsächlichen Gegenden, muss mit dem
Engagement auch eine aktive Partizipation an den räumlichen Auseinandersetzungen der betreffenden Orte einhergehen. Wir müssen sensibel dafür sein,
wie man diese Territorien betritt,
durchquert und wieder verlässt, wenn
unser Forschungsprozess und unser

Engagement beendet sind. Ist ein radika-
ler Eingriff in den Raum erforderlich,
müssen wir uns zudem nicht nur heute
engagieren, sondern auch darum bemü-
hen, neue zukünftig anwendbare Praktiken für den jeweiligen Ort zu entwickeln. Darüber hinaus hat ACTOPOLIS
Zagreb auch deutlich gemacht, dass das
Eingreifen in sozial komplexe Realitäten
eine Dynamik produktiver Konflikte mit
sich bringt. Es ist keineswegs einfach
nur eine „Kunstopia der Inklusion". Eine
ungeteilte Gemeinschaft, ein geeintes
Kollektiv ist ein verführerisches Hirnge-
spinst, das nur unter Ignorierung der
Differenzen erreichbar ist. Es war wichtig
zu erkennen, dass eine Zusammenarbeit
sich manchmal auch aus dem antagonis-
tischen Zusammenwirken der Akteur/
innen ergibt statt aus einer einvernehm-
lichen Version einer gemeinsam er-
dachten Utopie. Gemeinsam am Tisch
sitzen und reibungsfreie Aktionen zu
planen gilt nicht mehr als gemein-
schaftsbildend. Auch eine „konfliktge-
ladene Partizipation" sollte als relevan-
tes und produktives Konzept bürger-
schaftlichen Engagements im Alltagsleben einer Stadt anerkannt werden. Mehr
noch: Aufgrund ihrer Achtung von
Vielfalt und ihrer ehrlichen Aufgeschlos-
senheit gegenüber anderen und gegenüber Andersartigkeit sollte diese Partizipation besonders wertgeschätzt
werden – als Modus Operandi neuer
Subjektivität und Soziabilität in der Welt.

ANA DANA BEROŠ

Communities of Care

Communities of Care is an experiment-based workshop, designed for neighbourhood communities, committed to inventing, engineering, and sharing tools for everyday use that can help overcome a specific obstacle generated by the system (legal status and migration, marital status, labour conditions, systemic violence carried out by bureaucracy, legislation and the concept of state and nation, the institutionalisation of rights, etc.). In order to go beyond what is possible, we have to go further than what is currently imaginable, or even legal. In other words, we are invited to devise our political imagination beyond obedience.

Communities of Care *ist ein Experi-
mentalworkshop für nachbarschaft-
liche Gemeinschaften, der sich
mit der Erarbeitung, der Entwicklung
und dem gemeinsamen Einsatz
von Mitteln für den Alltagsgebrauch
befasst, die bei der Überwindung
spezieller systemimmanenter Hinder-
nisse (rechtlicher Status und Migration, Familienstand, Arbeitsbedingungen, systemische Gewalt durch
Bürokratie, Gesetzgebung und
das Konzept von Staat und Nation,
die Institutionalisierung von Rechten
usw.) hilfreich sein können. Um den
Rahmen des Möglichen zu sprengen,
müssen wir über das gegenwärtig
Vorstellbare hinausgehen oder sogar
die Grenzen der Legalität überschreiten. Mit anderen Worten: Wir
sind aufgefordert, unsere politische
Vorstellungskraft jenseits von Ge-
horsam weiterzuentwickeln.*

Project: Selma Banich → Format: workshop, intervention → Dates: April–May 2016 → Venue: Folka
neighbourhood, Zagreb → Participants: Selma Banich, Marija Borovičkić, Mila Čuljak, Ivana Rončević,
Ana Vilenica (artists and cultural workers); Ana Opalić (photographer); Matija Kralj (video);
Luka Juras (design); Ana Suntešić (public relations)

Connecting: Installation and Seminar for Walkers

Making a better city by walking

Spazierengehen als Engagement für eine bessere Stadt

Seminar for Walkers is an activist platform tasked with creating a new activist group to participate in a number of unusual themed city walks that are open to the general public, with the goal of getting to know the urban space of Zagreb and identifying and starting both small- and large-scale initiatives for its improvement.

Connecting: Within the programme, one public-space intervention is taking place to showcase possible temporary improvements of the public space through simple creative solutions. On the location of the wall dividing the public park and popular walkway in Zagreb's historic Upper Town, a connection has been created in the form of a temporary staircase over the wall in order to open up the possibility of a direct pedestrian link between the park and the walkway. This link is currently missing.

Das Seminar for Walkers (Seminar für Spaziergänger) ist eine aktive Plattform, an der sich engagierte Bürger/innen beteiligen können. Angeboten werden verschiedene Spaziergänge zu ungewöhnlichen Themen mit dem Ziel, den Zagreber Stadtraum zu erkunden und kleine und große Initiativen zur positiven Umgestaltung der Stadt auf den Weg zu bringen.

Connecting (Verbindung): Im Rahmen des Projekts findet eine Intervention im öffentlichen Raum statt, um anhand eines zeitlich begrenzten Beispiels aufzuzeigen, dass der Stadtraum durch einfache kreative Lösungen verbessert werden kann. Über einer Mauer, die einen Park in der historischen Zagreber Oberstadt von einem beliebten Spazierweg trennt, wird eine Fußgängertreppe gebaut, damit der Park direkt vom Spazierweg aus zugänglich ist. Eine solche Verbindung fehlt bislang.

Project: Saša Šimpraga → Format: installation, seminar for walkers → Dates: 2–11 April 2016 → Venue: Strossmayer Promenade, Zagreb → Collaborator: David Kabalin (architect) → Participants: Matija Kralj (video); Bojan Mrđenović (photographer); Luka Juras (design); Ana Suntešić (public relations)

Zagreb—Invisible Belonging

Full Range Society

What is your "Soundentity"?

Was ist deine „Soundentity"?

Full Range Society is a "composition-in-progress", an artwork that the Zagreb and international audience is able to experience in two acts: firstly as a spatial sound installation in a gallery venue, and secondly as an interactive web platform. The first act, entitled *Soundentity,* takes place in a fictional waiting room inside the Greta gallery, in the centre of Zagreb, where the audience participates in the anonymous filling out of a fictional survey form *FRS.001.* The second act is a web product based on a virtual, demographic *Soundmap of Europe.* The web project gives us an insight into the complexity of human relations within the communities we call states. By looking at population data, it is possible to observe the historical changes European countries have been through. As in the installation in the gallery space, the focus of the web project is on the transformation of data into sound.

Full Range Society ist eine „Komposition im Fluss", ein Kunstwerk, welches vom lokalen und internationalen Publikum in zwei Akten erlebt werden kann: zum einen als räumliche Klanginstallation in einer Galerie und zum anderen als interaktive Plattform im Internet. Der erste Akt trägt den Titel Soundentity und spielt in einem fiktiven Warteraum innerhalb der Galerie Greta im Zentrum Zagrebs, wo das Publikum an der fiktiven anonymen Umfrage FRS.001 teilnimmt. Der zweite Akt ist ein Internetprodukt, das auf einer virtuellen demografischen Soundmap of Europe (Klangkarte von Europa) basiert. Das Internetprojekt gibt einen Einblick in die Komplexität menschlicher Beziehungen innerhalb jener Gemeinschaften, die wir „Staaten" nennen. Anhand der Analyse von Bevölkerungsdaten ist zu erkennen, wie sehr sich die Länder Europas im Verlauf der Geschichte verändert haben. Ebenso wie bei der Installation in der Galerie liegt der Schwerpunkt des Internetprojekts auf der Umwandlung von Daten in Klänge.

Project: Bojan Gagić & Miodrag Gladović (Lightune.G) → Format: participatory audio installation, exhibition, web application → Dates: 5–10 July 2016 → Venue: Greta Gallery, Ilica 92, Zagreb → Participants: Ana Opalić (photographer); Matija Kralj (video); Draga Komparak (design); Ana Suntešić (public relations)

Spaces between (Living) Places

The forming of a new identity through the phenomenology of the "spaces between" the geographical, economic, and cultural coordinates of "living spaces"

Die Ausformung einer neuen Identität durch die Phänomenologie von „Räumen zwischen" den geografischen, ökonomischen und kulturellen Koordinaten von „Lebensräumen"

The art and research project entitled *Spaces between (Living) Places* examines the phenomenology of migrant and fluid identities and cultural and geographic living inter-spaces resulting from economic migrations. By using her own one-year migrant experience between Croatia and Germany and a series of interviews with other protagonists with similar biographies, the artist Tonka Maleković portrays a common collection of experiences of economic migration, the causes behind the recent mass departure from one's country of origin as well as the processes involved in constructing an identity and a sense of belonging to a new place, culture, and community.

Project: Tonka Maleković → Format: exhibition, research → Dates: 1–10 September 2016 →
Venue: Student Centre (SC) Gallery, Savska Cesta 25 → Collaborators: Petra Kelemen, Matija Kralj →
Participants: Ana Opalić, Damir Žižić (photographers); Matija Kralj, Neven Petrović (video);
Luka Juras (design); Ana Suntešić (public relations)

*Das Kunst- und Forschungsprojekt
Spaces between (Living) Places
untersucht die Phänomenologie der
im Übergang befindlichen Identität
von Migrant/innen und die aus
Wirtschaftsmigration resultierenden
kulturellen und geografischen
Lebenszwischenräume. Gestützt auf
ihre eigene einjährige Erfahrung als
Migrantin zwischen Kroatien und
Deutschland und mittels einer Reihe
von Interviews mit anderen Prota-
gonist/innen mit ähnlichen Biografien
porträtiert Tonka Maleković einen
gemeinsamen Erfahrungsschatz der
Wirtschaftsmigration. Sie wirft einen
Blick auf die Ursachen der jüngsten
Massenflucht aus den eigenen
Heimatländern und auf die Prozesse,
die bei der Identitätsfindung und
der Entstehung eines Zugehörigkeits-
gefühls zu einem neuen Ort, einer
neuen Kultur und einer neuen Gemeinschaft ablaufen.*

The Road to Belonging

Belonging as an emotional tool for reclaiming urban space

Zugehörigkeit als emotionales Instrument, um öffentlichen Raum zurückzufordern

In the election year of 2009, bulldozers announced the opening of the construction site Podbrežje, a new social housing project located in the underdeveloped southern area of New Zagreb. The project started with a long road and a massive parking lot that was supposed to serve the new apartment blocks. But the blocks were never built. On the other side of the road is a small village of fifteen family houses. Some of the houses are one hundred years old. The oldest man in the village moved in right after World War II. The road is a border between two realms of belonging. The project *The Road to Belonging* is a landscape intervention on the oversized and completely useless roundabout at the end of the dead road. Seven years ago, on the same site there was a garden with more than sixty trees, all wiped out during the construction work in 2009. The project aims to reconstruct the memory of the garden by planting a tree in the centre of the roundabout.

Im Wahljahr 2009 kündigten Bulldozer die Eröffnung einer Großbaustelle in Podbrežje an: Im unterentwickelten südlichen Teil Neu-Zagrebs sollten neue Sozialwohnungen entstehen. Als erstes wurden eine lange Straße zu den Wohnblocks und ein riesiger Parkplatz angelegt. Die Wohnblocks wurden jedoch nie gebaut. Auf der anderen Seite der Straße liegt eine kleine Siedlung mit 15 Einfamilienhäusern. Einige der Häuser sind 100 Jahre alt. Der älteste Bewohner der Siedlung zog direkt nach dem Zweiten Weltkrieg ein. Die Straße ist eine Grenze zwischen zwei Sphären der Zugehörigkeit. Das Projekt The Road to Belonging ist eine Landschaftsintervention auf dem übergroßen und komplett nutzlosen Kreisverkehr am Ende der nicht weitergebauten Straße. An dieser Stelle befand sich vor sieben Jahren noch ein Garten mit mehr als 60 Bäumen, die alle während der Bauphase im Jahr 2009 gefällt wurden. Mit dem Pflanzen eines Baumes auf der Mittelinsel des Kreisverkehrs soll der Garten in Erinnerung gerufen werden.

211 Project: Nikola Bojić → Date: Opening 8 June 2016 → Venue: Podbrežje, Radmanovačka Ulica 10, Zagreb → Participants: Damir Prizmić (app design and programming); Ana Opalić, Dinko Cepak (photographers); Matija Kralj, Neven Petrović (video); Luka Juras (design); Ana Suntešić (public relations)

OBERHAUSEN
ZAGREB
BELGRAD
SARAJEVO

BUCHAREST
ANKARA
HENS
MARDIN

ACTOPOLIS Organisational structure *Projektstruktur*

ACTOPOLIS|The Art of Action is a project of the Goethe-Institut and Urbane Künste Ruhr. *ACTOPOLIS|Die Kunst zu handeln ist ein Projekt des Goethe-Instituts und von Urbane Künste Ruhr.*

Concept *Konzept*
Angelika Fitz

Project Director *Projektleitung*
**Juliane Stegner,
Goethe-Institut Athen**

Artistic Directors
Künstlerische Leitung
**Katja Aßmann, Angelika Fitz,
Martin Fritz**

Curators *Kurator/innen*
Ana Dana Beroš, Danijela Dugandžić, geheimagentur, Ștefan Ghenciulescu/ Raluca Voinea, Elpida Karaba/ Glykeria Stathopoulou, Boba Mirjana Stojadinović, Pelin Tan

Project Coordinator
Projektkoordination
**Natalia Sartori,
Goethe-Institut Athen**

Project Team *Projektteam Urbane Künste Ruhr*
Carola Kemme (head of project management team *Leitung Projektmanagement***), Daniel Klemm (project management** *Projektmanagement***), Christina Danick (project management** *Projektmanagement***), Ulrike Ranft (technical planning** *Technische Fachplanung***), Aude Bertrand (marketing), Dijana Tanasić (head of press** *Leitung Presse***)**

Co-production *Koproduktion*
Goethe-Institut Ankara (Thomas Lier; Raimund Wördemann); Goethe-Institut Athen (Juliane Stegner); Goethe-Institut Belgrad (Matthias Müller-Wieferig); Goethe-Institut Bukarest (Beate Köhler; Evelin Hust);

Goethe-Institut Bosnien und Herzegowina (Charlotte Hermelink); Goethe-Institut Kroatien (Katrin Ostwald-Richter), TheaterOberhausen (Peter Carp)

Local Project Coordination
Koordination lokale Projekte
**Goethe-Institut
Ajla Eljšani-Arnautlija (Goethe-Institut Bosnien und Herzegowina), Oana Lapadatu (Goethe-Institut Bukarest), Zorica Milisavljević (Goethe-Institut Belgrad), Natalia Sartori (Goethe-Institut Athen), Emel Öztürk (Goethe-Institut Ankara), Jasmina Vukas (Goethe-Institut Kroatien)**

ACTOPOLIS exhibition
Ausstellung

Graphic design (exhibition)
Grafikdesign (Ausstellung)
NODE Berlin Oslo

Exhibition architecture
Ausstellungsarchitektur
Stadelmann Schmutz Wössner Architekten, Berlin

Translation and editing (exhibition texts)
Übersetzungen und Lektorat (Ausstellungstexte)
Tradukas GbR

Technical planning (exhibition)
Technische Fachplanung (Ausstellung)
Kultur Ruhr GmbH/ Urbane Künste Ruhr

The exhibition will travel to the following cities: Ankara, Athens, Belgrade, Bucharest, Istanbul, Izmir, Oberhausen, Sarajevo, Thessaloniki, Vienna, and Zagreb.
Die Ausstellung wird in folgenden Städten gezeigt: Ankara, Athen, Belgrad, Bukarest, Istanbul, Izmir, Oberhausen, Sarajevo, Thessaloniki, Wien und Zagreb.

www.actopolis.net

Editors *Herausgeber*
Goethe-Institut & Kultur Ruhr
GmbH/Urbane Künste Ruhr

Co-editors *Mitherausgeber*
Katja Aßmann, Angelika Fitz,
Martin Fritz

Edited by *Redaktion*
Martin Fritz

Editorial assistants
Redaktionsassistenz
Simon Cowper, Natalia Sartori

Translation *Übersetzung*
Tradukas GbR

Copyediting *Lektorat*
Tradukas GbR

Design *Gestaltung*
NODE Berlin Oslo

Lithography *Lithografie*
Norbert Dietsche, Perfektbild

Printing and binding
Druck und Bindung
DZA Druckerei zu Altenburg
GmbH

Funded by *Gefördert durch*

Federal Ministry for the
Environment, Nature Conservation,
Building and Nuclear Safety

Bibliographic information pub-
lished by the Deutsche Nationalbibliothek. The Deutsche
Nationalbibliothek lists this
publication in the Deutsche
Nationalbibliografie; detailed
bibliographic data are available on the Internet at
http://dnb.d-nb.de

*Bibliografische Information der
Deutschen Nationalbibliothek.
Die Deutsche National-
bibliothek verzeichnet diese
Publikation in der Deutschen
Nationalbibliografie; detaillierte
bibliografische Daten sind im
Internet über http://dnb.d-nb.de
abrufbar.*

jovis Verlag GmbH
Kurfürstenstraße 15/16
10785 Berlin

www.jovis.de

jovis books are available
worldwide in selected book-
stores. Please contact your
nearest bookseller or visit
www.jovis.de for information
about local distribution
in your area.

*jovis-Bücher sind weltweit
im ausgewählten Buchhandel
erhältlich. Informationen
zu unserem internationalen
Vertrieb erhalten Sie von
Ihrem Buchhändler oder unter
www.jovis.de.*

ISBN 978-3-86859-472-0